Robert John (Bob) Hunter was born in rural Meath in 1938 and was educated at Wesley College and Trinity College, Dublin. After graduation in 1960, he began research on the Ulster Plantation in the counties of Armagh and Cavan, 1608–41. This interest in the Plantation, and early modern Irish history generally, was to dominate his life.

In 1963 he was appointed Assistant Lecturer in History at Magee College, thus beginning an association with the city of Derry/Londonderry that was to continue for the rest of his life. The creation of what was to become the University of Ulster also saw him teaching regularly in Coleraine.

Through his meticulous research, he developed an encyclopaedic knowledge of his subject, traversing such themes as the development of towns, the role of the English planters, the history of trade and migration and the intellectual and cultural life of Ulster more generally.

Though his untimely death in 2007 was to cut short his ambitions for further writing, he was nevertheless to leave behind more than thirty articles, essays, reviews, etc., which were the result of painstaking study conducted with a careful eye for detail and relevance.

Brendan Scott (Ph.D.) is the author and editor of a number of books and articles dealing with the religion, culture and society of early modern Ireland. He is also the editor of the *Breifne* historical journal.

The Ulster
Port Books
1612–15

The Ulster Port Books 1612–15

Edited by R.J. Hunter

Prepared for publication
by Brendan Scott

Published in association with the R.J. Hunter Committee.
The Committee works to acknowledge the contribution R.J. Hunter made to
the study of our past by making more widely known the results of his research,
as well as giving limited support to others engaged in associated endeavours.

The Committee is grateful for the assistance of Dr Brendan Scott
in producing this volume.

First published 2012
by Ulster Historical Foundation
49 Malone Road, Belfast, BT9 6RY
www.ancestryireland.com
www.booksireland.org.uk

Cover design:
Map of the north of Ireland (F2012), from volume eight, Maps of Ireland, of the
Dartmouth collection of maps and plans, compiled for or by George Legge,
Master General of the Ordnance © National Maritime Museum, Greenwich, London

Printed by Nicholson & Bass Ltd.
Design by Cheah Design

CONTENTS

ACKNOWLEDGEMENTS   viii

EDITORIAL NOTES   ix

GLOSSARY OF TERMS   x

WEIGHTS AND MEASURES   x

INTRODUCTION   xi

1   The Port Books of Londonderry   1

2   The Port Books of Coleraine   55

3   The Port Books of Carrickfergus   89

4   The Port Books of the Lecale Ports   101

INDEX OF PEOPLE   114

INDEX OF SHIPS   120

MAP SECTION

1   Continental European ports mentioned   124
      in the Ulster Port Books

2   Londonderry: places mentioned in the Port Books   125

3   Coleraine: places mentioned in the Port Books   126

4   Carrickfergus: places mentioned in the Port Books   127

5   Lecale: places mentioned in the Port Books   128

ACKNOWLEDGEMENTS

I have no doubt that the work presented here is very different to what Robert Hunter would have produced had he completed this project – but I hope, nevertheless, that he would be pleased to see it finally ushered into publication.

My thanks go to the West Yorkshire Archive Service for permitting the Port Books in their possession to be reproduced here. I also wish to thank Laura Houghton, the R.J. Hunter Committee and Ian Montgomery of the Public Record Office of Northern Ireland (PRONI) for allowing me access to Robert Hunter's papers before they were fully available to the general public and for providing me with copies of Robert's transcripts. Dr William Roulston and Fintan Mullan of the Ulster Historical Foundation were extremely helpful while compiling this work, as was Dr Brian Trainor, for which I am hugely grateful. Thanks also to Professor Raymond Gillespie and Dr Susan Flavin for their suggestions and help. Dr Roulston also prepared the maps and the names' indexes. Professor Christopher Maginn also made helpful comments on the introduction.

Finally, my greatest debt as always is to my wife Tara, my parents, John and Rose, my sister Sinéad, my brother Martin, and my nieces and nephew for all of the support and kindness which they have shown to me over the years.

BRENDAN SCOTT

EDITORIAL NOTES

This is R.J. Hunter's edition of the Ulster Port Books found in the Temple Newsam MSS (West Yorkshire Archive Service), prepared for publication by Brendan Scott from Robert's handwritten transcription of the originals. Robert's transcription is followed here, except when he left a blank or a question mark beside a word or phrase in his transcription with the intention of revisiting it at a later point. In these few cases, Brendan Scott has checked the originals and made the necessary changes, but [?] denotes a word which remains illegible.

The 'f's in the folio columns, and occasionally in the lists of goods, were inserted by R.J. Hunter, to indicate a new folio in the original manuscripts. Occasionally Robert notes the folio number in his transcription – these are used here also.

The comments in the notes' columns are made mostly by Brendan Scott, who also records where Robert has made comments himself.

In the notes' columns, 'RJH' stands for Robert John Hunter.

The new year is taken to begin on 1 January, and not 25 March.

The entry numbers were added by R.J. Hunter.

Spelling has been modernised in most cases.

R.J. Hunter occasionally converted weights in the original manuscript to their equivalent poundage. His weights are retained in this edition.

Occasionally there are two figures in the taxation column. The second figure seems to be an imposition duty, normally on luxury items and raw material exports. This is why some consignments include this figure and not others.

GLOSSARY OF TERMS[1]

Abbreviations
bal – barrel
cdn – chaldron
cwt – hundred weight
dks/dkr – dicker
fkn – firkin
hhd – hogshead
pc – piece
yds – yards

WEIGHTS AND MEASURES

Wine
8 barrels = 1 tun
2 pipes/butts = 4 hogsheads

Beef
2 barrels = 1 hogshead
8 barrels = 1 ton

Linen
1 elle = 45 inches
48 lbs = 1 pack
1 piece = ½ cwt
1 dicker = 10 hides/skins

Paper
1 bale = 10 reams
1 ream = 480 sheets

Grain
Last = 2 English tons (principally a Dutch measure of grain)

Terms
Chaldron – measurement for coal.
Damask – rich fabric woven with a variety of designs and colours, and of a mixture of materials, such as silk wool, or silk and linen.
Dowlas – coarse linen cloth from Brittany.
Firkin – 32–36 gallons depending on commodity.
Fustian – strong cloth normally made of flax.
Raisins of the sun – raisins dried in the sun.
Rashes – smooth textile made of worsted or silk.
Butt = measure of wine, fish, etc., equal to a pipe.
Dicker = a measure of hides, normally 10 hides to a dicker.
Last = a measure of fish, equal to 12 barrels and of hides, equal to 20 dickers.
Madder = a dye which could also be used for medicinal purposes.

---

[1] Some of these are taken from A.M. Millard, 'Some useful weights and measures found in the London port books (imports only) for certain years between 1588 and 1640' and A.M. Millard, 'Glossary of some unusual words in the London port books (imports only) for certain years between 1588 and 1640' (PRONI D4446/A/6/5). Susan Flavin and Evan Jones (eds), *Bristol's trade with Ireland and the Continent, 1503–1601: the evidence of the Exchequer customs accounts* (Dublin, 2009), pp 943–66, also contains a very useful glossary.

INTRODUCTION

I

During semester one of the academic year, 1982–83, Robert Hunter was on study leave from the University of Ulster. The ultimate aim of this research sabbatical was, in Robert's words, the production of a 'calendar and edition of a uniquely-surviving group of Irish port books from the early seventeenth century'.[1] This collection is held by the West Yorkshire Archive Service, as part of the Temple Newsam MSS, among the papers of Sir Arthur Ingram, who was involved in the farm of the Irish customs in the early seventeenth century.[2] Having made a preliminary investigation in the early 1970s of these records, which were made up of the port books for Londonderry, Coleraine, Carrickfergus and the Lecale ports during the years 1612–15, Robert decided that they were important enough to justify the calendar mentioned above. He made photocopies of the port books and transcribed them in their entirety – initially copying them exactly as they were laid out and then later editing them and modernising the spelling for publication into a form which he felt would be most readable and accessible.[3]

Robert was forced to confront various difficulties with the port books, however, which ultimately stymied their publication. Raymond Gillespie has described the customs records of sixteenth-century Irish ports as being 'fragmentary and rendered almost useless by the exemptions given by the government to the port towns and individuals'.[4] For the seventeenth century, Robert found it difficult to identify some of the more obscure ports (possibly in the islands of Scotland), as well as some of the goods which were being imported and exported to and from Ulster. The biggest issue, however, was Robert's concern regarding the reliability of the port books, both in England and Ireland. Robert had discovered in some of the English port books, occasional differences in destinations and cargoes. The destinations were reasonably accurate, with Robert discovering only one discrepancy – a Welsh port book, detailing a ship from Londonderry which docked at Carnarvon in 1615, but for which there was no corresponding record in the Londonderry port book.[5]

Much more problematic, however, were the ships' cargo listings recorded in the port books, both in their place of origin and destination. Although often similar, when comparing the goods on a ship bound from Coleraine to Chester, for example, the goods listed in Coleraine could often be very different from the goods listed in Chester. Other entries again could not be compared due to the damaged state of the English books. Finally, many of the inventories listed in the port books merely state 'unnamed goods' or end in the frustrating and tantalising phrase, 'and other wares'.[6] Was this a sign of laziness on the part of the clerk assigned to record the goods, or do the divergent accounts recorded on both sides of the Irish Sea point to a system rife with smuggling and corruption?[7]

As it turned out, despite referring to his edition of the port books as forthcoming for many years, Robert, it seems, had never sought out a publisher, and his interest in the project waxed and waned throughout the 1970s. Indeed, as early as 1982–83, he seemed resigned to the fact that the poor economic climate would make their publication extremely unlikely, if not downright impossible.[8] Robert's edition of the port books would never be published in his lifetime.[9]

II

Port books were the records of trade kept by customs officials at the ports. As alluded to above, they may not always provide a total picture of a port's trade – smuggling and falsified returns make this unlikely.[10] And as Sven-Erik Åström has noted, the books of the seventeenth century were designed merely as a record of dues paid to the Crown, and were 'not meant … as a mirror of commercial trends or as a register of the volume and value of goods passing in and out of the country'. Moreover, the Crown had no expectation of customs revenue from Londonderry or Coleraine, as they had both been granted to the City of London as part of the Ulster Plantation scheme, so had no real need to record the figures from Londonderry.[11] Yet the port books nevertheless offer a valuable indication of the pattern of trade, the needs of the pioneer colonial society and the value set upon various goods in Ulster in the early seventeenth century.

Customs duties were assessed on commodities in accordance with fixed valuations. Lists of goods were drawn up, each given a specific value and the duty was assessed on that value. These lists, which were printed, were known as Books of Rates. In 1604, the administration of the customs in England was reformed, and a new Book of Rates issued. Shortly afterwards, the customs system in Ireland, which was disorganised and unprofitable, was reformed and received an overhaul.[12] In 1608, a Book of Rates for Ireland was promulgated in Dublin, this new rating system becoming the customs standard for the Ulster Plantation. The basic duty at this time was one shilling to the pound, that is, 5 per cent of the stated value of the goods.

In the sixteenth century, Gaelic Ireland was divided into a number of lordships, and many merchants did not engage in undertaking economic activity with more than one lordship.[13] It was felt by the merchants that to do so, and abide by the differing tariffs and customs imposed upon them by often competing lordships, would incur far more cost and trouble than it was worth. Outside the Pale, Waterford, Galway and the other port regions under English rule, Dublin Castle attempted in a fitful fashion to assert its interests upon the Gaelic lordships and the Old English earls, such as Desmond, but mostly to no avail. Pirating was also a constant source of worry and concern for the traders and merchants, with a number of incidents taking place during this period.[14] Once, however, the entire country came under of the rule of the British state in the early seventeenth century, and trading rights were resumed by the crown in 1613, all of the island was opened up to greater trading activity, as the transaction costs for wholesale trade for the merchants were now significantly reduced.[15]

Bucking European trends of economic distress in the early seventeenth century, the Irish economy actually improved and began to strengthen following the end of the Nine Years' War in 1603. Its close economic and political ties to England, which did not suffer as much in the economic downturn then engulfing Continental Europe, also sheltered Ireland economically.[16] The port towns grew dramatically in response to the growth in trade in the early seventeenth century, although the growth of towns such as Londonderry was relatively slow pre-1650.[17] Nevertheless, in Londonderry, trade seemed to pick up quicker and benefit from the plantation in a shorter timeframe than was the case with nearby Coleraine, whose growth actually seems to have retarded immediately following the plantation.[18] Sir Thomas Phillips, who, as a previous owner of Coleraine, perhaps had a vested interest, declared that prior to the plantation, 'the Scots resorted thether in great number, for every summer there came between 40 & 60 barkes and boats into the Band [Bann], which brought merchandizes & carried away timer and boards and other commodities such as the Country did yeeld'.[19] From June 1606 to March 1607, customs receipts at Coleraine and Ballyshannon combined (unfortunately the two ports are not differentiated between in the report) came to £35 3s. 10d. Nevertheless, Coleraine was believed by 1637 to have been the 'port of the greatest consequence in the kingdom for coast business'.[20] Similarly, in Derry by 1612–13, the customs had almost quadrupled in value to £130 11s. 8d.[21] The wide-reaching influence of Londonderry as a port can be illustrated by the fact that areas as far as Dungannon, north-west Fermanagh, Strabane (and presumably also Lifford) and much of north Donegal, used Derry as a trading centre.[22]

III

Ulster's close links with Britain but especially Scotland, are also evident throughout the port books. Michael Perceval-Maxwell has stated that 'there can be no question that it was the Scottish settlements that were largely responsible for the flourishing condition of commerce between Scotland and Ulster'.[23] The record of imports into Coleraine from 1 April to 30 September 1614 state that twenty-eight separate loads were registered as entering into the docks there (Table 1). Of these loads, at least three and possibly four, ships docked twice during this period.[24] So of these twenty-four (possibly twenty-five) boats, eighteen were from Scotland, three from Chester and one each from one of the Scottish Isles, London and Barnstaple. Of the thirty-eight ships which were recorded as docking at Coleraine between 6 April 1615 and 12 September 1615, two docked twice (Table 2). Twenty-seven boats came from Scotland, two each from France and Chester, and one from Barnstaple and London. The place of origin for seven of the ships was unaccounted for. Most of these ships, therefore, confined their trade to either side of the Irish Sea, normally carrying their wares from Scotland to Ulster.

Loads	Number of boats	How many boats used more than once	Origin of boats
28	24	4 Boat of William Gaulte; boat of Robert Borne; boat of John Taylor; boat of Duncan Alche/Leche.	18 – Scotland 3 – Chester 1 – Isles of Scotland 1 – London 1 – Barnstaple

Table 1: Coleraine Ingates 1 April 1614–30 September 1614

Loads	Number of boats	How many boats used more than once	Origin of boats
38		2 Boat of John Longe in twice; boat of Robert Forrest in twice.	27 – Scotland 7 – Unknown 2 – Chester 2 – France 1 – London 1 – Barnstaple

Table 2: Coleraine Ingates 6 April 1615–12 September 1615

Exports from Coleraine between 21 April and 20 September 1614 reveal a slightly different picture, however. Of thirteen shipments to leave Coleraine during this period, six went to Scotland, two to Chester, one to London and one to Barnstaple. But one went to Bilbao and another to an unspecified port in Spain (their loads containing salmon and pipe staves respectively, of which Spain was a major customer). The thirty-seven loads exported from Coleraine between 5 April 1615 and 27 September 1615 were made up of twenty-three to Scotland, seven to Chester, one apiece to Glasgow and Barnstaple, one which went stopped at both London and Chester, and three which travelled to Spain, the goods again being not only salmon, but also hides, both tanned and salted. Salt, including French salt, used in the preparation of hides was in high demand in Ulster and a regular feature in import lists, and the salted hides exported to Spain had possibly been treated with imported salt from the continent before being exported back to the continent again.[25]

The Lecale ports of County Down, which can sometimes be overlooked in favour of the larger ports such as Derry and Coleraine, also reveal a buzz of activity in the 1610s. This conglomeration of ports listed fifty-six exported loads between 29 January and 30 September 1614. Of these, three ships docked twice during this period, while one ship (*Trinity* of Ardglass), docked three times, possibly under two different captains.[26] Of their destinations, ten ships travelled to Kirkcudbright, ten to Ayr, nine to Workington, six to Whithorn, Wyre and Chester respectively, three to Largs, two each to Bristol and Liverpool and one to Tenby and Rosses respectively. Of these fifty-six loads from the Lecale ports, twenty-eight were from Ardglass, twenty from Strangford, six from Dundrum and two from Killough. Of thirty-one loads from Lecale ports during the period 26 March 1615–September 1615, eleven were from Ardglass, seven each from Ballintogher and Strangford, and three each from Dundrum and Killough. Ardglass was the busiest of the Lecale ports during this period, followed by Strangford.

The Lecale outgates from 3 October 1614 to 23 March 1615 record twenty-seven loads leaving for foreign ports – eight to Wyre, four each to Lancaster and Workington, three to Ayr, two each to R. Wyre, Beaumaris and Whithorn, and one each to Parton and Wales. Four of these boats were used twice during this period, with one of these ships using different captains during both of its journeys. One of the captains, John Boyde, docked three times in two different ships, the *Jelleflower* of Fairlie and the *Jelliflower* of Irvine. Despite the business of these ports, it was reported in October 1637 by Charles Monck, surveyor general of the customs, that more ships from English and foreign, i.e. mainland Europe, ports, docked at Londonderry than any other Ulster port.[27]

Place	Period	Number of loads	Total value of exports
Lecale	29 January 1614–30 September 1614	Fifty-six	£2,251 8s.
Lecale	3 October 1614–23 March 1615	Twenty-seven	£983 2s.
Lecale	26 March 1615–September 1615	Thirty-one	£1,650 8s. 4d.
Carrickfergus	3 October 1614 –16 September 1615	Forty-five	£3,170 13s. 8d.
Coleraine	21 April 1614–20 September 1614	Thirteen	£1,067 5s.

Table 3: Export values from Carrickfergus, Coleraine and the Lecale ports, 1614–1615

Place	Period	Number of loads	Total value of exports
Coleraine	15 March 1613–12 September 1615	Ninety-one	£3,485 5s. 13d.
Lecale	18 April 1614–25 April 1614	Two	£10 7s.
Lecale	26 November 1614–15 January 1615	Two	£20 6s. 8d.
Lecale	11 June 1615–14 September 1615	Five	£128 2s.

Table 4: Import values from Coleraine and the Lecale ports, 1613–1615

IV

It had been suggested by Oliver St John in 1614 that

> great good will come into this kingdom by transporting cattle and corn from hence into England; for this kingdom will be able to spare great quantities of both, which will bring money into it, and make this barbarous nation feel the sweets thereof, for the love of it will sooner effect civility than any other persuasion whatsoever.[28]

Indeed, livestock and grain were the main goods exported from the northern ports during this period. Of twenty-one recorded exports from the Lecale ports between October 1614 and March 1615, eight contained livestock, three carried hides, and eleven had oats and barley.[29] Again the fifty-two loads recorded as having left the Lecale ports between 29 January 1614 and 30 September 1614 were entirely made up of either livestock or grain. The most important export products from Derry were also those of an agricultural nature, as well as fish, and by the 1630s at least, timber. As has been noted elsewhere, 'livestock products, hides, sheepskins, wool, beef and tallow; grain, especially oats and rye and barley; linen yarn and salmon predominate in the early port books'.[30] So large were the numbers of cattle being exported across the Irish Sea in the early seventeenth century, that in 1625–26, measures were taken to prevent the export of cattle and cattle products, such as hides, from Ireland.[31] The planters were rarely the cattle farmers themselves, producing the livestock for sale on the British mainland – rather they were the middleman, procuring for sale the cattle so abundant in Ireland and making a hefty profit for their trouble.[32] As mentioned above, grain was an important export commodity which was extremely profitable for merchants during the early plantation period. The appearance of grain in the trade returns in the early seventeenth century points to an overhaul in customs duties rather than an innovation in trade and the further development of the Irish economy. It also seems to have been sold at a cheaper price than Scottish and English grain. But high rates of duty imposed by a protectionist Scottish council in 1618 put paid to much of this exportation, and also reduced the incentive to undertake arable farming in Ulster. Barring oats and other grainstuffs, the only other major non-pastoral product to be exported was linen yarn, which was mostly headed to Lancashire, Manchester in particular, where it was used in the production of fustian products.[33]

Other hides, such as stagskins, sealskins and goatskins were exported from Derry to France in March 1614. The timber trade, which began to grow and expand from the 1550s, experienced a significant but short-lived period of growth in the early seventeenth century.[34] It was reported that in Derry in May 1609 that 'all materials for building of ships (except tar) is there to be had in great plenty', and it was later hoped that Irish timber products may eventually be cheaper than those sold by the Dutch.[35] Charles Moncke reported in 1637 that the woods around Carrickfergus contained 'the best timber that ever I saw', and bemoaned the fact that such high quality timber was used to make pipe staves.[36] Other goods exported in large quantities from the northern ports in the early seventeenth century included large amounts of barrel staves, pipe staves and hogshead staves, these timber products travelling, as mentioned above, as far as Spain. Ireland has been identified as a major source of supply for products of this nature in the early seventeenth century, a source which was largely depleted by the end of that century.[37]

Initial imports to Londonderry included building materials associated with the construction of new buildings, towns and villages as part of the Ulster plantation. Large amounts of ridge tiles, tilestones, spades, chisels, iron tools, slates, nails, lead, door locks and unnamed 'household goods for the use of the plantation' were imported into Londonderry and Coleraine between 1612 and 1615. Once the houses and buildings had been constructed, they needed to be kept warm and comfortable, and glass for windows (described as glass 'allowed for the use of the plantation by warrant of Lord Treasurer' in April 1614), lanterns, candles, fire shovels, tongs, bellows were all imported from Britain, as well as vast amounts of coal and some slack.

A significant amount and wide variety of luxury food items were imported into the northern ports for the new settlers, including white candy, currants, prunes, figs, 'raisins of the sun' and Malaga raisins, indicating the relative prosperity of some of the settlers. There were also a large number of spices and other foodstuffs for added flavour, such as ginger, nutmeg, cinnamon, saffron, cloves, pepper, liquorice, sugar, salt and vinegar. Brass kettles, frying pans and drinking glasses were also imported. Large amounts of wine, especially from France, but some from Spain also, and Scottish whiskey was also imported into Ulster ports, indicating the Scottish origins of many planters.[38] Tobacco and pipes were also in high demand among the new settlers in Ulster, and by the 1680s, Irish ships were using the Isle of Man as a base for their tobacco smuggling operations.[39]

Despite the huge amount of beef being exported from Ireland, there was still some imported, along with some grain, salmon, herrings, cod, bacon, onions and apples. The appearance of salmon, herrings and cod, along with 'nets and ropes for fishing', in the list of imports implies an underdeveloped fishing industry, that now under the influence of the new settlers, was perhaps beginning to strengthen.[40] One aspect of trade which becomes clear, however, is the lack of regional specialisation of goods or produce throughout the sixteenth century. While the exportation of cloth and wool increased throughout that period, the importation of cloth from Scotland and England also rose accordingly. In 1611, it was recorded that linen yarn and wool were among the principal exports from Dublin, while linen and woollen cloth numbered among its main imports. This, as alluded to above, points to an inability on the part of the Irish, either of the Pale, or Gaelic Ireland, to process the raw materials themselves into usable products. As Raymond Gillespie has noted, this implies both an easy availability of land which precluded the need of the Gaelic Irish to diversify and complement their skills set, as well as the lowly status of tradesmen or craftsmen in the seventeenth century.[41]

The Scottish antecedents of many of the settlers in Ulster is plain to see in the large amounts of cloth being imported into the Ulster ports, including 'Scots grey cloth', 'Scotch hats', blue bonnets, blue cloth, broad cloths. But cloth from Yorkshire was also popular, along with some Genoa fustian, hats, stockings, 'coloured hats for children', silk, velvet, men's wool knit stockings, ribbon and shoes. Along with the cloth, large amounts of dye, soap[42] and starch was also imported. Dressed in the latest fashions using material from Britain and occasionally the continent, many of these planters had no intention of 'going native'. Another indication of new innovations introduced into Ireland by the planters can be seen in the importation of equine equipment such as stirrups, horseshoes, girdles, saddles, despite the fact that not many horses are recorded in Ulster's import records, with more exported than imported.

Books only appear once in the port books investigated as part of this study, and perhaps unsurprisingly given the reforming aspect of the plantation, they are religious in nature. On 23 October 1614, four bibles and four psalters were imported into Derry as part of a larger consignment. There does not seem to be any other mention of books entering the northern ports during this time, with only one mention in 1632 as part of a load from Chester to Derry.[43] Literacy was poor at this time, nevertheless, what is described as 'ordinary paper', and, more commonly, a form of writing paper called 'pott paper', receives mentions in the port books investigated here. They entered the port of Derry from Chester as part of a larger consignment on an unspecified date between 25 July and 12 August 1615.

On 10 July 1615, the city of London entered a consignment which illustrates some of the prevailing tensions associated with the plantation. By the beginning of the year, plans were being formulated by members of the O'Cahan family to mount a rebellion. The Dublin government was made aware of these plans, and were worried about the possibility of foreign intervention, or worse yet, the return of Hugh O'Neill. A series of arrests were made between February and June 1615, during the course of which, it was discovered that the first steps in the proposed rising were to have been the capture of Londonderry and Coleraine. On 1 May that year, the Irish Society in London,[44] alarmed by the threat to their interests in the Londonderry Plantation, raised money for arms to contribute to the defence of these towns. The consignment from the city of London, which docked at Londonderry on 15 July 1615, comprising a large variety and amount of weapons, gunpowder and shot, is the probable result of this fundraising. Gunpowder had also been imported into Londonderry in January and April 1615. Robert Hunter also believes that the arrival of these arms 'probably rendered the holding of the assizes in Londonderry on 31 July, at which several of the ringleaders were sentenced to execution, the more secure'.[45]

V

The port rolls for Londonderry, Coleraine, Carrickfergus and the Lecale ports are an underrated source which have been underutilised by historians of the early seventeenth century. As Robert Hunter himself stated,

> they can be used to establish the character of the merchant class of the merging plantation towns and the incipient commercialisation which was one of the characteristics of plantation. … They can also be used, as names are gradually identified, to indicate the hinterlands of the Ulster ports, for example, Strabane merchants trading through Derry. … The commodities exported illuminate the plantation economy; the enormous range of imports indicates that Ulster participated in the contemporary consumer society. The port books also provide fairly exact information about the places of origin of the ships that traded with Ulster and indicate the size of local Ulster merchant fleets.[46]

Many of these avenues of enquiry are beyond the remit of this short essay, but the work undertaken by Robert Hunter in transcribing and editing the Ulster port books should serve as an indispensable guide for those interested in pursuing these and other topics further and in greater detail.

[1] PRONI, D4446/C/1.

[2] West Yorkshire Archive Service, WYL 100/PO/7/I/1–4. The manuscript numbers are as follows: 100/PO/7/I/1 (Coleraine); 100/PO/7/I/2 (Lecale); 100/PO/7/I/3 (Carrickfergus); 100/PO/7/I/4 (Londonderry). See also Brian C. Donovan & David Edwards, *British sources for Irish history, 1485–1641: a guide to manuscripts in local, regional and specialised repositories in England, Scotland and Wales* (Dublin, 1997), pp 290–1; Victor Treadwell, 'The establishment of the farms of the Irish customs 1603–13' in *English Historical Review*, 93 (1978), pp 580–602; Hugh Kearney, *Strafford in Ireland, 1633–41: a study in absolutism* (Manchester, 1959; 2nd ed., Cambridge, 1989), pp 161–2.

[3] PRONI, D4446/C/1. Copies of the original transcripts ordered from what was then Leeds City Reference Library by Robert and which are now kept in PRONI are: D4446/B/6/1 (Carrickfergus); D4446/B/6/2 (Coleraine); D4446/B/6/3 (Lecale); D4446/B/6/4–5 (Londonderry). Robert's transcripts of these manuscripts can be found in D4446/A/6/20–21 (Londonderry); D4446/A/6/22 (Carrickfergus); D4446/A/6/28 (Coleraine); D4446/A/6/29 (Lecale). Leeds City Reference Library became part of the West Yorkshire Archive Service in 1982: http://www.archives.wyjs.org.uk/archives-leeds.asp, accessed 11/07/12.

[4] Raymond Gillespie, *The transformation of the Irish economy, 1550–1700* (2nd ed., Dundalk, 1998), p. 5.

[5] PRONI, D4446/C/1. For a study of trade from the English side, see Donald Woodward, *The trade of Elizabethan Chester* (Hull, 1970); idem, 'The overseas trade of Chester, 1600–1650' in *Transactions of the Historic society of Lancashire and Cheshire*, 122 (1970), pp 25–42.

[6] See in particular the large majority of cargoes moving through Londonderry between Michaelmas 1612 and Michaelmas 1613.

[7] PRONI, D4446/C/1. This was also the case with seventeenth-century records of trade between England and Scandinavia: Sven-Erik Åström, 'The reliability of the English port books' in *The Scandinavian Economic History Review*, xvi, no. 2 (1968), pp 125–136 at pp 133–5.

[8] PRONI, D4446/C/1; John Morrill, 'Introduction: Bob Hunter's Ulster' in John Morrill (ed.), *Ulster Transformed: essays on plantation and print culture c. 1590-1641* (Belfast, 2012). My thanks to Professor Morrill for sharing with me his wonderful assessment of Robert's life and work prior to publication.

[9] See his correspondence with Donald Woodward throughout the 1970s: PRONI, D4446/A/6/1. That Robert may have been interested in reviving the project in the 1990s is implied through the inclusion in his papers now held by PRONI of a memo sent around the history department at Magee in April 1991, informing the scholars there that the Royal Historical Society were seeking proposals to publish documentary sources as part of its Camden Series. Robert, however, does not seem to have pursued this avenue any further. He did, however, make his transcript of the port books available to his students, a number of whom wrote undergraduate theses based upon the port books, as well as to fellow scholars such as Donald Woodward, who referred to them in 'Irish Sea trades and shipping from the later middle ages to c. 1660' in M. McCaughan & J. Appleby (eds), *The Irish sea: aspects of maritime history* (Belfast, 1989), pp 35–44.

[10] The customs collector at Derry in the 1630s admitted that only 60 per cent of the legal duty on beef was paid: T.W. Moody, *The Londonderry plantation* (Belfast, 1939), p. 350. Numerous accounts of smuggling and piracy can be seen in John Appleby (ed.), *A calendar of material relating to Ireland from the high court of admiralty examinations, 1536–1641* (Dublin, 1992), pp 104–6, 126–39; *Cal. S.P. Ire., 1608–10*, p. 473; Woodward, 'Irish Sea trades and shipping from the later middle ages to c. 1660', p. 35; Charles Moncke, 'Report on the customs in the northern ports of Ireland, 1637' (unpublished, PRONI, 1974), unpaginated. See also Evan Jones, *Inside the illicit economy: reconstructing the smugglers' trade of sixteenth-century Bristol* (Ashgate, 2012).

[11] Åström, 'The reliability of the English port books'; Treadwell, 'The establishment of the farms of the Irish customs 1603–13', p. 598.

[12] See Treadwell, 'The establishment of the farms of the Irish customs 1603–13'.

[13] For more on Gaelic trade, see Mary O'Dowd, 'Gaelic economy and society' in Ciaran Brady & Raymond Gillespie (eds), *Natives and newcomers: essays on the making of Irish colonial society* (Dublin, 1986), pp 120–47 at pp 130–32.

[14] Moody, *The Londonderry plantation*, pp 351–2.

[15] Gillespie, *The transformation of the Irish economy, 1550–1700*, p. 23; Treadwell, 'The establishment of the farms of the Irish customs 1603–13', pp 580–1.

[16] Aidan Clarke, 'The Irish economy, 1600–60' in T.W. Moody, F.X. Martin & F.J. Byrne (eds), *A new history of Ireland III: early modern Ireland, 1534–1691* (Oxford, 1976), pp 168–84 at p. 168.

[17] Gillespie, *The transformation of the Irish economy, 1550–1700*, p. 28. Derry was erected as a port and a military outpost in 1604: Treadwell, 'The establishment of the farms of the Irish customs 1603–13', p. 588; R.J. Hunter, 'Ulster Plantation towns' in D.W. Harkness & Mary O'Dowd (eds), *The Town in Ireland: Historical studies XIII* (Belfast, 1981), pp 55–80 at p. 56.

[18] Michael Perceval-Maxwell, *The Scottish migration to Ulster in the reign of James I* (London, 1973), p. 291; R.J. Hunter, 'The fishmongers' company of London and the Londonderry plantation, 1609–41' in Gerard O'Brien (ed.), *Derry and Londonderry: history and society* (Dublin, 1999), pp 205–58.

[19] Quoted in Perceval-Maxwell, *The Scottish migration to Ulster in the reign of James I*, p. 291; T.W. Moody, 'Sir Thomas Phillips of Limavady, servitor' in *Irish Historical Studies*, 3 (1938–39), pp 251–72.

[20] Moody, *The Londonderry plantation*, p. 348.

[21] Perceval-Maxwell, *The Scottish migration to Ulster in the reign of James I*, p. 293.

[22] Hunter, 'Ulster Plantation towns', p. 68.

[23] Perceval-Maxwell, *The Scottish migration to Ulster in the reign of James I*, p. 301.

[24] The boat belonging to 'Duncan Alche' and 'Duncan Leche' may the same one, but as these boats do not seem to have personalised names, or at least were not recorded using their monikers, it is difficult to say.

[25] Hunter, 'Ulster Plantation towns', p. 73. One load of butter and oats left Derry for Norway on 27 February 1615. Butter has been reckoned to be the most important export from Belfast in the seventeenth century: Jean Agnew, *Belfast merchant families in the seventeenth century* (Dublin, 1996), p. 105.

[26] This may actually be the same person – John Flynne and John Boye a Felyn. There were two main types of ships docking and departing from the Ulster ports – those hired, along with a captain, by a merchant to transport goods for them, or those captained by the man who also the merchant, which would have been cheaper.

[27] Hunter, 'Ulster Plantation towns', p. 78.

[28] *Cal. S.P. Ire., 1611–14*, pp 501–2; Donald Woodward, 'The Anglo-Irish livestock trade in the seventeenth century' in *Irish Historical Studies*, 72 (1973), pp 489–523 at p. 490.

[29] Traders do not seem to have specialised in any particular cargo. John Boyde, for example, exported twenty-five cows from Strangford to Workington on the *Jelleflower* of Fairlie on 3 October 1614, and then exported sixty barrels of oats from Portaferry to Wyre on 1 November 1614.

[30] Hunter, 'Ulster Plantation towns', p. 77. Fish had been a major Irish export in the sixteenth century, particularly from Wexford and south Munster, but this witnessed a major decline during the seventeenth century: Woodward, 'Irish Sea trades and shipping from the later middle ages to *c.* 1660', pp 35, 37.

[31] Clarke, 'The Irish economy, 1600–60', p. 177. For some figures on the export of livestock from all of the Irish ports in the early seventeenth century, see Woodward, 'The Anglo-Irish livestock trade in the seventeenth century', pp 515–17. Sheep were later to become a major export, with the produce of 1.5 million to 2 million sheep exported from Ireland on the eve of the 1641 rising: Woodward, 'Irish Sea trades and shipping from the later middle ages to *c.* 1660', p. 38.

[32] Clarke, 'The Irish economy, 1600–60', p. 177. The settlers claimed in 1610 that they were better off selling cattle and corn as they had neither the space nor the inclination to develop these industries further: *Cal. S.P. Ire., 1608–10*, p. 526.

[33] Clarke, 'The Irish economy, 1600–60', p. 176; Gillespie, *The transformation of the Irish economy, 1550–1700*, p. 33; Perceval-Maxwell, *The Scottish migration to Ulster in the reign of James I*, pp 294–5.

[34] Gillespie, *The transformation of the Irish economy, 1550–1700*, p. 34.

[35] *Cal. S.P. Ire., 1608–10*, p. 209; *Cal. S.P. Ire., 1611–14*, p. 227.

[36] Moncke, 'Report on the customs in the northern ports of Ireland, 1637'.

[37] Kenneth Nicholls, 'Woodland cover in pre-modern Ireland' in Patrick J. Duffy, David Edwards & Elizabeth Fitzpatrick (eds), *Gaelic Ireland, c.1250–c.1650: land, lordship & settlement* (Dublin, 2001), pp 181–206 at p. 199. See also *Cal. S.P. Ire., 1608–10*, p. 209.

[38] Perceval-Maxwell, *The Scottish migration to Ulster in the reign of James I*, pp 301–2. Some English beer was also imported. For more on the Irish wine trade, see H.F. Kearney, 'The Irish wine trade, 1614–15' in *Irish Historical Studies*, 36 (1955), pp 400–42.

[39] Gillespie, *The transformation of the Irish economy, 1550–1700*, p. 53.

[40] However, salmon was being exported from Derry to as far away as Spain.

[41] Gillespie, *The transformation of the Irish economy, 1550–1700*, pp 7–8. As Ireland had no mint, it was important to ensure that its exports were always in surplus in order to provide ready cash. This constant monetary requirement was another possible reason why Ireland exported unprocessed goods: Raymond Gillespie, 'The Irish economy at war, 1641–1652' in Jane H. Ohlmeyer (ed.), *Ireland: from independence to occupation* (Cambridge, 1995), pp 160–180 at pp 162–3; idem, 'Meal and money: the harvest crisis of 1621–4' in E.M. Crawford (ed.), *Famine: the Irish experience* (Edinburgh, 1989), pp 75–95.

[42] The Salters Company in Derry discussed the possibility of manufacturing soap from wood-ash and oil imported from Spain. It was believed by one of the Salters' agents in particular, that enough soap could be made to supply the whole of Ireland, but the idea never seems to have been acted upon and it came to naught: Moody, *The Londonderry plantation*, p. 344.

[43] Moody, *The Londonderry plantation*, p. 347.

[44] A standing committee of the City Council of London which was set up for the general management of the lands assigned to them, roughly co-terminus with modern-day County Londonderry.

[45] Raymond Gillespie, *Conspiracy: Ulster plots and plotters in 1615* (Belfast, 1987); Robert Hunter, 'PRONI Education Facsimile No. 169: Plantations'. Gunpowder had also been imported into Coleraine in June 1614.

[46] PRONI, D4446/C/1.

The Port Books
of Londonderry

Number	Folio	Date	Ship	Captain – Forename	Captain – Surname	Place – From	Place – To	Merchant Forename
1	f	3 Oct. 1612	*Post* of Leith	John	Steward	Londonderry	France	Hugh
2		6 Oct. 1612	Small barque of Scotland	William	Pattison	Inwards		William
3		23 Jan. 1613	*Joane*	Edward	Motherwell	Inwards		Edward
4		23 Jan. 1613	*Katherin* of Renfrew	John	Jackson	Inwards		John
5		25 Jan. 1613	*Blessing* of [missing]	John	Jinningham	Inwards		Hugh
6		26 Jan. 1613	*Margaret* of Irvine	Abraham	Hoy	Inwards		Abraham
7		20 Feb. 1613	*Grace of God* of Dumbarton	Peter	Donnell		Outwards	Peter
8		24 Feb. 1613	*Joane*	Edward	Motherwell		Outwards	Edward
9		28 Feb. 1613	*Robarte* of Dumbarton	John	Land	Inwards		John
10	f	2 Mar. 1613	*Grace of God*	Hugh	Ballentine	Inwards		Hugh
11		20 Mar. 1613	Small barque of Liverpool	George	Farroll	Inwards		George
12		4 Apr. 1613	Small barque of Liverpool	George	Farroll		Outwards	George
13		13 Apr. 1613	*Margaret*	Abraham	Hoy		Outwards	Abraham
14		17 Apr. 1613	*Robarte* of Dumbarton	John	Gland		Outwards	John
15		17 Apr. 1613	*Margaret* of Kirkcaldy	Hugh	Bohell			Hugh
16		17 Apr. 1613	*Jennet*	Robert	Kenningham		Outwards	William
17		17 Apr. 1613	*Vangarde*	William	Nisbett	Inwards		William
18		26 Apr. 1613	*Bride* of Hilbre	John	Hamlett	Inwards		Henry
19		5 May 1613	*Blessing* of [blank]	John	Kenningham	Inwards		Hugh
20	f	17 May 1613	*Blessing of God* of Leith			Inwards		John
21		20 May 1613	*Grace of God*	Peter	Donnell		Outwards – Scotland	Peter
22		26 May 1613	*Katherine*	John	Boyde		Outwards	John
23		27 May 1613	*Hope* of Dublin			Inwards		Maximilian
24		27 May 1613	Small boat of Scotland	Robert	Cohone	Inwards		Robert
25		27 May 1613	*Margaret*			Inwards		James
26		5 June 1613	Small boat of Scotland	Robert	Cohone			Hugh
27		22 June 1613	*Jennet*					Robert
28		22 June 1613	*Peeter*	Wybrand	Alpherte	Inwards		Wybrand
29		26 June 1613	*Bride* of Hilbre	John	Hamlett	Inwards		John
30		28 June 1613	Small boat of Scotland	Walter	Steward	Inwards		Walter
31	f	1 July 1613	*Bride* of Hilbre	John	Hamlet		Outwards	Hugh
32		8 July 1613	Small boat of Scotland	John	Boyde	Inwards		John
33		10 July 1613	*Peeter*	Wybrand	Alpherte		Outwards	Wybrand
34		24 July 1613	*John* of Renfrew	Adam	[blank]		Outwards	Adam
35		2 Aug. 1613	*Man* of Dumbarton	John	Gland		Outwards	John
36		26 Aug. 1613	Small barque of Scotland	Adam	Moderwell	Inwards		Adam
37		27 Aug. 1613	*Elizabeth* of Londonderry				Outwards – France	Andrew
38		7 Sep. 1613	*Grace of God* of Burntisland			Inwards?		Richard
39		10 Sep. 1613	*Margerie* of Chester	Robert	Ormes	Inwards		Christopher
		10 Sep. 1613	*Margerie* of Chester	Robert	Ormes	Inwards		Mr

Merchant Surname	Where Merchant is from	Goods	Total Value	Tax	Notes
Hamelton		Unnamed goods – £181 10s.	£181 10s.	£9 1s. 6d.; £2 5s. 4d.	
Pattison		Unnamed goods – £5.	£5	5s.; 1s. 3d.	
Motherwell		Unnamed goods – £18 5s.	£18 5s.	18s. 3d.; 4s. 6 3/4d.	
Boyles		Unnamed goods – £8 10s. 2d.	£8 10s. 2d.	8s. 6d.; 2s. 1 1/2d.	
Hammelton		40 tuns French wine – £12.	£12		
Hoy		Unnamed goods – £4 10s.	£4 10s.	4s. 6d.; 1s. 1 1/2d.	
Donnell		Unnamed goods – £7.	£7	7s.; 1s. 9d.	
Motherwell		Unnamed goods – £33.	£33	£1 13s.	
Land		Unnamed goods – £13 9s. 8d.	£13 9s. 8d.	3s. 4d.	
Ballentine		Unnamed goods – £6.	£6	6s.; 1s. 6d.	
Farroll		Unnamed goods – £8 4s.	£8 4s.	8s. 2d.	
Farroll		Unnamed goods – £63 6s. 8d.	£63 6s. 8d.	£3 3s. 4d.	
Hoy		Unnamed goods – £5.	£5	5s.; 1s. 3d.	
Gland		Unnamed goods – £25.	£25	£1 5s.; 6s. 3d.	
Hamelton		39 1/2 tuns French wine – £11 7s.; goods – £2 10s.	No entry	2s. 6d.; 7 1/2 d.	
Cunningham		Unnamed goods – £28.	£28	£1 8s.; 7s.	
Nisbett		3 hhd wine – 4s. 6d.; goods – £7 2s. 9d.	No entry	7s. 1d.; 1s. 9 1/4d.	
Sadler		Unnamed goods – £4 4s.	No entry	4s. 2 1/2d.	
Hamelton		Unnamed goods – £33 3s. 4d.	No entry	£1 13s. 4d.; 8s. 3 1/2d.	
Poore		Unnamed goods – £119 15s.	£119 5s.	£5 19s. 9d.; £1 9s. 11 1/4d.	No captain named.
Donnell		Unnamed goods – £3 10s.	£3 10s.	3s. 6d.; 10 1/2d.	
Boyde		Unnamed goods – £12.	£12	12s.; 3s.	
Van de Leure		Unnamed goods – £4 10s.	£4 10s.	4s. 6d.; 1s 1 1/2d.	No captain named.
Cohone		Unnamed goods – £5 5s.	£5 5s.	5s. 3d.; 1s. 3 3/4d.	
Greeneoake		Unnamed goods – £2 9s.	£2 9s.	2s. 5d.	No captain named.
Tompson		Unnamed goods – £15.	£15	15s.; 3s. 9d.	
Burne		Unnamed goods – £3 10s.	£3 10s.	3s. 6d.; 10 1/2d.	No captain named.
Alpherte		Unnamed goods – £34 6s. 8d.	£34 6s. 8d.	£1 14s. 4d.; 8s. [page damaged]	
Hamlett		Unnamed goods – £3 10s.	£3 10s.	3s. 6d.	
Steward		Unnamed goods – £2 2s.	£2 2s.	2s. 1d.; 6 1/4d.	
Thompson		Unnamed goods – £26 13s. 4d.	£26 13s. 4d.	£1 6s. 8d.; 6s. 8d.	
Boyde		Unnamed goods – £8 3s. 2d.	£8 3s. 2d.	8s. 2d.; 2s. 0 1/2d.	
Alpherte		Unnamed goods – £13 10s.	£13 10s.	13s. 6d.; 3s. 4 1/2d.	
[blank]		Unnamed goods – £27 15s.	£27 15s.	£1 7s. 9d.; 6s. 11 1/4d.	
Gland		Unnamed goods – £9 15s.	£9 15s.	9s. 9d.; 2s. 5 1/4d.	
Moderwell		Unnamed goods – £8 18s. 1d.	£8 18s. 1d.	8s. 10d.; 2s. 2 1/2d.	
Dickes		Unnamed goods – £47.	£47	£2 7s.; 11s. 9d.	No captain named.
Fitzsimons		Unnamed goods – £32.	£32	£1 12s.	No captain named. No indication whether goods are inward or outward.
Felles		2 hhd French wine – 1s. 6d.; unnamed goods – 10s. 8d.			
Walter		14 hhd French wine – 10s. 6d.; 6 broad cloths – £2; unnamed goods – £42 8s. 4d.			No total value or tax noted.

Number	Folio	Date	Ship	Captain – Forename	Captain – Surname	Place – From	Place – To	Merchant Forename
40	f	14 Sep. 1613	Small boat of Scotland	John	Blanne		Outwards	John
41		14 Sep. 1613	*Blessing*				Outwards	Robert
42		27 Sep. 1613	*Grace of God*	Thomas	Smitar		Outwards	Thomas

The account of the customs arising due at port Londonderry for goods landed inwards and ripped outwards since Michaelmas 1613 to 24 March 1614 (TN/P07/1/46)

Number	Folio	Date	Ship	Captain – Forename	Captain – Surname	Place – From	Place – To	Merchant Forename
43	f	13 Oct. 1613	Boat of Scotland	Peter	Donnell		Outwards	Peter
44		2 Nov. 1613	Small boat of Scotland	John	Smithe	Inwards		John
45		10 Nov. 1613	*Margaret* of Bristol	Henry	Ellis	Inwards		John
46		11 Nov. 1613	Small boat of Scotland	David	Mullan	Inwards		David
47		12 Nov. 1613	Barque of Liverpool	George	Farroll	Inwards		George
48		13 Nov. 1613	*John* of Renfrew	Adam	Moderwell	Inwards		Adam
49		13 Nov. 1613	*Bride* of Hilbre	John	Hamlett	Inwards		Henry
		13 Nov. 1613	*Bride* of Hilbre	John	Hamlett	Inwards		George
50		15 Nov. 1613	Small barque of Scotland	John	Smithe		Outwards	Archibald
		15 Nov. 1613	Small barque of Scotland	John	Smithe		Outwards	John
		15 Nov. 1613	Small barque of Scotland	John	Smithe		Outwards	Hugh
51	f	16 Nov. 1613	*Greyhownd* of Londonderry			Inwards		John
52		26 Nov. 1613	*Martine*				Outwards	Robert
53		29 Nov. 1613	*Margaret* of Bristol	Henry	Ellis		Outwards	Henry
54		2 Dec. 1613	*Speedwell* of Liverpool	George	Farroll		Outwards	George
55		4 Dec. 1613	Small barque of Scotland	John	Smithe		Outwards	John
56		6 Dec. 1613	*Bride* of Hilbre	John	Hamlett		Outwards – Chester	Henry
57		8 Dec. 1613	*Stone* of Renfrew	Adam	Motherwell			Adam
58		18 Dec. 1613	*Guifte of God* of Irvine	William	Gaulte	Inwards		William
59		20 Dec. 1613	*Guifte* of Dumbarton	John	Thomas			John
60		29 Dec. 1613	*Jennet* of Scotland	Robert	Burne		Outwards	Robert
61	f	29 Dec. 1613	*Guifte of God* of Irvine	William	Galte		Outwards	William
62		20 Jan. 1614	*Poste* of Londonderry	John	Steward			Robert
63		21 Jan. 1614	*Elizabethe* of Londonderry	Robert	Shaw			Andrew
64		26 Jan. 1614	*William* of Renfrew	Andrew	Coheran	Inwards		Andrew
65		30 Jan. 1614	*Poste* of Londonderry	John	Steward		Outwards – France	John
66		7 Feb. 1614	*Greyhound* of Londonderry	Martin	Brooks		Outwards	John
67		16 Feb. 1614	*Guifte of God* of Dumbarton	Robert	Linseie		Outwards	Mr
		16 Feb. 1614	*Guifte of God* of Dumbarton	Robert	Linseie		Outwards	Ringing
		16 Feb. 1614	*Guifte of God* of Dumbarton	Robert	Linseie		Outwards	Robert
		16 Feb. 1614	*Guifte of God* of Dumbarton	Robert	Linseie		Outwards	Saunder
68		19 Feb. 1614	*Bride* of Hilbre	John	Hamlet	Inwards – Chester		William

Merchant Surname	Where Merchant is from	Goods	Total Value	Tax	Notes
Blanne		Unnamed goods – £8 5s.	£8 5s.	8s. 3d.; 2s. 0 3/4d.	
Byas	Edinburgh	Unnamed goods – £543 2s. 6d.	£543 2s. 6d.	£27 3s. 1 1/2d.; £6 19s. 9 3/8d.	No captain named.
Fitzsimmons		Unnamed goods – £333.	£333	£16 13s.	
Donnell		Unnamed goods – £53 8s. 4d.	£53 8s. 4d.	£2 13s. 5d.; 13s. 4d.	
Smithe		Unnamed goods – £41 1s. 8d.	£41 1s. 8d.	£2 1s. 1d.; 10s. 3 1/4d.	
Pitts		Unnamed goods – £31 18s. 9d.	£31 18s. 9d.	£1 11s. 11 1/4d.	
Mullan		Unnamed goods – £6 6s. 7d.	£6 6s. 7d.	6s. 4d.; 1s. 7d.	
Farroll		Unnamed goods – £48 17s. 4d.	£48 17s. 4d.	£2 8s. 10d.	
Moderwell		Unnamed goods – £18 8s. 8d.	£18 8s. 8d.	18s. 5d.; 4s. 7 1/4d.	
Sadler		Unnamed goods – £36 14s.; 2 Northern dozens reckoned 1 cloth – 6s. 8d.			
Hamond		Unnamed goods – £37 7s. 2d.	£74 1s. 2d.	£3 14s. 0 1/2d.	An entry for 5 broad cloths – £1 13s. 4d. – not clear whose it is – possibly George Hamond.
Russell		Unnamed goods – £9 5s. 8d.			
Smithe		Unnamed goods – £56 9s. 6d.			
Nelson		Unnamed goods – £22 14s. 6d.	£88 9s. 8d.	£4 8s. 6d.; £1 2s. 1 1/2d.	
Banckes		5 pipes wine – 7s. 6d.; unnamed goods – £448 6s. 8d.		£22 8s. 4d.	No total value given or captain named.
Evine		Unnamed goods – £62 10s.	£62 10s.	£3 2s. 6d.; 15s. 7 1/2 d.	No captain named.
Ellis		Unnamed goods – £12.	£12	12s.	
Farroll		Unnamed goods – £54 8s. 4d.	£54 8s. 4d.	£2 14s. 5d.	
Smithe		Unnamed goods – £37 15s.	£37 15s.	£1 17s. 9d.; 9s. 5 1/4d.	
Sadler		Unnamed goods – £98 13s. 4d.	£98 13s. 4d.	£4 18s. 8d.	
Motherwell		Unnamed goods – £129 12s. 6d.	£129 12s. 6d.	£6 9s. 7 1/2d.; £1 12s. 4 3/4d.	
Gaulte		Unnamed goods – £6 8s. 4d.	£6 8s. 4d.	6s. 5d.; 1s. 7 1/4d.	
Thomas		Unnamed goods – £7 12s.	£7 12s.	7s. 7 1/4d.; 1s. 10 3/4d.	
Burne		Unnamed goods – £41.	£41	£2 1s.; 10s. 3d.	
Galte		Unnamed goods – £5 6s. 8d.	£5 6s. 8d.	5s. 4d.; 1s. 4d.	
Byas		34 1/2 tuns French wine – £10 7s.; unnamed goods – £53 6s. 8d.		£2 13s. 4d.; 13s. 4d.	No total value given.
Dickes		9 tuns French wine – £2 14s.	£2 14s.		No tax noted.
Coheran		Unnamed goods – £31 3s. 10d.	£31 3s. 10d.	£1 11s. 2d.; 7s. 9 1/2d.	
Steward		Unnamed goods – £417 10s.	£417 10s.	£20 17s. 6d.; £5 4s. 4 1/2d.	
Banckes		Unnamed goods – £419 3s. 9d.	£419 3s. 9d.	£20 19s. 2 1/4d.	
Bias		Unnamed goods – £90.			
English		Unnamed goods – £5.			
Russell		Unnamed goods – £3 7s. 6d.			
Steward		Unnamed goods – £38 6s. 8d.	£136 14s. 2d.	£6 16s. 8 1/2d.; £1 14s. 2d.	
Parry		Unnamed goods – £22 15s. 3d.	£22 15s. 3d.	£1 s. 9d.	

Number	Folio	Date	Ship	Captain – Forename	Captain – Surname	Place – From	Place – To	Merchant Forename
69	f	23 Feb. 1614	Small boat of Scotland	Robert	Cohoone	Inwards		William
70		23 Feb. 1614	Small boat of Scotland	Robert	Morison	Inwards		Robert
71		25 Feb. 1614	Small boat of Renfrew	Thomas	Jackson	Inwards		Thomas
72		26 Feb. 1614	Small boat of Scotland	Robert	Cuningham	Inwards		Robert
73		26 Feb. 1614	Small boat of Scotland	Robert	Berne	Inwards		Robert
74		1 Mar. 1614	Small boat of Lough Foyle	John	Cambell		Outwards	John
75		8 Mar. 1614	*John* of Plymouth	John	Pyke	Inwards		John
76		8 Mar. 1614	*Bride* of Hilbre	John	Hamlett		Outwards – Chester	William
		8 Mar. 1614	*Bride* of Hilbre	John	Hamlett		Outwards – Chester	Jesse
		8 Mar. 1614	*Bride* of Hilbre	John	Hamlett		Outwards – Chester	Henry
		8 Mar. 1614	*Bride* of Hilbre	John	Hamlett		Outwards – Chester	Raphe
		8 Mar. 1614	*Bride* of Hilbre	John	Hamlett		Outwards – Chester	John
77	f	10 Mar. 1614	*Robarte* of Dumbarton	Robert	Cohoone		Outwards	William
78		11 Mar. 1614	Small boat of Largs	John	Henry	Inwards		John
79		12 Mar. 1614	*Jennett* of Mongavlin	Robert	Cuningham	Inwards		Robert
80		13 Mar. 1614	Small boat of Scotland	Robert	Morrison			Robert
81		13 Mar. 1614	*Greyhound* of Londonderry – 70 tons				Outwards – Norway	Wybrand

The half year's account of the customs arising due at port Londonderry from 25 March 1614 to 29 September 1614 (TN/P07/1/4C)

Number	Folio	Date	Ship	Captain – Forename	Captain – Surname	Place – From	Place – To	Merchant Forename
82	f	25 Mar. 1614	*Jennet* – 6 tons	Robert	Burne		Outwards – Glasgow	William
		25 Mar. 1614	*Jennet* – 6 tons	Robert	Burne		Outwards – Glasgow	Sir George
83		25 Mar. 1614	*William*	Andrew	Cokeran		Outwards – Coleraine	Alexander
84		4 Apr. 1614	*John* of Plymouth	John	Pyke		Outwards – Plymouth	John
		4 Apr. 1614	*John* of Plymouth	John	Pyke		Outwards – Plymouth	Alexander
85		8 Apr. 1614	*Katherine* of Renfrew – 8 tons	Adam	Ogle	Inwards		Earl of
86		13 Apr. 1614	*Katherine* of Saltcoats – 4 tons	Adam	Lodimer			Adam
87		13 Apr. 1614	*Jennet* of Saltcoats – 4 tons	John	Kaile	Inwards		John
88		13 Apr. 1614	*Thomas* of Saltcoats – 3 tons	Michael	Legate	Inwards		Michael
89		13 Apr. 1614	*Grace of God* of the Wemyss – 5 tons	Hugh	Ballentine	Inwards		Hugh
90		14 Apr. 1614	*Good Fortune* of Ayr – 34 tons	John	Slois	Inwards		John

Merchant Surname	Where Merchant is from	Goods	Total Value	Tax	Notes
Cunningham		Unnamed goods – £11 9s. 8d.	£11 9s. 8d.	11s. 5d.; 2s. 10d.	
Morison		Unnamed goods – £6 1s. 4d.	£6 1s. 4d.	6s. 0 3/4d.; 1s. 6d.	
Jackson		Unnamed goods – £3.	£3	3s.; 9d.	
Cuningham		Unnamed goods – £6 1s. 4d.	£6 1s. 4d.	6s. 1d.; 1s. 6d.	
Berne		Unnamed goods – £16 5s. 4d.	£16 5s. 4d.	16s. 5d.; 4s. 1 1/4d.	
Cambell		Unnamed goods – £39 6s. 8d.	£39 6s. 8d.	£1 19s. 4d.; 9s. 10d.	
Pyke		Unnamed goods – £16 15s.	£16 15s.	16s. 9d.	
Mather		Unnamed goods – £6 5s.			
Smithe		Unnamed goods – £106 13s. 4d.			
Sadler		Unnamed goods – £53 6s. 8d.			
Borroughs		Unnamed goods – £10 13s. 4d.			
Stocton		Unnamed goods – £65 9s. 2d.	£242 7s. 6d.	£12 2s. 4 1/2d.	RJH wrote the following in the margin of his xerox copy of the original port books – 'Footnotes needed on condition of Derry book. Give in another footnote the local Chester book entry to show how many variations there were'.
Cuningham		Unnamed goods – £172 2s. 8d.	£172 2s. 8d.	£8 12s. 1d.; £2 3s.	
Henry		Unnamed goods – £4.	£4	4s.; 1s.	
Cuningham		Unnamed goods – £1 10s.	£1 10s.	1s. 6d.; 4 1/2d.	
Morrison		Unnamed goods – £8.	£8	8s.; 2s.	
Oldfers		Unnamed goods – £67 6s. 8d.	£67 6s. 8d.	£3 7s. 4d.; 16s. 10d.	No captain named.
Hamelton		Unnamed goods – £71		18s.	
Hamelton		Unnamed goods – £9 2s. 6d.		£81 6d.; £4 1s.; £1 3d.	
Steward		Unnamed goods – £39 13s. 4d.	£39 13s. 4d.	£1 19s. 8d.; 9s. 11d.	The following is noted for this entry: Goods are to be shipped from thence [Coleraine] in a barque for Chester.
Pyke		Unnamed goods – £28.			
Steynings		Unnamed goods – £38 8s. 4d.	£38 8s. 4d.	£1 18s. 5d.	
Abercorn		Unnamed goods – £9 4s. 8d.	£9 4s. 8d.	9s. 2d.; 2s. 3d.	
Lodimer		Unnamed goods – £1 2s. 6d.	£1 2s. 6d.	1s. 1 1/2d.; 3d.	There is no indication whether this shipment is inwards or outwards.
Kaile		Unnamed goods – £1 2s. 6d.	£1 2s. 6d.	1s. 1 1/2d.; 3d.	
Legate		Unnamed goods – £1 2s. 6d.	£1 2s. 6d.	1s. 1 1/2d.; 3d.	
Ballentine		Unnamed goods – £10.	£10	10s.; 2s. 6d.	
Poore		22 1/2 tuns French wine – £6 15s.; unnamed goods – £10.		10s.; 2s. 6d.	Total missing.

Number	Folio	Date	Ship	Captain – Forename	Captain – Surname	Place – From	Place – To	Merchant Forename
91	f	16 Apr. 1614	*Hopwell* of Dumbarton	Saunder	Yeonen	Inwards		Saunder
92		18 Apr. 1614	*John* of Dumbarton	John	Folesdale	Inwards		John
93		19 Apr. 1614	*Jones* of Fairlie – 14 tons	Humphrey	Simson	Inwards		Humphrey
94		20 Apr. 1614	*Margaret* of Largs – 4 tons	James	Bradshawe	Inwards		Ringing
95		21 Apr. 1614	*Grace of God* of Largs – 7 tons	John	Foster	Inwards		John
96		23 Apr. 1614	*Good Fortune* of Ayr – 34 tons	John	Slois		Outwards – Ayr	John
97		28 Apr. 1614	Small boat of Greenock – 12 tons	James	Lion	Inwards		James
98		28 Apr. 1614	Small boat of Saltcoats – 8 tons	John	Larriman	Inwards		John
99		2 May 1614	*John* of Dumbarton	John	Simple	Inwards		John
100		2 May 1614	*Jennet* of Saltcoats	John	Lodimer		Outwards – Ayr	John
101		7 May 1614	*John* of Renfrew – 16 tons	Adam	Moderwell		Outwards – Chester	Hugh
102	f	7 May 1614	*Hopwell* of Dumbarton – 12 tons	Alexander	Even		Outwards – Scotland	John
103		13 May 1614	*Greyhound* of Londonderry – 18 tons	Martin	Brookes	Inwards		John
104		13 May 1614	*Peeter* of Londonderry – 70 tons	Wybrand	Oldfers	Inwards		Wybrand
105		16 May 1614	*Seaflower* of London	John	Zacharie	Inwards		City of
		16 May 1614	*Seaflower* of London	John	Zacharie	Inwards		George
106		17 May 1614	*George* of Renfrew – 8 tons	John	Boide	Inwards		John
107		20 May 1614	*Bonadventure* of Largs	Robert	Fleming		Outwards	Sir James
108		23 May 1614	Small boat of Scotland	Patrick	Cambell		Outwards – Scotland	John
109		23 May 1614	*Jenett* of Saltcoats – 5 tons	Robert	Blacke			Robert
110		23 May 1614	*Katherin* of Saltcoats – 5 tons	Adam	Lodimer	Inwards		Adam
111		23 May 1614	*Guifte of God* of Saltcoats – 5 tons	John	Smithe	Inwards		John
112		23 May 1614	*Jennet* of Saltcoats – 5 tons	William	Gregge	Inwards		William
113	f	24 May 1614	*Grace* of Chester – 24 tons	William	Smithe	Inwards		George
		24 May 1614	*Grace* of Chester – 24 tons	William	Smithe	Inwards		William
114		26 May 1614	Small boat of Scotland – 5 tons	Thomas	Lion	Inwards		Thomas
115		27 May 1614	Small boat of Scotland	Thomas	Lyon		Outwards	John
116		28 May 1614	*Peeter* of Londonderry – 70 tons	Wibrand	Oldfers		Outwards – Norway	Wibrand
117		30 May 1614	*Robarte* of Dumbarton – 8 tons	Robert	Cohone	Inwards		John
		30 May 1614	*Robarte* of Dumbarton – 8 tons	Robert	Cohone	Inwards		William

Merchant Surname	Where Merchant is from	Goods	Total Value	Tax	Notes
Yeonen		Unnamed goods – 8s.	8s.	5d.; 1d.	RJH believed that captain's surname should read 'Yeoven'.
Folesdale		Unnamed goods – £22.	£22	£1 2s.; 5s. 6d.	
Simson		Unnamed goods – £5 5s.	£5 5s.	5s. 3d.; 1s. 3 3/4d.	
Boide		Unnamed goods – £8 14s. 10d.	£8 14s. 10d.	8s. 8d.; 2s. 2d.	
Foster		Unnamed goods – £2 12s. 6d.	£2 12s. 6d.	2s. 7 1/2d.; 7 3/4d.	
Poore		Unnamed goods – £80.	£80	£4; £1.	
Lion		Unnamed goods – £3 15s. 4d.	£3 15s. 4d.	3s. 9d.; 11 1/4d.	
Larriman		Unnamed goods – £2 12s. 6d.	£2 12s. 6d.	2s. 7 1/2d.; 7 3/4d.	
Simple		Unnamed goods – £18 16s. 2d.	£18 16s. 2d.	18s. 9 1/2d.; 4s. 8 1/4d.	
Poore		Unnamed goods – £12.	£12	12s.; 3s.	
Tomson		Unnamed goods – £213 6s. 8d.	£213 6s. 8d.	£10 13s. 4d.; £2 13s. 4d.	
Wilson		Unnamed goods – £12 19s. 11 1/2d.	£12 19s. 11 1/2d.	13s.; 3s. 3d.	
Banckes		14 butts sack – £1 1s.; unnamed goods – £38.		£1 18s.	No total given. Tax only on unnamed goods.
Oldfers		Unnamed goods – £100.	£100	£5; £1 5s.	
London		Unnamed goods – £40.			
Hamond		Unnamed goods – £44 4s. 2d.	£84 4s. 2d.	£4 4s. 2 1/2d.	
Boide		Unnamed goods – £6 8s.	£6 8s.	6s. 4 3/4d.; 1s. 7 1/4d.	
Keningham		Unnamed goods – £53 6s. 8d.	£53 6s. 8d.	£2 13s. 4d.; 13s. 4d.	
Haye		Unnamed goods – £40.	£40	£2 10s.	
Blacke		Unnamed goods – £1 17s. 6d.	£1 17s. 6d.	1s. 10 1/2d.; 5 1/2d.	
Lodimer		Unnamed goods – £1 17s. 6d.	£1 17s. 6d.	1s. 10 1/2d.; 5 1/2d.	
Smithe		Unnamed goods – £1 17s. 6d.	£1 17s. 6d.	1s. 10 1/2d.; 5 1/2d.	
Gregge		Unnamed goods – £1 17s. 6d.	£1 17s. 6d.	1s. 10 1/2d.; 5 1/2d.	
Hamond		Unnamed goods – £12.			
Smithe		Unnamed goods – £3 15s.	£15 15s.	15s. 9d.	
Lion		Unnamed goods – £1 17s. 6d.	£1 17s. 6d.	1s. 10 1/2d.; 5 1/2d.	
Haye		Unnamed goods – £16.	£16	16s.; 4s.	
Oldfers		Unnamed goods – £176 13s. 4d.	£176 13s. 4d.	£8 16s. 8d.; £2 4s. 2d.	
Balie		Unnamed goods – £6.			
Keningham		Unnamed goods – £39 15s. 4d.			

Number	Folio	Date	Ship	Captain – Forename	Captain – Surname	Place – From	Place – To	Merchant Forename
		30 May 1614	*Robarte* of Dumbarton – 8 tons	Robert	Cohone	Inwards		Hugh
118		30 May 1614	Small boat of Scotland	John	Wilson	Inwards		John
119		3 June 1614	*Greyhound* of Londonderry – 18 tons	Martin	Brookes		Outwards – Ayr	John
120		4 June 1614	*Grace* of Chester – 24 tons	William	Smithe		Outwards – Chester	William
121		6 June 1614	*Poste* of Leith – 70 tons	John	Steward	Inwards		John
122		6 June 1614	*Sondaie* of [blank]	Patrick	Horton		Outwards	Josp
123		7 June 1614	Small boat of Scotland	Thomas	Montforte	Inwards		Thomas
124	f	8 June 1614	Small boat of Scotland	John	Wilson		Outwards – Glasgow	John
125		9 June 1614	*Bride* of Londonderry – 30 tons	John	Hamlett	Inwards		Jesse
		9 June 1614	*Bride* of Londonderry – 30 tons	John	Hamlett	Inwards		Giles
		9 June 1614	*Bride* of Londonderry – 30 tons	John	Hamlett	Inwards		Henry
126		14 June 1614	*George* of Renfrew – 8 tons	John	Bride		Outwards – Renfrew	Ringing
		14 June 1614	*George* of Renfrew – 8 tons	John	Bride		Outwards – Renfrew	Earl of
127		14 June 1614	Small boat of Scotland	Thomas	Mawberrey		Outwards	Thomas
128		14 June 1614	*Elizabeth* of Londonderry – 14 tons				Outwards – Chester	Andrew
129		17 June 1614	*Guifte of God* – 16 tons	Thomas	Montford		Outwards – Chester	Thomas
130		22 June 1614	*Bride* of Londonderry – 30 tons	John	Hamlet		Outwards – Chester	Michael
		22 June 1614	*Bride* of Londonderry – 30 tons	John	Hamlet		Outwards – Chester	Henry
		22 June 1614	*Bride* of Londonderry – 30 tons	John	Hamlet		Outwards – Chester	William
		22 June 1614	*Bride* of Londonderry – 30 tons	John	Hamlet		Outwards – Chester	Jesse
131		25 June 1614	*Carvaile* of Coleraine – 40 tons	John	Betson		Outwards – Chester	George
		25 June 1614	*Carvaile* of Coleraine – 40 tons	John	Betson		Outwards – Chester	William
		25 June 1614	*Carvaile* of Coleraine – 40 tons	John	Betson		Outwards – Chester	Robert
132	f	27 June 1614	*Swallow* of Dumbarton – 20 tons	Peter	Williamson		Outwards – Chester	Jesse
133		27 June 1614	*Elizabethe* of London – 60 tons	Thomas	Piercson	Inwards		Thomas
134		30 June 1614	*Good Fortune* of Ayr – 34 tons	John	Slois	Inwards		John
135		8 July 1614	*Margret* of Greenock – 10 tons	John	Lion	Inwards		James
136		8 July 1614	*Isable* of Greenock – 9 tons	Robert	Forrester	Inwards		Robert
137		9 July 1614	*Hopewell* of Dumbarton – 12 tons	Saunder	Yeven		Outwards	Saunder

Merchant Surname	Where Merchant is from	Goods	Total Value	Tax	Notes
Cohone		Unnamed goods – £3 8s. 8d.	£49 4s.	£2 9s. 2d.; 12s. 3 1/2d.	
Wilson		Unnamed goods – £4 17s. 6d.	£4 17s. 6d.	4s. 10 1/2d.; 1s. 2 1/2d.	
Bankes		Unnamed goods – £106 13s. 4d.	£106 13s. 4d.	£5 6s. 8d.	
Smithe		Unnamed goods – £4.	£4	4s. 10 1/2d.; 1s. 2 1/2d.	
Poore		Unnamed goods – £80.	£80	£4; £1.	
Chillin		Unnamed goods – £48 1s. 8d.	£48 1s. 8d.	£2 8s. 1d.	
Montforte		Unnamed goods – £4 10s.	£4 10s.	4s. 6d.; 1s. 1 1/2d.	
Wilson		Unnamed goods – £13 6s. 8d.	£13 6s. 8d.	13s. 4d.; 3s. 4d.	
Smithe		Unnamed goods – £33 6s. 9d.; 2 broad cloths – 13s. 4d.; 2 kerseys – 4s. 5d.			
Baker		Unnamed goods – £29 10s. 4d.			
Sadler		Unnamed goods – £32 8s.; 1 broad cloth – 6s. 8d.	£95 5s. 1d.	£4 15s. 3d.	
Boide		Unnamed goods – £36 16s. 11d.			
Abercorn		Unnamed goods – £7 13s. 4d.	£44 10s. 3d.	£2 4s. 6d.; 11s. 1 1/2d.	
Mawberrey		Unnamed goods – £1 17s. 6d.	£1 17s. 6d.	1s. 10 1/2d.; 5 1/2 d.	.
Dickes		Unnamed goods – £84 6s. 8d.	£84 6s. 8d.	£4 4s. 4d.; £1 1s. 1d.	
Montford		Unnamed goods – £72.	£72	£3 12s.	
Graves		Unnamed goods – £13 6s. 8d.			
Sadler		Unnamed goods – £124.			
Parry		Unnamed goods – £21 2s. 4d.			
Smithe		Unnamed goods – £13 6s. 8d.	£171 15s. 8d.	£8 11s. 9d.	
Hamond		Unnamed goods – £20.			
Boulton		Unnamed goods – £13 9s. 10d.			
Nunne		Unnamed goods – £1 13s. 4d.	£35 3s. 2d.	£1 15s. 2d.	
Smithe		Unnamed goods – £133 6s. 8d.	£133 6s. 8d.	£6 13s. 4d.	
Piercson		Unnamed goods – £18 15s.	£18 15s.	18s. 9d.	
Poore		Unnamed goods – £25.	£25	£1 5s.; 6s. 3d.	
Lion		Unnamed goods – £3 3s.	£3 3s.	3s. 1 1/2d.; 9 1/2d.	
Forrester		Unnamed goods – £2 9s.	£2 9s.	2s. 5d.; 7 1/4d.	
Yeven		Unnamed goods – £12 15s.	£12 15s.	12s. 9d.; 3s. 2 1/4d.	

Number	Folio	Date	Ship	Captain – Forename	Captain – Surname	Place – From	Place – To	Merchant Forename
138		14 July 1614	*Isable* of Glasgow – 7 tons	James	Gaie	Inwards		James
139		15 July 1614	*Guifte of God* of Strabane – 20 tons	Robert	Linseie	Inwards		Robert
140		18 July 1614	*Guifte of God* of Saltcoats – 5 tons			Inwards		John
141		20 July 1614	*John* of Renfrew – 6 tons	Ringing	Hunter		Outwards	Ningen
142		21 July 1614	*Peeter* of Londonderry – 70 tons	Wibrand	Oldfers	Inwards		Wibrand
143	f	22 July 1614	*Hopewell* of Ayr – 18 tons	Saunder	Locon	Inwards		Saunder
144		23 July 1614	Small boat of Scotland – 6 tons	Hugh	Ballentine	Inwards		Hugh
145		23 July 1614	*Greyhound* of Londonderry – 18 tons	Patrick	Mordocke	Inwards		John
146		23 July 1614	*William* of Renfrew – 8 tons	William	Snap		Outwards	William
		23 July 1614	*William* of Renfrew – 8 tons	William	Snap		Outwards	John
147		25 July 1614	*William* of Renfrew – 7 tons	Andrew	Cokeran	Inwards		Andrew
		25 July 1614	*William* of Renfrew – 7 tons	Andrew	Cokeran	Inwards		Earl of
148		25 July 1614	*Jennet* of Saltcoats – 6 tons	William	Gregge	Inwards		William
149		25 July 1614	*John* of Renfrew – 20 tons	Adam	Moderwell	Inwards		Hugh
		29 July 1614	*John* of Renfrew – 20 tons	Adam	Moderwell	Inwards		Hugh
150		26 July 1614	*Jennet* of Saltcoats – 6 tons	Francis	Rosse	Inwards		Francis
151		28 July 1614	*Mayflower* of London – 25 tons	Peter	Peate		Outwards – Chester	Jesse
		28 July 1614	*Mayflower* of London – 25 tons	Peter	Peate		Outwards – Chester	George
		28 July 1614	*Mayflower* of London – 25 tons	Peter	Peate		Outwards – Chester	Brute
152	f	29 July 1614	*Hopewell* of Largs – 14 tons	David	Mullan	Inwards		David
153		30 July 1614	*Hopewell* of Ayr – 18 tons	Saunder	Locon		Outwards	Saunder
		30 July 1614	*Hopewell* of Ayr – 18 tons	Saunder	Locon		Outwards	John
154		3 Aug. 1614	*John* of Renfrew – 20 tons	Adam	Moderwell		Outwards – Glasgow	John
		3 Aug. 1614	*John* of Renfrew – 20 tons	Adam	Moderwell		Outwards – Glasgow	Robert
155		3 Aug. 1614	*Guifte of God* of Ayr	Thomas	Montford	Inwards		Thomas
156		8 Aug. 1614	*William* of Renfrew – 7 tons	Andrew	Cokeran		Outwards	Andrew
157		10 Aug. 1614	*Grace of God* – 30 tons	Thomas	Sunter	Inwards		Thomas
158		13 Aug. 1614	*Greyhound* of Londonderry – 18 tons	John	Slois		Outwards – Rouen	John

Merchant Surname	Where Merchant is from	Goods	Total Value	Tax	Notes
Gaie		Unnamed goods – £2 2s.	£2 2s.	2s.; 6d.	
Linseie		Unnamed goods – £4 18s.	£4 18s.	4s. 10 3/4d.; 1s. 2 1/2d.	
Smith		Unnamed goods – £1 8s.	£1 8s.	1s. 5d.; 4d.	No captain named.
Inglishe		Unnamed goods – £10.	£10	£1; 2s. 6d.	
Oldfers		Unnamed goods – £100.	£100	£5; £1 5s.	
Locon		4 1/2 tuns French wine – £1 7s.; unnamed goods – £4 2s. 8d.		4s. 1 1/2d.; 1s. 0 1/4d.	
Ballentine		Unnamed goods – £1 10s.	£1 10s.	1s. 6d.; 4 1/2d.	
Bankes		Unnamed goods – £5 12s.	£5 12s.	5s. 7d.	
Snap		Unnamed goods – £2 10s.			
Scot		Unnamed goods – £10 12s. 6d.	£13 2s. 6d.	13s. 1 1/2d.; 3s. 3 1/4d.	
Cokeran		Unnamed goods – £2 3s. 8d.			
Abercorn		Unnamed goods – £2 1s. 4d.	£4 5s.	4s. 3d.; 1s. 0 3/4d.	
Gregge		Unnamed goods – £1 13s. 4d.	£1 13s. 4d.	1s. 8d.; 5d.	
Tomson		Unnamed goods – £34 14s. 8d.	£34 14s. 8d.	£1 14s. 8d.; 8s. 8d.	
Tomson		11 2/3 broad cloths – £8 9s. 2d			No total value or tax listed.
Rosse		Unnamed goods – £1 5s.	£1 5s.	1s. 3d.; 3 3/4d.	
Smithe		Unnamed goods – £140.			
Hamond		Unnamed goods – £4 8s. 10d.			
Hamond		Unnamed goods – £16 13s. 4d.	£161 2s. 2d.	£8 1s. 1d.	
Mullan		Unnamed goods – £3 19s. 6d.; 2 broad cloths – £1 9s.	£3 19s. 6d.	3s. 11 1/2d.; 11 3/4d.	The broad cloths do not seem to have been taxed.
Locon		Unnamed goods – £34 16s. 8d.			
Poore		Unnamed goods – £7 10s.	£42 6s. 8d.	£2 2s. 4d.; 10s. 7d.	
Wilson		Unnamed goods – £25.			
Russell		Unnamed goods – £12.	£37	£1 17s.; 9s. 3d.	
Montford		Unnamed goods – £4.	£1	4s. 1s.	
Cokeran		Unnamed goods – £6 10s.	£6 10s.	6s. 6d.; 1s. 7 1/2d.	
Sunter		Unnamed goods – £7 10s.	£7 10s.	7s. 6d.; 1s. 10 1/2d.	
Poore		Unnamed goods – £135.	£135	£6 15s.; £1 13s. 9d.	

Number	Folio	Date	Ship	Captain – Forename	Captain – Surname	Place – From	Place – To	Merchant Forename
159		13 Aug. 1614	*Peeter* of Londonderry – 70 tons	Wibrand	Oldfers		Outwards – Norway	Wybrand
160	f	15 Aug. 1614	*Grace of God* of Rothesay – 6 tons	William	Steward	Inwards		William
161		18 Aug. 1614	*John* of Renfrew – 10 tons	William	Leeche	Inwards		William
162		18 Aug. 1614	*John* of Dumbarton – 12 tons	Peter	Donnell	Inwards		Peter
163		19 Aug. 1614	*Roberte* of Dumbarton – 6 tons	John	Gland		Outwards – Dumbarton	John
		19 Aug. 1614	*Roberte* of Dumbarton – 6 tons	John	Gland		Outwards – Dumbarton	Sir James
		24 Aug. 1614	*Roberte* of Dumbarton – 6 tons	John	Gland		Outwards – Dumbarton	John
164		22 Aug. 1614	*Hopewell* of Dumbarton – 12 tons	Saunder	Yeoven	Inwards		Sir John
165		22 Aug. 1614	*Swallow* of Dumbarton – 20 tons	Peter	Williamson	Inwards		Jesse
166		22 Aug. 1614	*Bride* of Londonderry – 30 tons	John	Hamlett	Inwards		Jesse
		22 Aug. 1614	*Bride* of Londonderry – 30 tons	John	Hamlett	Inwards		Henry
		22 Aug. 1614	*Bride* of Londonderry – 30 tons	John	Hamlett	Inwards		Richard
		22 Aug. 1614	*Bride* of Londonderry – 30 tons	John	Hamlett	Inwards		Moses
		22 Aug. 1614	*Bride* of Londonderry – 30 tons	John	Hamlett	Inwards		William
		22 Aug. 1614	*Bride* of Londonderry – 30 tons	John	Hamlett	Inwards		Humphrey
		22 Aug. 1614	*Bride* of Londonderry – 30 tons	John	Hamlett	Inwards		William
		22 Aug. 1614	*Bride* of Londonderry – 30 tons	John	Hamlett	Inwards		George
167		22 Aug. 1614	*Steven* of Liverpool – 30 tons	Giles	Brookes	Inwards		Giles
		29 Aug. 1614	*Steven* of Liverpool – 30 tons	Giles	Brookes	Inwards		Giles
168		23 Aug. 1614	*Guifte of God* of Strabane – 20 tons	Robert	Linseie		Outwards – Clyde	Earl of
		23 Aug. 1614	*Guifte of God* of Strabane – 20 tons	Robert	Linseie		Outwards – Clyde	Mathew
169		29 Aug. 1614	*Hopewell* of Leith – 70 tons	David	Coborne	Inwards		John
170		29 Aug. 1614	*Mary and James* of Dartmouth – 15 tons	Edward	Hardy	Inwards		City of
171		30 Aug. 1614	*Hopewell* of Leith – 70 tons	David	Coborne		Outwards – Bilbao	John
172		1 Sep. 1614	*Mary and James* of Dartmouth – 15 tons	Edward	Hardy		Outwards – Dartmouth	Edward
173		1 Sep. 1614	*Grace of God* of Burntisland – 30 tons	Thomas	Sunter		Outwards – Bilbao	John
174		5 Sep. 1614	*Steven* of Liverpool – 30 tons	Giles	Brookes		Outwards – Liverpool	Giles

Merchant Surname	Where Merchant is from	Goods	Total Value	Tax	Notes
Oldfers		Unnamed goods – £144.	£144	£7 4s.; £1 16s.	
Steward		Unnamed goods – £7 13s. 4d.	£7 13s. 4d.	7s. 8d.; 1s. 11d.	
Leeche		Unnamed goods – £1 19s.	£1 19s.	1s. 11d.; 5 3/4d.	
Donnell		Unnamed goods – £2.	£2	2s.; 6d.	
Gland		Unnamed goods – £3 5s.			
Keningham		Unnamed goods – £30.	£33 5s.	£1 13s. 3d.; 8s. 3 3/4d.	
Gland		Unnamed goods – £4.	£4	4s.; 1s.	
Stewarde		Unnamed goods – £10.	£10	10s.; 2s. 6d.	
Smithe		Unnamed goods – £3 10s.	£3 10s.	3s. 6d.	
Smithe		Unnamed goods – £21 7s. 7d.; 3 single Northern dozens – 10s.			
Sadler		Unnamed goods – £1 10s.			
Stanton		Unnamed goods – £41 17s. 5d.; 1/2 short cloth – 3s. 4d.			
Dalbye		Unnamed goods – £10.			
Lanckforde		Unnamed goods – £25 18s.			
Lee		Unnamed goods – £14 11s. 8d.			
Parry		Unnamed goods – £13 19s. 11d.			
Hamond		Unnamed goods – £5; 2 single Northern dozens – 6s. 8d.	£134 4s. 7d.	£6 14s. 2d.	
Brookes		Unnamed goods – £42 10s.	£42 10s.	£2 2s. 6d.	
Brookes		8 butts sack – 12s.	12s.		
Abercorn		Unnamed goods – £186 13s. 4d.			
Linseie		Unnamed goods – £10 7s. 6d.	£197 10d.	£9 17s. 0 1/2d.; £2 9s. 3d.	
Poore		Unnamed goods – £80.	£80	£4; £1.	
London		Unnamed goods – £118 7s. 4d.	£118 7s. 4d.	£5 18s. 4d.	
Poore		Unnamed goods – £675.	£675	£33 15s.; £8 8s. 9d.	
Hardy		Unnamed goods – £35 5s.	£35 5s.	£1 15s. 3d.	
Pierson		Unnamed goods – £234.	£234	£11 14s.; £2 18s. 6d.	
Brookes		Unnamed goods – £18.	£18	18s.	

Number	Folio	Date	Ship	Captain – Forename	Captain – Surname	Place – From	Place – To	Merchant Forename
175	f	5 Sep. 1614	Small boat of Scotland – 6 tons	John	Steward		Outwards – Ayr	Hugh
176		12 Sep. 1614	*Bride* of Londonderry – 30 tons	John	Hamlett		Outwards – Chester	Moses
		12 Sep. 1614	*Bride* of Londonderry – 30 tons	John	Hamlett		Outwards – Chester	Jesse
		12 Sep. 1614	*Bride* of Londonderry – 30 tons	John	Hamlett		Outwards – Chester	Henry
		12 Sep. 1614	*Bride* of Londonderry – 30 tons	John	Hamlett		Outwards – Chester	George
		16 Sep. 1614	*Bride* of Londonderry – 30 tons	John	Hamlett		Outwards – Chester	Jesse
		16 Sep. 1614	*Bride* of Londonderry – 30 tons	John	Hamlett		Outwards – Chester	William
		16 Sep. 1614	*Bride* of Londonderry – 30 tons	John	Hamlett		Outwards – Chester	George
177		14 Sep. 1614	*Hopewell* of Dumbarton – 12 tons	Saunder	Yeoven		Outwards	Saunder
		14 Sep. 1614	*Hopewell* of Dumbarton – 12 tons	Saunder	Yeoven		Outwards	James
178		14 Sep. 1614	Small boat of Scotland – 18 tons	William	Leeche		Outwards	Henry
179		21 Sep. 1614	*Guifte of God* of Strabane – 20 tons	Mathew	Linseye	Inwards		Mathew
180		24 Sep. 1614	*Consent* of London – 40 tons	Thomas	Evans		Outwards – London	John
181	f	25 Sep. 1614	Small boat of Scotland – 16 tons	Peter	Donnell		Outwards	Earl of
		25 Sep. 1614	Small boat of Scotland	Peter	Donnell		Outwards	William
		25 Sep. 1614	Small boat of Scotland – 16 tons	Peter	Donnell		Outwards	John

Portus London Derry. The whole year's account of the customs arising due in this port from Michaelmas 1614 to Michaelmas 1615 kept by Thomas Dolman for the farmers (TN/P07/1/4d)

Ingates

Number	Folio	Date	Ship	Captain – Forename	Captain – Surname	Place – From	Place – To	Merchant Forename
182	f	3 Oct. 1614	*Carvaile* of Coleraine – 50 tons	John	Bettson	Inwards		John
		4 Oct. 1614	*Carvaile* of Coleraine – 50 tons	John	Bettson	Inwards		Brute
183		4 Oct. 1614	*Peeter* of Londonderry – 70 tons	Wibrand	Oldfers	Inwards		Wibrand
184		4 Oct. 1614	*William* of Renfrew – 8 tons	Andrew	Cokeran	Inwards		Andrew
185	f	11 Oct. 1614	*John* of Dumbarton – 14 tons	John	Simple	Inwards		John

Merchant Surname	Where Merchant is from	Goods	Total Value	Tax	Notes
Hamelton		Unnamed goods – £34.	£34	£1 14s.; 8s. 6d.	
Dalbye		Unnamed goods – £6 13s. 4d.			
Smithe		Unnamed goods – £52 6s. 8d.			
Sadler		Unnamed goods – £9 10s.			
Hamond		Unnamed goods – £5.	£73 10s.	£3 13s. 6d.	
Smithe		Unnamed goods – £8 6s. 8d.			
Boulton		Unnamed goods – £24 14s. 2d.			
Hamond		Unnamed goods – £1 13s. 4d.	£34 14s. 2d.	£1 14s. 5d.	
Yeoven		Unnamed goods – £10.			
Stewarde		Unnamed goods – 15s.	£10 15s.	10s. 9d.; 2s. 8 1/4d.	
Noble		Unnamed goods – £12.	£12	12s.; 3s.	
Linsey		Unnamed goods – £2 5s.	£2 5s.	2s. 3d.; 6 3/4d.	Surnames as given.
Rowley		Unnamed goods – £345.	£345	£17 5s.	
Abercorn		Unnamed goods – £12 11s. 8d.			
Keningham Hamelton		Unnamed goods – £71 16s. 2d. Unnamed goods – £7 2s. 6d.	£91 10s. 4d.	£4 11s. 6d.; £1 2s. 10 1/2d.	
Bettson		40 tons coal – £10.	£10	10s.	
Hamond		Small wares – £36; hats – £10; friezes – £11; fustians and sackcloth – £10; stockings – £10; 1 pc. black stuff – £3.	£80	£4	
Oldfers		3000 Meiboroughe deals – £120; 1/2 last tar great bounde – £1 13s. 4d.	£121 13s. 4d.	£6 1s. 8d.; £1 10s. 5d.	
Cokeran		6 cwt iron – £3; 6 iron French pots – 10s.; 10 hhd salt – £2; 10 fkn soap – £5; 100 ells woollen cloth – £12 10s.; 1/2 cwt madder & 1/2 cwt alum – 18s. 4d.; 48 gallons aquavite – £3 4s.; 100 lbs grains – £3 14s. 8d.; 4 bushels apples – 1s. 4d.; 1 great brass pot – 4s.; 1 fkn nuts – 6d.; 80 yds linen cloth – £6 13s. 4d.; 2 doz. woolcards – 3s. 4d.; 1/2 cwt wrought iron – 5s.; 2 small kettles/7 lbs – 3s. 9d.	£38 8s. 3d.	£1 18s. 5d.; 9s. 7 1/4d.	
Simple		12 tons coal – £3; 1 bal wrought iron – £2 10s.; 128 lbs fat madder –	£15 2s. 8d.	15s. 1 1/2d.; 3s. 9 1/4d.	

Number	Folio	Date	Ship	Captain – Forename	Captain – Surname	Place – From	Place – To	Merchant Forename
186		19 Oct. 1614	*Margaret* of Renfrew – 8 tons	John	Enry	Inwards		John
		19 Oct. 1614	*Margaret* of Renfrew – 8 tons	John	Enry	Inwards		John
		19 Oct. 1614	*Margaret* of Renfrew – 8 tons	John	Enry	Inwards		William
		19 Oct. 1614	*Margaret* of Renfrew – 8 tons	John	Enry	Inwards		William
		24 Oct. 1614	*Margaret* of Renfrew – 8 tons	John	Enry	Inwards		John
187	f	23 Oct. 1614	*Bride* of Londonderry – 30 tons	John	Hamlett	Inwards		Richard
		23 Oct. 1614	*Bride* of Londonderry – 30 tons	John	Hamlett	Inwards		Jesse
		23 Oct. 1614	*Bride* of Londonderry – 30 tons	John	Hamlett	Inwards		Tristram
		23 Oct. 1614	*Bride* of Londonderry – 30 tons	John	Hamlett	Inwards		William
		23 Oct. 1614	*Bride* of Londonderry – 30 tons	John	Hamlett	Inwards		George
		23 Oct. 1614	*Bride* of Londonderry – 30 tons	John	Hamlett	Inwards		William
		23 Oct. 1614	*Bride* of Londonderry – 30 tons	John	Hamlett	Inwards		Michael
188	f	30 Oct. 1614	*Margaret* of [blank] – 8 tons	David	Crookewood	Inwards		Robert
189		4 Nov. 1614	*Guifte of God* of Glasgow – 10 tons	John	Wilson	Inwards		John
190		16 Nov. 1614	*Margaret* of Barnstaple – 16 tons	William	Verchilde	Inwards		Foulkes

Merchant Surname	Where Merchant is from	Goods	Total Value	Tax	Notes
		£1; 90 lbs alum – 17s.; 2 fkn soap – £1; 1 doz. pair gloves at 20d. per pair – £1; 2 doz. girdles – 4s.; 1 doz. purses – 3s.; 8 bushels apples – 2s. 8d.; 6 yds stuff – 15s.; 80 yds linen cloth – £3 6s. 8d.; 16 yds Welsh frieze – 16s.; 4 gallons aquavite – 5s. 4d.; 1 doz. cups – 3s.			
Eury		4 tons coal – £1; 12 yds Scots grey cloth – 12.			This load was valued and taxed separately from the rest of the consignment.
Strong		80 ells linen cloth – £3 6s. 8d.; 2 pair small plades – £1 12s.; 32 lbs alum – 5s 8d.; 12 bal salt – £1 4s.			
Steward		2 hhd salt – 8s.; 1 hhd onions – 2s. 8d.; 1 hhd apples – 2s. 8d.			
Nisbett		1 hhd onions – 2s. 8d.; 30 ells grey cloth – £2 10s.; 30 ells blue cloth – £3.	£14 6s. 4d.	14s. 3d.; 3s. 3 3/4d.	
Eury		1 bal aquavite – £2 13s. 4d.	£2 13s. 4d.	2s. 8d.; 8d.	
Sadler		10 tons coal – £2 10s.; 30 yds frieze £1 10s.; 3 broad cloths – £1.			
Smithe		2 pc. frieze, 78 goads cotton, 2 doz. unlined hats, other small wares – £16 7s. 8d.; 12 yds double bays – £1 12s.; 3 Yorkshire single dozens – 10s.; 3 kerseys – 6s. 8d.			
Berrisford		1 1/2 doz. children's hats – 15s.; 16 1/2 doz. unlined hats – £16 10s.; 4 doz. parcel lined hats – £5 6s. 8d.; 6 doz. hat bands – £1 4s.			
Langforde		6 cwt hops – £6; 6 doz. green glasses – 4s.; 1 doz. lanterns – 8s.; 17 ells Holland – £1 2s. 8d.; 1 pc Genoa fustian – 7s. 6d.; 6 doz. pair gloves – 12s.; 1 doz. silk garters – £1 8s.; 4 Bibles and 4 Psalters – 15s.; 4 pair boots – £1; 8 pair shoes – 8s.			
Hamond		2 grs course knives, 1 pc. say, other small wares – £53 2s. 2d.			
Parry		1 cwt wrought tin – £3.			
Graves		3 single Northern dozens – 10s.	£114 2s. 8d.	£8 9d.	
Woodroofe		3 nags – £6; 7 cows – £5 5s.	£11 5s.	11s. 3d.; 2s. 9 3/4d.	
Wilson		24 Scots gallons aquavite – £6; 24 ells linen cloth – £3 12s.; 40 yds woollen cloth – £6; 2 lasts salt – £2 8s.	£18	18s.; 4s. 6d.	
Downe		2 tons Spanish iron – £20; 1 ton English iron – £10; 3 hhd French vinegar – £1 15s.; 2 3/4 cwt. Madeira sugar – £9 3s. 4d.; 1 cwt. white powder sugar – £3 6s. 8d.; 1 bal & 3 fkn soap – £3 10s.; 26 bal French salt – £2 12s.; 1 cwt cotton weeke – £2 10s.; 33 yds Dowlas – £3 6s.; 10 doz. tin spoons and other small wares – £5; 40 yds			

Number	Folio	Date	Ship	Captain – Forename	Captain – Surname	Place – From	Place – To	Merchant Forename
191		23 Nov. 1614	*Jennet* of Irvine	Robert	Bourne	Inwards		Robert
192		30 Nov. 1614	*John* of Glasgow – 24 tons	William	Walt			
193	f	28 Dec. 1614	*John* of Renfrew – 20 tons	Adam	Moderwell			Adam
		28 Dec. 1614	*John* of Renfrew – 20 tons	Adam	Moderwell			George
194		21 Jan. 1615	*Blessing* of Glasgow – 45 tons	Duncan	Simple			Duncan
195		27 Jan. 1615	*Guifte of God* of Strabane – 20 tons	Matthew	Linsey			Matthew
196		27 Jan. 1615	*John* of Dumbarton – 20 tons	Peter	Donnell			Archibald
		27 Jan. 1615	*John* of Dumbarton – 20 tons	Peter	Donnell			David
		27 Jan. 1615	*John* of Dumbarton – 20 tons	Peter	Donnell			Hugh
197	f	27 Jan. 1615	*Greyhounde* of Londonderry – 24 tons	John	Slone			John
	f	2 Feb. 1615	*Greyhounde* of Londonderry – 24 tons	John	Slone			John
198		27 Jan. 1615	*Elizabeth* of Londonderry – 15 tons	John	Stewarde			Andrew
	f	27 Jan. 1615	*Elizabeth* of Londonderry – 15 tons	John	Stewarde			Alexander
199		27 Jan. 1615	*William* of Renfrew – 7 tons	Andrew	Cokeran			Andrew

Merchant Surname	Where Merchant is from	Goods	Total Value	Tax	Notes
		canvas – £2; 23 yds fine Dowlas – £2 13s.; 132 yds Dowlas – £6 12s.; 66 yds Dowlas – £3 11s. 6d.; 40 lbs pepper – £3 6s. 8d.; 14 lbs cinnamon – £2 6s. 8d. [f] 1 cwt currants – £1 10s.; 1 cwt prunes – 10s.; 160 yds coloured bays – £14 13s. 4d.; 12 bragen skillets – £1 6s.; 12 chopping hooks – 12s.; 24 iron shovels – £1 16s.; 12 hatchets, 12 coffer locks and other small wares – £1 10s.; 43 lbs pewter – £1 3s.; 2 great saws – 12s.; 2 smaller saws – 8s.; 120 doz. earthen pots – £8; 700 middle sort Newland fish – £5 16s. 8d.	£119 10s. 6d.	£5 19s. 6d.	
Bourne		30 gallons aquavite – £2 13s. 4d.; 1 cwt iron – 10s.; 30 yds woollen cloth – £3 15s.; 40 yds linen cloth – £1 10s.; 1/2 cwt fat madder – 8s.	£8 16s. 4d.	8s. 9 1/2d.; 2s. 2 1/4d.	
		1 tun French wine – 6s.; 40 bal salt – £4.		4s.; 1s.	Total not given.
Moderwell		10 tons coal – £2 10s.; 60 gallons aquavite – £4; 20 yds linen cloth – £1 13s. 4d.			
Orre		40 gallons aquavite – £3; 80 lbs alum – 14s. 3d.; 20 lbs fat madder – 3s.; 1/2 cwt rough hemp – 5s.; 5 doz. horse-shoes – 12s. 6d.; 12 yds woollen cloth – £1; 8 yds linen cloth – 13s. 4d.; 1 bal pitch – 3s. 4d.	£14 14s. 9d.	14s. 11d.; 3s. 9d.	
Simple		5 tons coal – £1 5s.	£1 5s.	1s. 3d.; 3 3/4d.	
Linsey		12 tons coal – £3; 1 ton salt – 16s.	£3 16s.	3s. 9 1/2d.; 11 1/4d.	
Harbinson		8 tons coal – £2; 100 yds woollen cloth – £10; 100 yds linen cloth – £4 13s. 4d.			
Mencriffe		5 cwt iron – £2 10s.; 2 1/2 lasts salt – £3.			
Tomson		48 gallons aquavite – £4; 12 iron pots – £1; 2 brewing kettles – £10.	£37 3s. 4d.	£1 17s. 2d.; 9s. 3 1/2d.	
Poore		17 tuns French wine – £5 2s.; 16 lbs loaf sugar – 10s.; 30 lbs whale bone – 15s.; 1 cwt prunes – 5s.	£1 10s.	1s. 6d.; 4 1/2d.	
Poore		5 tuns French wine – £1 10s.			
Dikes		14 tons coal – £3 10s.; 5 cwt iron – £2 10s.; 1 cwt fat madder – 16s. 8d.; 1 brass kettle/40 lbs – £1 1s. 5d.; 1 cwt alum – £1.	£8 18s. 1d.	8s. 10 3/4d.; 2s. 2 1/2d.	
Stewarde		20 gallons aquavite – £1 13s. 4d.; 60 yds linen cloth – £2 5s.; 2 grs knives – £1 2s.; 15 yds course lawn – £1 2s. 6d.	£6 2s. 10d.	6s. 1 1/2d.; 1s. 6 1/2d.	
Cokeran		2 tons coal – 10s.; 3 cwt iron – £1 10s.; 18 English gallons aquavite – £1 10s.; 2 hhd salt – 8s.; 10 doz. horse-shoes – £1 5s.; 20 lbs aniseeds –	£10 5s. 5d.	10s. 3d.; 2s. 6 3/4d.	

Number	Folio	Date	Ship	Captain – Forename	Captain – Surname	Place – From	Place – To	Merchant Forename
200	f	27 Jan. 1615	*Swallow* of Dumbarton – 20 tons	Peter	Williamson			John
201		30 Jan. 1615	*Roberte* of Dumbarton – 5 tons	Robert	Cohone			William
202	f	31 Jan. 1615	*John* of Dumbarton – 14 tons	John	Smithe			John
		31 Jan. 1615	*John* of Dumbarton – 14 tons	John	Smithe			David
203		1 Feb. 1615	Small boat of Largs	John	Ore			John
204		2 Feb. 1615	Small boat of Irvine	Theophilus	Smiter			Theophilus
205	f	15 Feb. 1615	*Margaret* of Renfrew – 8 tons	James	Eury			James
		15 Feb. 1615	*Margaret* of Renfrew – 8 tons	James	Eury			John

Merchant Surname	Where Merchant is from	Goods	Total Value	Tax	Notes
		5s. 4d.; 20 yds linen cloth – £2; 2 bal onions – 2s. 8d.; 12 yds grey cloth – £1 4s.; 1/2 hhd white salt – 2s. 8d.; [?] barrel staves – 10s.; [f] 10 gallons aquavite – 16s. 8d.; 4 lbs aniseeds – 1s. 1d.			
Cambell		12 tons coal – £3; 2 1/2 tons herring – £15; 4 cwt iron – £2; 40 yds linen cloth – £2; 30 yds woollen cloth – £3 15s.; 8 bal salt – 16s.	£29 11s.	£1 9s. 6d.; 7s. 4 1/2d.	
Kenningham		20 bal salt – £2; 120 yds grey cloth – £10; 120 yds linen cloth – £6; 30 small brass kettles/2 cwt – £6; 4 brass brewing kettles 40 lbs each – £4 5s.; 22 iron pots – £1 16s. 8d.; 4 brass pots 40 lbs each – £4 5s.; 1/2 tons iron – £5; 1 cwt crop madder – £1 6s. 8d.; 1 cwt alum – £1; 1/2 cwt aniseeds – 15s.; 1/2 ld grains – £1 9s.; 10 lbs pepper – 16s. 8d.; 1 doz. wool cards – 10s.; hats hatbands pins points buttons knives and white starch – £4; 1 bal soap – £2; 1/2 bal orchid – 10s.; 20 yds woollen cloth – £4; 10 gallons aquavite – 16s. 8d.	£56 12s.	£2 16s. 7d.; 14s. 1 3/4d.	
Smithe		8 tons coal – £2; 96 lbs alum – 17s. 1d.; 1/2 bal soap – £1; 12 lbs gunpowder – 2s. 10d.; 1 ton salt – 16s.; 16 lbs white starch – 2s. 10d.; 4 doz. coarse gloves – 8s.; 8 gallons aquavite – 13s. 4d.; 1 brass brewing kettle/80 lbs – £2 2s. 10d.			
Morrison		1/2 bal soap – £1; 60 lbs fat madder – 8s. 11d.; 160 lbs iron – 14s. 3d.; brass pans/10 lbs – 5s. 4d.; 1 small bal wrought iron – £1 4s.; 10 yds woollen cloth – 16s. 8d.; 30 yds course linen cloth – £1; 6 lbs aniseeds – 1s. 7d.; 2 iron pots – 3s. 4d.; 14 lbs lead – 10d.	£13 17s. 10d.	13s. 10 3/4d.; 3s. 6d.	
Ore		5 tons coal – £1 5s.; 1 bal herring – 15s.; 1 cwt iron – 10s.	£2 10s.	2s. 6d.; 7 1/2d.	
Smiter		6 tons coal – £1 10s.; 28 gallons aquavite – £2 6s. 8d.; 20 ells grey cloth – £2.	£5 16s. 8d.	5s. 10d.; 1s. 5 1/2d.	
Eury		16 gallons aquavite – £1 6s. 8d.; 20 yd woollen cloth – £1 13s. 4d.; 1 ton salt – 16s.; 320 lbs iron – £1 8s. 6d.; 1/2 cwt rough hemp – 5s.; 1 brass kettle – £1 10s.; 1 doz. door locks – 12s.; 1 doz. horse locks – 12s.			
Strong		1 cwt cropp madder – £1 6s. 8d.; 1/2 cwt alum – 10s.; bone lace – £1; 2 half pc fustians – 15s.; 4 grs knives – £3 12s.; 14 yds blue cloth – £1 15s.; 10 yds grey cloth – £1; 18 doz. combs – 9s.; 100 yds linen cloth – £6 13s. 4d.; 1 doz. wool cards – 10s.; 2 doz. bridles – 10s.; 2 doz. stirrup-leathers with some stirrups – 13s. 4d.			

Number	Folio	Date	Ship	Captain – Forename	Captain – Surname	Place – From	Place – To	Merchant Forename
		15 Feb. 1615	*Margaret* of Renfrew – 8 tons	James	Eury			William
		15 Feb. 1615	*Margaret* of Renfrew – 8 tons	James	Eury			Robert
		15 Feb. 1615	*Margaret* of Renfrew – 8 tons	James	Eury			John
		15 Feb. 1615	*Margaret* of Renfrew – 8 tons	James	Eury			Patrick
		15 Feb. 1615	*Margaret* of Renfrew – 8 tons	James	Eury			George
	f	24 Feb. 1615	*Margaret* of Renfrew – 8 tons	James	Eury			John
206		15 Feb. 1615	*Hopwell* of Ayr – 20 tons	John	Barkely			John
207	f	15 Feb. 1615	*Joane* of Renfrew – 5 tons	Ringen	Hunter			Ringen
208		20 Feb. 1615	Small boat of Scotland	John	Harvy			John
209		20 Feb. 1615	Small boat of Scotland	David	Crookwoode			David
210		20 Feb. 1615	*Margaret* of Clyde (a small boat)	Robert	Morrison			Robert
		20 Feb. 1615	*Margaret* of Clyde (a small boat)	Robert	Morrison			John
211		20 Feb. 1615	*Margaret* of Irvine – 5 tons	James	Morrison			James
212		3 Mar. 1615	*Hopwell* of Largs – 5 tons	Matthew	Wilson			Matthew
213	f	3 Mar. 1615	*Edward* of Hilbre – 30 tons	John	Hamlett			John

Merchant Surname	Where Merchant is from	Goods	Total Value	Tax	Notes
Hamelton		8 yds grey cloth – 13s. 4d.; 1/2 ton salt – 8s.; 1 1/2 bal onions – 2s.			
Booke		128 lbs cropp madder – £1 10s. 5d.; 48 lbs alum – 8s. 6d.; 5 doz. purses – 5s.; 4 doz. gloves – 12s.; 1 pair [?] – 16s. 8d.; 40 yds linen cloth – £2 13s. 4d.; 400 lbs iron – £1 15s. 8d.; 4 bal salt – 8s.			
Hamill		80 lbs cropp madder – 19s.; 32 lbs alum – 5s. 8d.; 1 pair pladdes – 16s. 8d.; 5 hats – £1; 60 ells linen cloth – £2 5s.; 8 yds linen cloth – 16s.; 24 yds grey cloth – £1 16s.; 20 [RJH suggests yds should be here] parchment lace – £1 3s. 4d.; 2 doz. scissors – 3s. 4d.; [f] 17 Scots daggers – 17s.; 2 doz. knives – 5s. 4d.; 9 pair spurs – 2s. 3d.; 96 yds coarse woollen cloth – £1 12s.; 13 yds linsey–wolsey – 13s.; 2 doz. belts – 8s.; 6 lbs indigo – £1 4s.; bone lace – 15s.; 2 1/2 doz. blue bonnets – £1 10s.			
Forsithe		4 yds grey cloth – 6s. 8d.; 50 ells linen cloth – £3 6s. 8d.; 1 doz. spurs – 5s.; 2 grs knives – £2 8s.; 48 yds bone lace – 8s.; 3 pc. [?] lawn – 10s.; 10 bridles with snaffles – 10s.; 2 doz. [?] pins – 6s.; 2 grs leather points – 6d.			
Leather		6 skins Spanish leather – £1 10s.			
Loggie		Locks, bands, spoons, aquavite, fish and other goods – £20.	£80 13s. 2d.	£4 8s.; £1 2d.	
		7 hhd French wine – 10s. 6d.; 14 tons coal – £3 10s.; 1 bal soap – £2; 1 cwt white starch – £1; 800 lbs iron – £3 11s. 5d.; 56 gallons aquavite – £3 14s.; 80 yds woollen cloth – £10; 12 lbs gunpowder – 2s. 10d.; 3 stone flax – 4s. 3d.; 3 lbs pudding tobacco – £1 10s.; 24 gallons honey – £1 2s. 6d.	£26 15s. 8d.	£1 6s. 9d.; 6s. 8 1/4d.	No merchant listed.
Hunter		1 ton 3 hhd salt – £1 8s.; 8 gallons aquavite – 13s. 4d.; 1 cwt alum – £1; 1 cwt fat madder – 16s. 8d.; 60 yds linen cloth – £5; 20 yds woollen cloth – £1 13s. 4d.; 20 lbs brass – 10s. 8d.; 6 iron pots – 10s.	£11 12s.	11s. 7d.; 2s. 10 3/4d.	
Harvy		5 tons coal – £1 5s.	£1 5s.	1s. 3d.; 3 3/4d.	
Crookwoode		5 tons coal – £1 5s.	£1 5s.	1s. 3d.; 3 3/4d.	
Morrison		1 1/2 ld codfish – £3.			
Keningham		80 codfish – £1 6s. 8d.	£4 6s. 8d.	4s. 4d.; 1s. 1d.	
Morrison		5 tons coal – £1 5s.	£1 5s.	1s. 3d.; 3 3/4d.	
Wilson		5 tons coal – £1 5s.; codfish – £1 10s.	£2 15s.	2s. 9d.; 8 1/4d.	
Hamlett		6 tons coal – £1 10s.			

Number	Folio	Date	Ship	Captain – Forename	Captain – Surname	Place – From	Place – To	Merchant Forename
		3 Mar. 1615	*Edward* of Hilbre – 30 tons	John	Hamlett			Jesse
		3 Mar. 1615	*Edward* of Hilbre – 30 tons	John	Hamlett			John
		3 Mar. 1615	*Edward* of Hilbre – 30 tons	John	Hamlett			John
		3 Mar. 1615	*Edward* of Hilbre – 30 tons	John	Hamlett			David
		3 Mar. 1615	*Edward* of Hilbre – 30 tons	John	Hamlett			Richard
		3 Mar. 1615	*Edward* of Hilbre – 30 tons	John	Hamlett			William
214	f	6 Mar. 1615	*Blessing* of Burntisland – 45 tons	David	Barran			William
215		6 Mar. 1615	*Hopwell* of Dumbarton – 12 tons	Saunder	Yeoven			Saunder
216		6 Mar. 1615	*Grace of God* of Greenock – 10 tons	John	Hunter			John
217		9 Mar. 1615	*William* of Dumbarton – 6 tons	Allen	Ellison			Allen
218		23 Mar. 1615	*Thomas* of Renfrew – 7 tons	Thomas	Jacson			Thomas
219	f	6 Mar. 1615	*Hopwell* of Renfrew – 6 tons	John	Bonde[?]			David
Outgates								
220	f	8 Oct. 1614	*Blessing* of Leith – 56 tons	David	Barran	Londonderry	Diepe	John
221		2 Nov. 1614	*Bride* of Londonderry – 30 tons	John	Hamlett	Londonderry	Chester	Jesse
		2 Nov. 1614	*Bride* of Londonderry – 30 tons	John	Hamlett	Londonderry	Chester	William

Merchant Surname	Where Merchant is from	Goods	Total Value	Tax	Notes
Smithe		2 pc. grey frieze, 81 goads Kendal cottons, 2 doz. unlined hats and other small wares – £26; 36 yds double bays – £2 14s.; 3 Yorkshire dozens – 13s. 4d.; 4 pc. kersey – 8s. 10d.			
Rowley		8 doz. unlined hats – £8; 6 doz. parcel lined hats – £7 10s.			
Leach		1 cwt. sugar, 5 pc. Genoa fustians, 1 pc. Bolton fustian and other wares – £39 5s. 8d.; 1 single Yorkshire dozen – 3s. 4d.			
Evans		1 grs course knives – £1 10s.; 2 half pc. English fustians – £1; 36 yds three thread grogham – £1 6s. 8d.; 2 doz. unlined hats – £2; 1/2 cwt wrought iron – 5s.; 5 cwt wrought tin – £15; 2 Yorkshire single dozens – 6s. 8d.			
Stanton		101 yds double bays – £7 11s. 6d.; small wares – £19 10s.; 115 yds broad cloth reckoned 3 short cloths – £1 6s. 8d.; 36 single Devonshire dozens – £3.			
Parry		5 doz. unlined hats – £5; 5 fkn soap – £2 10s.; 80 lbs Malaga raisins – 9s. 6d.; 4 cwt lead – £1 6s. 8d.; 35 yds huswifes cloth – £2 10d.; 1/2 grs box combs – 2s. 6d.; 1 bal nails – £4.	£148 12s. 4d.	£7 8s. 7d.	
Rogers		2 tuns French wine – 12s.; 400 bal salt – £40; 8 bal meal – £2; small wares – £20.	£62	£3 2s.; 15s. 6d.	
Even		1 hhd French wine – 1s. 6d.; 3 hhd salt – 12s.; 192 lbs iron – 8s. 6d.; 4 gallons aquavite – 6s. 8d.; 6 yds blue cloth – 9s.; 64 lbs lead – 3s. 9d.	£1 19s. 11d.	2s.; 6d.	
Hunter		10 tons coal – £2 10s.	£2 10s.	2s. 6d.; 7 1/2d.	
Ellison		1 ton coal – 5s.; 20 gallons aquavite £1 13s. 4d.; 10 iron pots – 16s.; 8d.; 96 lbs pitch – 4s.; 6 locks – 4s.; 1 fkn onions – 4d.	£3 3s. 4d.	3s. 2d.; 9 1/2d.	
Jacson		24 bal salt – £2 8s.	£2 8s.	2s. 4 1/2d.; 7d.	
Wemes		1 hhd vinegar – 11s. 8d.; 2 cwt prunes – £1; 4 doz. iron pots – £4; 1 hhd and 2 bal drinking glasses – 13s. 4d.; 240 lbs iron – 10s. 8d.; 14 gallons aquavite – £1 3s. 4d.; 7 bal salt – 14s.; 1 doz. glass bottles – 6s. 8d.	£8 19s. 8d.	9s.; 2s. 3d.	
Poore		54 tons salmon – £486; 10 dickers hides – £50; 7 1/2 cwt tallow – £7 10s.; 1 cwt yarn – £3 6s. 8d.	£546 16s. 8d.	£27 6s. 10d.; £6 16s. 8 1/2d.	
Smithe		15 dickers hides – £75; 5 dickers kips – £16 13s. 4d.; 3 hhd salmon – £6 15s.			
Langforde		20 cwt tallow – £20; 2 tons 1 bal 1 fkn salmon – £19 8s.; 1 ton beef – £16; 188 lbs yarn – £5 11s. 10d.			

Number	Folio	Date	Ship	Captain – Forename	Captain – Surname	Place – From	Place – To	Merchant Forename
		2 Nov. 1614	*Bride* of Londonderry – 30 tons	John	Hamlett	Londonderry	Chester	William
		2 Nov. 1614	*Bride* of Londonderry – 30 tons	John	Hamlett	Londonderry	Chester	Henry
		2 Nov. 1614	*Bride* of Londonderry – 30 tons	John	Hamlett	Londonderry	Chester	Richard
222	f	5 Nov. 1614	*John* of Dumbarton – 14 tons	John	Smithe	Londonderry	Scotland	John
223		9 Nov. 1614	*William* of Renfrew – 8 tons	Andrew	Cockran	Londonderry	Renfrew	Andrew
		9 Nov. 1614	*William* of Renfrew – 8 tons	Andrew	Cockran	Londonderry	Renfrew	Thomas
		9 Nov. 1614	*William* of Renfrew – 8 tons	Andrew	Cockran	Londonderry	Renfrew	John
		9 Nov. 1614	*William* of Renfrew – 8 tons	Andrew	Cockran	Londonderry	Renfrew	John
		9 Nov. 1614	*William* of Renfrew – 8 tons	Andrew	Cockran	Londonderry	Renfrew	Thomas
		9 Nov. 1614	*William* of Renfrew – 8 tons	Andrew	Cockran	Londonderry	Renfrew	John
224	f	14 Nov. 1614	*Guifte of God* of Strabane – 20 tons	Robert	Linseye	Londonderry	Clyde	Earl of
		14 Nov. 1614	*Guifte of God* of Strabane – 20 tons	Robert	Linseye	Londonderry	Clyde	Hugh
		14 Nov. 1614	*Guifte of God* of Strabane – 20 tons	Robert	Linseye	Londonderry	Clyde	Robert
225		28 Nov. 1614	*Margaret* of Southend (Kintyre) – 7 tons	David	Crookwood	Londonderry	Southend	John
226		6 Dec. 1614	*John* of Glasgow – 24 tons	James	Mellin	Londonderry	England	William
227		6 Dec. 1614	*Margaret* of Renfrew – 8 tons	John	Enry	Londonderry	Renfrew	John
228	f	9 Dec. 1614	*Henry* of Londonderry – 12 tons	Henry	Robinson	Londonderry	Glasgow	Henry
		9 Dec. 1614	*Henry* of Londonderry – 12 tons	Henry	Robinson	Londonderry	Glasgow	John
		9 Dec. 1614	*Henry* of Londonderry – 12 tons	Henry	Robinson	Londonderry	Glasgow	John
		9 Dec. 1614	*Henry* of Londonderry – 12 tons	Henry	Robinson	Londonderry	Glasgow	William
229		30 Dec. 1614	*Margaret* of Barnstaple – 18 tons	William	Verchilde	Londonderry	Barnstaple	Foulkes

Merchant Surname	Where Merchant is from	Goods	Total Value	Tax	Notes
Parry		1 pack yarn – £13 6s. 8d.; 2 bal salmon – £2 5s.; 3 cwt tallow – £3; 6 bal beef – £12; 7 dickers hides – £35; 3 dickers kips – £10; 300 sheepskins – £2 5s.			
Sadler		3 cwt rough tallow – £6; 3 dickers hides – £15.			
Sadler		6 bal beef – £12; 1 dicker hides – £5; 1/2 dicker kips – £1 13s. 4d.			
Smithe		2 1/2 dickers hides – £12 10s.; 16 cows – £8; 6 horses vocat garrons – £3 12s.; 7 bal beef – £14; 16 bal oats – £10 13s. 4d.; 224 lbs cheese – 16s. 8d.; 100 sheepskins – 15s.; 80 lbs tallow – 10s.	£50 17s.	£2 10s. 9d.; 12s. 8 1/4d.	
Cokeran		4 cwt cheese – £1 6s. 8d.; 5 bal beef – £10; 50 sheepskins – 7s. 6d.; 50 lambskins – 5s.; 2 dickers hides – £10.			
McMare		1 hhd beef – £4.			
Bersban		5 cwt cheese – £1 13s. 4d.; 3 cwt butter – £2.			
Bibbie		4 bal malt – £2 13s. 4d.; 2 cwt cheese – 13s. 4d.			
Redgate		1 1/2 dicker hides – £7 10s.; 50 sheepskins – 7s. 6d.			
Fleming		3 cwt cheese – £1.	£41 16s. 8d.	£2 1s. 10d.; 10s. 5 1/2d.	
Abercorn		32 hhd beef – £128; 5 1/2 cwt tallow – £5 10s.; 6 dickers hides – £30; 10 bal oats – £13 6s. 8d.			
Coen		95 sheepskins and goatskins – 15s.; 22 hides – £11.			
Linsey		4 hhd beef – £16.	£204 11s. 8d.	£10 4s. 7d.; £2 11s. 1 3/4d.	
Keningham		80 bal oats – £53 6s. 8d.; 2 hides – £1; 1 hhd beef – £4.	£58 6s. 8d.	£2 18s. 4d.; 14s. 7d.	
Watt		156 bal beef – £312; 32 cwt tallow – £32; 16 dickers hides – £80.	£424	£21 4s.; £5 6s.	
Strong		10 dickers hides – £50; 10 dickers kips – £33 6s. 8d.; 24 bal beef – £48; 2 cwt tallow – £2.	£133 6s. 8d.	£6 13s. 4d.; £1 13s. 4d.	
Robinson		1 ton beef – £16; 1 cwt Meiboroughe deals – £4; 2 dicker hides – £10.			
Bawby		10 hides – £5; 2 beeves – £1 6s. 8d.			
Luggie		2 bal beef – £4; 1 hhd oatmeal – £1 6s. 8d.; 3 dickers hides – £15; 50 sheepskins – 7s. 8d.			
Somerell		8 hides – £4.	£61 10s.	£3 1s. 0 1/2d.; 15s. 3d.	
Downe		8 tons beef – £128; 2 tons 7 bal pork – £46; 7 cwt 70 lbs rendered tallow – £7 12s. 6d.; 42 hides – £21; 1 hhd train oil – £1; 1/2 cwt linen yarn – £1 13s. 4d.	£205 5s. 10d.	£10 5s. 3 1/2d.	

Number	Folio	Date	Ship	Captain – Forename	Captain – Surname	Place – From	Place – To	Merchant Forename
230		5 Jan. 1615	*Guifte of God* of Glasgow – 8 tons	John	Wilson	Londonderry	Glasgow	John
231	f	12 Jan. 1615	*Jennet* of Irvine – 9 tons	Robert	Bourne	Londonderry	Irvine	Robert
232		10 Feb. 1615	*Blessing* of Glasgow – 45 tons	Duncan	Simple	Londonderry	Chester	Jesse
		10 Feb. 1615	*Blessing* of Glasgow – 45 tons	Duncan	Simple	Londonderry	Chester	Henry
		10 Feb. 1615	*Blessing* of Glasgow – 45 tons	Duncan	Simple	Londonderry	Chester	William
233		27 Feb. 1615	*Peeter* of Londonderry – 70 tons	Wibrand	Oldphers	Londonderry	Norway	Wibrand
234		27 Feb. 1615	Two small boats of Scotland	William & John	Ballentine & Ore	Londonderry	Scotland	John
235		27 Feb. 1615	*Jennet* of Renfrew – 16 tons	Andrew	Knockes	Londonderry	Renfrew	Andrew
236	f	27 Feb. 1615	*Mary Grace* of Burntisland – 40 tons	John	Browne	Londonderry	Plymouth	William
237		27 Feb. 1615	*John* of Renfrew – 20 tons	Adam	Moderwell	Londonderry	Renfrew	Adam
		27 Feb. 1615	*John* of Renfrew – 20 tons	Adam	Moderwell	Londonderry	Renfrew	John
		27 Feb. 1615	*John* of Renfrew – 20 tons	Adam	Moderwell	Londonderry	Renfrew	Andrew
238		27 Feb. 1615	*William* of Renfrew – 8 tons	Andrew	Cokeran	Londonderry	Renfrew	Andrew
		27 Feb. 1615	*William* of Renfrew – 8 tons	Andrew	Cokeran	Londonderry	Renfrew	William
		27 Feb. 1615	*William* of Renfrew – 8 tons	Andrew	Cokeran	Londonderry	Renfrew	Alexander
239	f	7 Mar. 1615	*Greyhound* of Londonderry	Patrick	Murdach	Londonderry	France	John
240		10 Mar. 1615	*Margaret* of Southend Kintyre	David	Cirkwood	Londonderry	Southend	David
241		11 Mar. 1615	*John* of Dumbarton – 14 tons	John	Smith	Londonderry	Dumbarton	John
242		13 Mar. 1615	*John* of Renfrew	Ringen	Hunter	Londonderry	Renfrew	Ringen
243	f	13 Mar. 1615	*Jennet* of Mongavlin	Walter	Ore	Londonderry	Scotland	John

Merchant Surname	Where Merchant is from	Goods	Total Value	Tax	Notes
Wilson		30 bal beef – £60; 10 dickers hides – £50; 640 lbs tallow – £5 14s. 3d.; 2 doz. sheepskins – 3s.	£115 17s. 3d.	£5 15s. 10d.; £1 8s. 11 1/2d.	
Bourne		12 bal beef – £24; 36 hides – £18; 1 1/2 cwt rough tallow – £1 10s.	£43 10s.	£2 3s. 6d.; 10s. 10 1/2d.	
Smithe		15 dickers hides – £75; 10 dickers hides vocat kips – £50; 8 hhd beef – £32; 20 cwt tallow – £20.			
Sadler		8 dickers hides – £40; 4 dickers hides vocat kips – £20; 16 tons beef – £256; 20 cwt tallow – £20.			
Langford		8 tons beef – £128; 30 cwt tallow – £30.	£671	£33 11s.	
Oldphers		15 bal butter – £20; 100 bal oats – £66 13s. 4d.	£86 13s. 4d.	£4 6s. 8d.; £1 1s. 8d.	
Cambell		140 bal oats – £93 6s. 8d.	£93 6s. 8d.	£4 13s. 4d.; £1 3s. 4d.	Two captains listed, William Ballentine & John Ore.
Knockes		120 bal oats – £80.	£80	£4; £1.	
Rogers		12 tons beef – £192; 21 cwt tallow – £21; 80 hides – £40; 80 hides vocat kips – £40; 1 hhd 1 bal salmon – £3 7s. 6d.; 1 1/2 bal pork – £3; 100 sheepskins – 15s.	£300 2s. 6d.	£15 1 1/2d.; £3 15s. 0 1/2d.	
Moderwell		140 bal oats – £93 6s. 8d.			
Browne		160 goatskins – £1; 1 dicker hides – £5.			
Cohone		2 dickers hides – £10.	£109 6s. 8d.	£5 9s. 4d.; £1 7s. 4d.	
Cokeran		3 dickers hides – £15; 24 deal boards – 16s.; 6 bal oatmeal – £4.			
Hamelton		6 bal oatmeal – £4; 2 hhd beef – £8; 15 hides – £7 10s.; 1/2 cwt tallow – 10s.			
Steward		1 ton beef – £16; 4 dickers hides – £20.	£75 16s.	£3 15s. 9 1/2d.; 18s. 11 1/4d.	
Banckes		60 dickers hides – £300; 7 dickers hides vocat kips – £35; 52 cwt tallow – £52; 1 bal 4 fkn butter – £2 13s. 4d.; 7 cleanes wool – £18 6s.; 5 cwt lqr 5 lbs candles – £9 17s. 8d.; 76 lbs brass – £2 8d.; 16 stagskins – £2 13s. 4d.; 60 sealskins – £5; 3 martinskins – 15s.; 20 goatskins – 2s. 2d.	£428 8s. 2d.	£21 8s. 4 1/2d.	
Cirkwood		40 bal oats – £26 13s. 4d.; 3 hhd beef – £12; 1 hhd butter – £2 13s. 4d.; 640 lbs cheese – £1 18s. 1d.	£43 4s. 9d.	£2 3s. 2 3/4d.; 10s. 9 1/2d.	
Smith		40 hhd oats – £53 6s. 8d.; 2 dickers hides – £10.	£63 6s. 8d.	£3 3s. 4d.; 15s. 10d.	
Hunter		30 bal oats – £20; 7 bal oatmeal – £4 13s. 4d.; 1 dicker hides – £5; 416 lbs tallow – £2 5s. 8d.	£31 19s.	£1 11s. 11d.; 7s. 11 3/4d.	
Beton		40 bal oats – £26 13s. 4d.; 7 hides – £3 15s.; 40 sheepskins – 5s.; 48 lambskins – 4s.; 1 bal beef – £2; 1 bal oatmeal – 13s. 4d.; 1 cwt tallow – £1.	£34 10s. 8d.	£1 14s. 6d.; 8s. 7 1/2d.	

Number	Folio	Date	Ship	Captain – Forename	Captain – Surname	Place – From	Place – To	Merchant Forename
244		13 Mar. 1615	*Roberte* of Dumbarton	Robert	Chohone	Londonderry	Dumbarton	William
245		13 Mar. 1615	*Grace of God* of Greenock	John	Hunter	Londonderry	Scotland	John
246		14 Mar. 1615	Small boat of Greenock	Gabriell	Hone	Londonderry	Scotland	Gabriell
247	f	14 Mar. 1615	Small boat of Scotland	James	Bleare	Londonderry	Scotland	Robert
248		16 Mar. 1615	*Elizabeth* of Londonderry – 15 tons	John	Penny	Londonderry	Chester	Brute
		16 Mar. 1615	*Elizabeth* of Londonderry – 15 tons	John	Penny	Londonderry	Chester	George
249		24 Mar. 1615	*Edwarde* of Hilbre	John	Hamlet	Londonderry	Chester	Jesse
		24 Mar. 1615	*Edwarde* of Hilbre	John	Hamlet	Londonderry	Chester	George
Ingates								
250		4 Apr. 1615	*Bride* of Londonderry – 20 tons	George	Woodroofe		Londonderry	Richard
		4 Apr. 1615	*Bride* of Londonderry – 20 tons	George	Woodroofe		Londonderry	George
251		14 Apr. 1615	*Peeter* of Londonderry – 70 tons	Wibrand	Oldphers		Londonderry	Wibrand
252		18 Apr. 1615	*Roberte* of Renfrew – 8 tons	Robert	Landles		Londonderry	Robert
253		21 Apr. 1615	*Roberte* of Renfrew – 8 tons	Robert	Robinson		Londonderry	John
254		24 Apr. 1615	*William* of Northam – 10 tons	William	Jefferye		Londonderry	William
255	f	24 Apr. 1615	*Thomas* of Clyde – 6 tons	Thomas	Lan		Londonderry	Thomas
256		25 Apr. 1615	*Jonathan* of Saltcoats – 12 tons	John	Browne		Londonderry	Sir James
257		25 Apr. 1615	*Jennet* of Dumbarton – 4 tons	Thomas	Morrison		Londonderry	Thomas
258		27 Apr. 1615	*John* of Renfrew – 6 tons	Andrew	Cokeran		Londonderry	Andrew
		27 Apr. 1615	*John* of Renfrew – 6 tons	Andrew	Cokeran		Londonderry	Alexander

Merchant Surname	Where Merchant is from	Goods	Total Value	Tax	Notes
Kenningham		240 hides – £120; 120 hides vocat kips – £60; 300 goatskins – £2; 100 sheepskins – 15s.; 7 bal beef – £14; 4 cwt tallow – £4; 1/2 bal butter – 13s. 4d.; 16 foxskins – £1 6s. 8d.; 4 otter skins – 10s.; 3 marten skins – 15s.	£204	£10 4s.; £2 11s.	
Bartly		3 tons beef – £48; 3 dickers hides – £15; 2 cwt tallow – £2; 50 sheepskins – 7s. 6d.	£65 7s. 6d.	£3 5s. 4 1/2d.; 16s. 4d.	
Hone		40 bal oats – £26 13s. 4d.; 7 hides – £3 15s.; 2 bal oatmeal – £1 6s. 8d.	£31 15s.	£1 11s. 9d.; 7s. 11 1/4d.	
Porter		2 dickers hides – £10.	£10	10s.; 2s. 6d.	
Hamond		6 dickers hides – £30; 3 tons beef – £48; 1 pack yarn – £13 6s. 8d.			
Hamond		5 dickers hides – £25; 6 bal beef – £12; 5 cwt tallow – £5.	£133 6s. 8d.	£6 13s. 4d.	
Smithe		5 dickers hides – £25.			
Hamond		1 1/2 packs yarn – £20; 3 1/2 cwt tallow – £3 10s.	£48 10s.	£2 8s. 6d.	
Sadler		10 tons coal – £2 10s.; 5 doz. unlined hats – £5; 16 yds coarse kersey – £1 12s.			
Hamond		2 doz. stock locks – 6s.; 1 doz. woolcards – 10s.	£9 18s.	9s. 10 3/4d.	
Oldphers		3000 Meiboroughe deals – £100.	£100	£5; £1 5s.	
Landlers		2 tons coal – 10s.	10s.	6d.; 1 1/2d.	
Loggie		5 hhd French salt – £1.	£1	1s.; 3d.	
Jefferye		1 pipe Canary wine – 1s. 6d.; 30 doz. earthen ware – £4 10s.; 2 hhd vinegar – £1 3s. 4d.; 7 cwt lead – £2 6s. 8d.; 1/2 ton iron – £5; 60 yds woollen cloth – £7 10s.; 2 bal apples – 2s.; wrought pewter – £3; 20 lbs loaf sugar – £1; 3 fkn soap – £1 10s.; 1 cwt Castile soap – £1 17s. 4d.			
Lan		3 tons coal – 15s.	15s.	9d.; 2 1/4d.	
Keningham		12 tons coal – £3; 2 bal Spanish salt – 5s. 4d.	£3 5s. 4d.	3s. 3d.; 9 3/4d.	
Morrison		4 cows – £2.	£2	2s.; 6d.	
Cokeran		4 hhd biscuit – £3 6s. 8d.; 16 English gallons aquavite – £1 6s. 8d.; 2 tons coal – 10s.			
Steward		40 lbs brass – £1 1s. 5d.; 80 lbs cropp madder – 19s.; 2 grs coarse knives – £2 10s.; 1 grs thread points – 10s.; 1/2 cwt alum – 10s.; 1/2 cwt loggwood – 5s.; 1/2 grs thread buttons – 2s. 6d.; 60 yds linen cloth – £3 10s.; 3 doz. pair playing cards – 5s.; 6 doz. wood combs – 1s. 8d.			

Number	Folio	Date	Ship	Captain – Forename	Captain – Surname	Place – From	Place – To	Merchant Forename
		27 Apr. 1615	*John* of Renfrew – 6 tons	Andrew	Cokeran		Londonderry	John
	f	27 Apr. 1615	*John* of Renfrew – 6 tons	Andrew	Cokeran		Londonderry	William
		27 Apr. 1615	*John* of Renfrew – 6 tons	Andrew	Cokeran		Londonderry	John
		27 Apr. 1615	*John* of Renfrew – 6 tons	Andrew	Cokeran		Londonderry	George
259		27 Apr. 1615	*John* of Renfrew – 6 tons	Adam	Moderwell		Londonderry	William
260		27 Apr. 1615	*Jennet* of Glasgow – 12 tons	John	Moderill		Londonderry	Sir William
261		1 May 1615	*John* of Glasgow – 6 tons	John	Wilson		Londonderry	John
262		8 May 1615	*Grace of God* of Burntisland – 40 tons	Thomas	Sunter		Londonderry	William
	f	12 May 1615	*Grace of God* of Burntisland – 40 tons	Thomas	Sunter		Londonderry	William
263		8 May 1615	Small boat of Scotland – 8 tons	James	Rogers		Londonderry	James
264		8 May 1615	*Roberte* of Dumbarton – 5 tons	Robert	Cohone		Londonderry	Robert
		8 May 1615	*Roberte* of Dumbarton – 5 tons	Robert	Cohone		Londonderry	William
265		9 May 1615	*Mary* of Neston – 16 tons	William	Rider		Londonderry	William
		9 May 1615	*Mary* of Neston – 16 tons	William	Rider		Londonderry	William
		9 May 1615	*Mary* of Neston – 16 tons	William	Rider		Londonderry	Walter
266		9 May 1615	Small boat of Scotland – 6 tons	John	Warden		Londonderry	John
267	f	9 May 1615	*Grace of God* of Irvine – 4 tons	Walter	Stewarde		Londonderry	Walter
268		9 May 1615	*Guifte of God* of Strabane – 20 tons	Robert	Linseye		Londonderry	Robert
269		10 May 1615	*Michaell* of Parton – 20 tons	Thomas	Saunderson		Londonderry	Thomas
270		12 May 1615	*Henry* of Ayr – 12 tons	James	Melon		Londonderry	John
		12 May 1615	*Henry* of Ayr – 12 tons	James	Melon		Londonderry	Sir John
		12 May 1615	*Henry* of Ayr – 12 tons	James	Melon		Londonderry	John

Merchant Surname	Where Merchant is from	Goods	Total Value	Tax	Notes
Strong		1/2 grs bridles with bits – £1 10s.; 4 doz. spurs – 10s.; leather points – 5s.; 14 yds stick – 14s.; 48 yds linen cloth – £3 12s.			
Booke		Gartering – £2.			
Browne		Nets and ropes with other provision for the fishings – nil.			
Orre		1 1/2 cwt crop madder – £2; 1 1/2 cwt alum – £1 10s.; 1 cwt hemp – 10s.; 9 yds grey cloth – 18s.; 1/2 cwt biscuit – 3s.; 16 gallons aquavite – £1 6s. 8d.; 22 lbs gunpowder – 5s. 2d.; 10 dippings for the fishing – £1; 1/2 doz. stock locks – 6s.; 1 doz. spade heads – 3s.; 48 lbs cordage – 4s. 3d.; 6 iron ladles – 1s. 6d.; 16 yds sackcloth – 10s. 8d.	£32 7s. 2d.	£1 2s. 4d.; 8s. 1d.	
Watt		3 hhd French wine – 4s. 6d.	4s. 6d.		
Stewarde		8 tons coal – £2.	£2	2s.; 6d.	
Wilson		24 bal French salt – £2 8s.	£2 8s.	2s. 4 3/4d.; 7 1/4d.	
Rogers		34 tuns French wine – £10 4s.			
Rogers		6 tuns French wine – £1 16s.			
Rogers		7 tons coal – £1 15s.	£1 15s.	1s. 9d.; 5 1/4d.	
Cohone		4 tons coal – £1.			
Keningham		1 last French salt – £1 4s.	£2 4s.	2s. 2 1/2d.; 6 1/2d.	
Rider		4 tons coal – £1.			
Denall		2 hhd vinegar – £1 3s. 4d.; 4 cwt hops – £4; 8 fkn soap – £4; 6 doz. unlined hats – £6; 6 doz. woollen stockings – £7 4s.; 6 whole pc fustian – £6; 2 pc kersey – 4s. 5d.; 24 yds flannel – 16s.; 20 yds frieze – £1; 20 yds Bridgewater red kersey reckoned at 1 2/3 kersey – 3s. 8d.			
Tuckey		4 doz. snaffles; 3 doz. stirrups, 2 doz. bits and other small wares – £15.			
Warden		4 tons coal – £1.	£1	1s.; 3d.	
Stewarde		4 tons coal – £1.	£1	1s. 3d.	
Linsey		20 tons coal – £5.	£5	5s.; 1s. 3d.	
Saunderson		20 tons coal – £5; 10 bal white salt – £1 6s. 8d.	£6 6s. 8d.	6s. 4d.	
Thomson		80 ells woollen cloth – £9 6s. 8d.			
Stewarde		640 lbs iron – £2 17s. 1 1/2d.			
Kenedie		Aniseeds and hops – £3; 15 bal French salt – £1 10s.			

Number	Folio	Date	Ship	Captain – Forename	Captain – Surname	Place – From	Place – To	Merchant Forename
		12 May 1615	*Henry* of Ayr – 12 tons	James	Melon		Londonderry	Henry
271		12 May 1615	*Jennet* of Renfrew – 16 tons	Adam	Knockes		Londonderry	Adam
272	f	12 May 1615	*Elizabeth* of Londonderry – 15 tons	John	Penny		Londonderry	Thomas
		12 May 1615	*Elizabeth* of Londonderry – 15 tons	John	Penny		Londonderry	John
		12 May 1615	*Elizabeth* of Londonderry – 15 tons	John	Penny		Londonderry	Brute
273		13 May 1615	*Margaret* of Renfrew – 10 tons	James	Eury		Londonderry	James
274	f	19 May 1615	*Daniell* of Leith – 70 tons	James	Leycocke		Londonderry	James
	f	8 July 1615	*Daniell* of Leith – 70 tons	James	Leycocke		Londonderry	James
275		22 May 1615	*Guifte of God* of Irvine – 35 tons	John	Deene		Londonderry	John
	f	5 June 1615	*Guifte of God* of Irvine – 35 tons	John	Deene		Londonderry	John
276		22 May 1615	*John* of Renfrew – 20 tons	Adam	Moderwell		Londonderry	Adam
277		31 May 1615	*Hopewell* of Ayr – 20 tons	John	Wilson		Londonderry	John
278		2 June 1615	Small boat of Clyde – 6 tons	Thomas	Long		Londonderry	John
279		2 June 1615	Small boat of Clyde – 6 tons	James	Wray		Londonderry	James
280	f	6 June 1615	Jennet of Mongavlin – 4 tons	Robert	Keningham		Londonderry	Robert
281		12 June 1615	*Bride* of Londonderry – 30 tons	John	Hamlett		Londonderry	Richard
		12 June 1615	*Bride* of Londonderry – 30 tons	John	Hamlett		Londonderry	Jesse
		12 June 1615	*Bride* of Londonderry – 30 tons	John	Hamlett		Londonderry	Thomas
		12 June 1615	*Bride* of Londonderry – 30 tons	John	Hamlett		Londonderry	Harry
		12 June 1615	*Bride* of Londonderry – 30 tons	John	Hamlett		Londonderry	Brute
	f	14 June 1615	*Bride* of Londonderry – 30 tons	John	Hamlett		Londonderry	George

Merchant Surname	Where Merchant is from	Goods	Total Value	Tax	Notes
Osbone		2 tuns French wine – 12s.	£16 13s. 9 1/2d.	16s. 8d.; 4s. 2d.	
Knockes		13 tons coal – £3 5s.; 24 gallons aquavite – £2.	£5 5s.	5s. 3d.; 1s. 3 3/4d.	
Canning		1 pack bedding, 1 fkn nails – provision; 4 northern dozens – 13s. 4d.			
Barkeley		10 yds northern cloth – £2 10s.; 10 yds red cloth – £1; 16 lbs blue starch – 8s.; 6 doz. knives – 15s.; 1 Devonshire kersey and 1 Hampshire kersey – 4s. 5d.	£4 13s.	4s. 7 1/2d.; 1s. 1 3/4d.	
Hamond		12 tons coal – £3; 1 bal nails – £4; hats – £15; stockings – £3; Manchester stuff – £3; madder and other dyeing stuff – £6; currants, raisins and other grocery ware – £10; paper, gartering, points, buttons, pins and other small wares – £10.	£54	£2 14s.	
Eury		6 tons coal – £1 10s.; 2 tons French salt – £1 12s.; 16 gallons aquavite – £1 6s. 8d.; 1 hhd Spanish salt – 5s. 4d.	£4 14s.	4s. 8d.; 1s. 2d.	
Leycocke		450 bal Spanish salt – £60; 50 lbs tobacco – £16 13s. 4d.; 3 lbs Spanish silk – £3; 2 cwt Raisins of the sun – £1 16s.; 7 1/2 tuns Spanish wine – £2 5s.	£81 9s. 4d.	£4 1s. 5 1/2d.; £1 4 1/4d.	
Leycocke		11 1/2 tuns Spanish wine – £3 9s.			
Deene		10 tons coal – £2 10s.; 3 tons salt – £2 8s.; 40 gallons aquavite – £3 6s. 8d.	£8 4s. 8d.	8s. 2d.; 2s. 0 1/2d.	
Deene		5 tuns French wine – £1 10s.			
Moderwell		20 tons coal – £5.	£5	5s.; 1s. 3d.	
Dutton		10 tons coal – £2 10s.	£2 10s.	2s. 6d.	
Long		4 tons coal – £1.	£1	1s.; 3d.	
Wray		4 tons coal – £1.	£1	1s.; 3d.	
Keningham		4 tons coal – £1 2s. 6d.	£1 2s. 6d.	1s. 1 1/2d.; 3 1/4d.	
Sadler		10 tons coal – £2 10s.			
Smithe		Divers small wares – £10 14s. 11d.			
Williams		6 saddles with furniture – £4 15s.			
Trafforde		5 1/2 doz. unlined hats – £5 10s.			
Hamond		3 doz. hats lined with taffeta – £6; 1 doz. unlined hats – £1.			
Hamond		4 bal nails – £16; 1 cwt hops – £1; 1 doz. pair bellows – 8s.; 6 fire shovels and tongs – 12s.			

Number	Folio	Date	Ship	Captain – Forename	Captain – Surname	Place – From	Place – To	Merchant Forename
	f	16 June 1615	*Bride* of Londonderry – 30 tons	John	Hamlett		Londonderry	John
	f	20 June 1615	*Bride* of Londonderry – 30 tons	John	Hamlett		Londonderry	Moses
282		13 June 1615	*John* of Dumbarton – 12 tons	Peter	Donnell		Londonderry	Peter
		13 June 1615	*John* of Dumbarton – 12 tons	Peter	Donnell		Londonderry	William
		13 June 1615	*John* of Dumbarton – 12 tons	Peter	Donnell		Londonderry	John
283	f	13 June 1615	*Unicorne* of Chester – 20 tons	William	Smithe		Londonderry	William
		13 June 1615	*Unicorne* of Chester – 20 tons	William	Smithe		Londonderry	Laurence
	f	16 June 1615	*Unicorne* of Chester – 20 tons	William	Smithe		Londonderry	Laurence
284		14 June 1615	*John* of Dumbarton – 6 tons	John	Gland		Londonderry	John
285		15 June 1615	*Blessing* of Burntisland – 45 tons	Robert	Gardner		Londonderry	Robert
286		19 June 1615	*Providence* of Dumbarton – 40 tons	William	Curethe		Londonderry	Jesse
287		20 June 1615	*Hopwell* of Dumbarton – 8 tons	Saunder	Euen		Londonderry	Saunder
288		20 June 1615	Small boat of Scotland – 4 tons	Edward	Wilson		Londonderry	Edward
289	f	20 June 1615	Small boat of Scotland – 5 tons	James	Guye		Londonderry	James
290		20 June 1615	*William* of Clyde – 6 tons	Robert	Lion		Londonderry	Robert
291		20 June 1615	*Guifte of God* of Saltcoats – 20 tons	Robert	Blacke		Londonderry	Robert
292		20 June 1615	Small boat of Scotland – 6 tons	Alen	Allison		Londonderry	Alen
		20 June 1615	Small boat of Scotland – 6 tons	Alen	Allison		Londonderry	William
293		23 June 1615	*Peter* of Londonderry – 70 tons	Wibrand	Oldphers		Londonderry	Wibrand
294	f	26 June 1615	Small boat of Scotland – 8 tons	William	Orre		Londonderry	William
295		26 June 1615	Small boat of Scotland – 8 tons	James	Rogers		Londonderry	James
296		27 June 1615	Small boat of Scotland – 8 tons	Andrew	Cokran		Londonderry	Andrew

Merchant Surname	Where Merchant is from	Goods	Total Value	Tax	Notes
Hatton		5 cwt lead – £1 13s. 4d.; 8 bal white salt – £1 1s. 4d.			
Dalbye		3 chests Burgundy glass – £6.	£59 4s. 7d.	£2 19s. 2 1/2d.	
Donnell		10 tons coal – £2 10s.; 1 ton salt – 16s.; 2 doz. chest locks – 6s.			
Keningham		3 cwt hops – £3; 1 bal soap – £2.			
Baudie		8 saddles – £4; 10 yds coarse stamell cloth – £2; 4 doz. bridles and bits – £2 8s.; 10 yds says – £2.	£19 12s.	19s. 7d.; 4s. 11d.	
Smithe		14 tons coal – £3 10s.			
Holland		1 tun beer – £2; 2 bal soap – £4; 1 1/2 cwt hops – £1 10s.; 2 doz. unlined hats – £2; small wares – £5; 2 hhd vinegar – £1 3s. 4d.; 3 Yorkshire single dozens – 10s.	£28 15s. 4d.	£1 8s. 3d.	
Holland		2 half pc stuffs – £1 3s.; 3 Devonshire kerseys – 6s. 8d.; 4 grs gartering – £1 16s.; 2 doz. woollen stockings – £2 8s.; 1 doz. French bodies – 15s.; 6 half pc fustian – £3.			
Gland		4 tons coal – £1; 6 iron pots – 10s.; 6 brass kettles/56 lbs – £1 10s.; 8 stock locks and 8 pair hinges – 12s.; 20 ells pladding – 10s.; 10 ells grey cloth – £1; 4 ells blue cloth – 8s.	£5 10s.	5s. 6d.; 1s. 4 1/2d.	
Gardner		340 bal French salt – £34; 1 tun French wine – 6s.	£34	£1 14s.; 8s. 6d.	
Smithe		300 bal French salt – £30; 3 hhd vinegar – £1 15s.	£31 15s.	£1 11s. 9d.	
Euen		5 tons coal – £1 5s.; 48 English gallons aquavite – £3 11s.; 1 hhd French wine – 1s. 6d.; 24 yds linen cloth – £1 4s.; 8 iron pots – 13s. 4d.; 2 kettles and 3 brass pots/28 lbs – 15s.	£7 8s. 4d.	7s. 5d.; 1s. 10 1/4d.	
Wilson		2 millstones – £6 13s. 4d.	£6 13s. 4d.	6s. 8d.; 1s. 8d.	
Guye		4 tons coal – £1.	£1	1s.; 3d.	
Lyon		4 tons coal – £1.	£1	1s.; 3d.	Surnames as given.
Blacke		14 tons coal – £3 10s.	£3 10s.	3s. 6d.; 10 1/2d.	
Allison		7 English gallons aquavite – 11s. 8d.; 3 iron pots – 5s.; 6 locks – 4s.			
Keningham		1 last French salt – £1 4s.	£2 4s. 8d.	2s. 2 3/4d.; 6 1/2d.	
Oldphers		3000 deal boards – £100.	£100	£5; £1 5s.	
Orre		6 tons coal – £1 10s.	£1 10s.	1s. 6d.; 4 1/2d.	
Rogers		6 tons coal – £1 10s.	£1 10s.	1s. 6d.; 4 1/2d.	
Cokran		3 tons coal – 15s.; 20 gallons aquavite £1 13s. 4d.; 1/2 cwt hops – 10s.;			

Number	Folio	Date	Ship	Captain – Forename	Captain – Surname	Place – From	Place – To	Merchant Forename
		27 June 1615	Small boat of Scotland – 8 tons	Andrew	Cokran		Londonderry	John
		27 June 1615	Small boat of Scotland – 8 tons	Andrew	Cokran		Londonderry	John
		27 June 1615	Small boat of Scotland – 8 tons	Andrew	Cokran		Londonderry	Matthew
		27 June 1615	Small boat of Scotland – 8 tons	Andrew	Cokran		Londonderry	James
297	f	3 July 1615	*Blessinge* of Glasgow – 50 tons	Duncan	Simple		Londonderry	Henry & Jesse
298		5 July 1615	*William* of Northam – 10 tons	William	Jeffery		Londonderry	William
299		5 July 1615	*Daisie* of Barnstaple – 10 tons	Thomas	Berriman		Londonderry	Thomas
300		10 July 1615	*Seaflower* of London – 50 tons	John	Zachary		Londonderry	William
		10 July 1615	*Seaflower* of London – 50 tons	John	Zachary		Londonderry	Peter
		10 July 1615	*Seaflower* of London – 50 tons	John	Zachary		Londonderry	Giles
	f	10 July 1615	*Seaflower* of London – 50 tons	John	Zachary		Londonderry	George
		10 July 1615	*Seaflower* of London – 50 tons	John	Zachary		Londonderry	George
		10 July 1615	*Seaflower* of London – 50 tons	John	Zachary		Londonderry	City of

Merchant Surname	Where Merchant is from	Goods	Total Value	Tax	Notes
Watson		24 lbs aniseeds – 6s. 5d.; 1 bal French salt.			
Loggie		3 bal 1 hhd wheat meal – £1 5s.; 3 gallons aquavite – 5s.; 1 bal sickle and hooks – 13s. 4d.; 2 saddles – 13s. 4d.; 1 great grs thread points – 10s.; 1 great grs thread buttons – 5s.; 2 bal French salt – 4s.			
		5 1/2 hhd French wine – 8s.; 3d.; 2 bal 2 fkn soap – £5; 2 1/2 doz. horsemen's staves – £2 5s.; 2 cwt hops – £2; 2 doz. scythes – £2 8s.; 2 doz. hooks – £1 16s.			
Tomson		20 gallons aquavite – £1 13s. 4d.			
Steward		2 doz. horsemen's staves – £1 16s.; 1 fkn soap – 10s.	£24 10s. 9d.	£1 4s. 6d.; 6s. 1 1/2d.	
Sadler & Smith		30 tuns French wine – £4 10s.; 5 tons wheat meal – £10; 3 tuns vinegar – £7; 2 tons prunes – £20; 2 tons drinking glasses – £5.	£42	£2 2s.	There were two merchants listed for this shipment.
Jeffery		160 doz. ridge tile – £12; 2 tierces canary wine – 6d.; 1 hhd vinegar – 11s. 8d.; 3 doz. kersey stockings – £1 16s.	£14 7s. 8d.	14s. 4 1/2d.	
Berriman		1 butt Spanish wine – 1s. 6d.; 120 doz. ridge tile – £9; 3 cwt white soap – £4 4s.; 132 lbs black soap – £1; 40 yds grey woollen cloth – £3.	£17 4s.	17s. 2d.	
Barrow		2 tuns vinegar – £4 13s. 4d.; 5 hhd aquavite – £20; 5 cwt prunes – £2 10s.; 16 half fkn soap – £4; 1/2 cwt powder blue – £1 8s.; 6 gallons candy oil – 10s.; 9 grs tobacco pipes – £1 10s.; 2 cwt liquorice – 10s.			
Benson		12 bal soap – £24; 1 tun aquavite – £16.			
Baker		One small barrel of shag, falling-bands, cobweb lawn and loom work – £30.			
Hamond		16 cwt iron ware – £1 10s.; 1 cwt frying pans – 10s.; 9 iron pots with one iron kettle – 16s. 8d.; 1 puncion with crockery ware – £6 13s. 4d.; 5 grs trenchers – 10s.; 1 maune iron ware – £3; 3 bal soap – £6; 3 iron mortars with pestles – 6s. 8d.; 1 iron beam – £1.			
Swetenham		2 cwt starch – £2; 1 fkn indigo – £10; 2 cwt raisins of the sun – £1 16s.; 3 cwt currants – £4 10s.; 2 cwt Castile soap – £3 14s. 8d.; 15 gallons salad oil – £1 5s.; 4 pcs raisins – £2; 1 3/4 cwt coil rope – 7s. 6d.; 1 cwt steel – 15s.; 16 cwt (58 bars) iron – £8.			
London		11 bal nails – £44; 6 coils (4 cwt) tarred rope – £2; 94 calivers, 94 headpieces and 94 flaxes and touchboxes – £46 4s. 4d.; 1 musket	£374 14s. 2d.	£18 14s. 7 1/2d.	

Number	Folio	Date	Ship	Captain – Forename	Captain – Surname	Place – From	Place – To	Merchant Forename
		24 July 1615	*Seaflower* of London – 50 tons	John	Zachary		Londonderry	Nicholas
301		11 July 1615	*Swallow* of Dumbarton – 20 tons	Peter	Williamson		Londonderry	Hugh
302		13 July 1615	Small boat of Scotland – 5 tons	John	Williams		Londonderry	John
303	f	13 July 1615	Small boat of Scotland – 8 tons	John	Love		Londonderry	John
304		14 July 1615	*Jonathan* of Largs – 6 tons	John	Heade		Londonderry	John
305		14 July 1615	*Mary Grace* of Burntisland – 45 tons	John	Browne		Londonderry	John
306		15 July 1615	*Hopwell* of Renfrew – 7 tons	John	Boide		Londonderry	John
307		24 July 1615	*Faulcon* of Barnstaple – 15 tons	Roger	Cressy		Londonderry	Roger
308	f	24 July 1615	*Trinitie* of Chester – 30 tons	Robert	Gill		Londonderry	Robert
		24 July 1615	*Trinitie* of Chester – 30 tons	Robert	Gill		Londonderry	Jesse
		24 July 1615	*Trinitie* of Chester – 30 tons	Robert	Gill		Londonderry	George
		24 July 1615	*Trinitie* of Chester – 30 tons	Robert	Gill		Londonderry	Robert
309		24 July 1615	*Sara* of Chester – 20 tons	Richard	Reymond		Londonderry	Richard
		24 July 1615	*Sara* of Chester – 20 tons	Richard	Reymond		Londonderry	William
		24 July 1615	*Sara* of Chester – 20 tons	Richard	Reymond		Londonderry	Henry
		24 July 1615	*Sara* of Chester – 20 tons	Richard	Reymond		Londonderry	John
310	f	30 July 1615	*Salamander* of Irvine – 30 tons	Archibald	George		Londonderry	Hugh

Merchant Surname	Where Merchant is from	Goods	Total Value	Tax	Notes
Leate		with [?] and bandelier – £1 2s.; 48 cosletts – £24; 48 pikes and headpieces – £15 12s.; 144 swords – £13 6s. 8d.; 6 bal gunpowder – £8; 2 bal matches – £3 14s. 8d.; 2 little bal caliver shot – 13s. 4d. 6 3/4 cwt hops – £6 15s.; 12 fkn 7 bal soap – £20; 6 hhd aquavite – £24; 2 fkn nails – £2.			
Tomson		20 tons coal – £5.	£5	5s.; 1s. 3d.	
Williams		3 tons coal – 15s.	15s.	9d.; 2 1/4d.	
Love		6 tons coal – £1 10s.	£1 10s.	1s. 6d.; 4 1/2d.	
Heade		6 tons coal – £1 10s.	£1 10s.	1s. 6d.; 4 1/2d.	
Poore		250 bal French salt – £25; 9 pc French serge – £40; 51 bal wheat meal – £12 15s.; 6 doz. wool cards – £3; 12 pair hand bellows – 13s. 4d.; 5 iron pots – 8s. 4d.; 1/2 cwt starch – 10s.	£82 6s. 8d.	£4 2s. 4d.; £1 7d.	
Boide		6 tons coal – £1 10s.; 12 gallons aquavite – £1; 1/2 cwt cropp madder – 13s. 4d.; 24 lbs alum – 4s. 3d.	£3 7s. 7d.	3s. 4d.; 10d.	
Cressy		150 doz. ridge tile – £11 5s.; 20 doz. earthen ware – £1 10s.; 2 tuns wine – 6s.; 15 cwt iron – £7 10s.; stone pitch – £1 5s.; 3 cwt lead – £1; 1 cwt currants – £1 10s.; 2 pcs raisins – £1; 1 cwt black soap – 18s. 8d.; 1 cwt white soap – £1 17s. 4d.	£27 16s.	£1 7s. 9d.	
Gill		14 tons coal – £3 10s.			
Smithe		8 reams pot paper, 4 doz. coarse-made garters – 3 boulls browne thread and other wares – £13 12s.; 2 Yorkshire single dozens – 6s. 8d.			
Hamond		4 cwt frying pans, 4 cwt wrought iron, 3 pcs raisins and other wares – £11 10s. 6d.			
Tomson		4 cwt hops, 2 fkn soap, 1/2 cwt raisins and other wares – £10 4s. 11d.	£38 17s. 5d.	10s. 3d.; 2s. 6 3/4d. £1 18s. 10 1/2d.; 2s. 6 3/4d.	
Reimond		10 tons coal – £2 10s.			Surnames as given.
Parry		18 yds says, 2 ends Genoa fustian, 2 doz. [lbs] inkle and other wares – £24 2s. 11d.; 20 bal malt – £2 10s.; 2 hhd aquavite – £8; 4 single Northern dozens – 13s. 4d.			
Carter		1 hhd aquavite, 1 cwt aniseed, 1/2 cwt grains and other small wares – £22 11s.			
Davis		3 tuns beer – £6.	£65 13s. 11d.	£3 5s. 8d.	
Tomson		100 bal French salt – £10; 1 hhd vinegar – 11s. 8d.	£10 11s. 8d.	10s. 7d.; 2s. 7 3/4d.	

Number	Folio	Date	Ship	Captain – Forename	Captain – Surname	Place – From	Place – To	Merchant Forename
311		1 Aug. 1615	*Margaret* of Ayr – 25 tons	Alexander	Dicker		Londonderry	Alexander
		1 Aug. 1615	*Margaret* of Ayr – 25 tons	Alexander	Dicker		Londonderry	John
312		4 Aug. 1615	Small boat of Scotland – 14 tons	John	Miller		Londonderry	John
313		4 Aug. 1615	*Good Fortune* of Irvine – 35 tons	Alan	Deloppe		Londonderry	Alan
314		10 Aug. 1615	*Henry* of Londonderry – 10 tons	Henry	Robinson		Londonderry	Henry
		10 Aug. 1615	*Henry* of Londonderry – 10 tons	Henry	Robinson		Londonderry	Robert
315	f	10 Aug. 1615	*Jhon* of Glasgow – 15 tons	John	Smithe		Londonderry	John
316		13 Aug. 1615	Small boat of Scotland – 10 tons	Adam	Moderwell		Londonderry	Adam
317		19 Aug. 1615	*Bride* of Londonderry – 30 tons	John	Hamlett		Londonderry	Richard
		19 Aug. 1615	*Bride* of Londonderry – 30 tons	John	Hamlett		Londonderry	Jesse
		19 Aug. 1615	*Bride* of Londonderry – 30 tons	John	Hamlett		Londonderry	John
		19 Aug. 1615	*Bride* of Londonderry – 30 tons	John	Hamlett		Londonderry	Richard
318		19 Aug. 1615	*Peeter* of Londonderry – 70 tons	Wibrand	Oldphers		Londonderry	Wibrand
319	f	23 Aug. 1615	*Greyhound* of Londonderry – 25 tons	Patrick	Mordach		Londonderry	John
320		25 Aug. 1615	Small boat of Scotland – 8 tons	Andrew	Cockran		Londonderry	Andrew

Merchant Surname	Where Merchant is from	Goods	Total Value	Tax	Notes
Dicker		20 tons coal – £5; 40 yds woollen cloth – £3 6s. 8d.			
Bartley		3 cwt hops – £3.	£11 6s. 8d.	11s. 4d.; 2s. 10d.	
Miller		12 tons coal – £3.	£3	3s.; 9d.	
Deloppe		28 tons coal – £7.	£7	7s.; 1s. 9d.	
Robinson		6 tons coal – £1 10s.			
Royle		12 iron pots – £1; alum and madder – 13s. 4d.; 12 doz. coarse knives – £1 10s.; 8 half pcs fustian – £4; 18 pair woolcards – 15s.; 20 ells pladding – £1 6s. 8d.; 6 blue bonnets – 5s.; 1 grs combs – 3s. 4d.	£13 3s. 4d.	13s. 2d.; 3s. 3 1/2d.	
Smithe		12 tons coal – £3.	£3	3s.; 9d.	
Moderwell		8 tons coal – £2.	£2	2s.; 6d.	
Sadler		10 tons coal – £2 10s.; 4 cwt hops – £4.			
Smithe		6 doz. unlined hats, 3 doz. children's hats, 36000 pins and other small wares – £17 16s.			
Onion		4 grs coarse knives – £6; 1 cwt loaf sugar – £3 6s. 8d.; 2 bal white salt – 5s. 4d.; 4 doz. coarse hats – £4; 40 yds single bays – £2; 4 single northern dozens – 13s. 4d.; 4 pcs kersey – 8s. 10d.; 3 pcs remnants of kersey – £1; 20 bal malt – £2 10s.; 10 bal meal – £2 10s.			
Stanton		150 goads cotton – £6; 8 doz. unlined hats – £8.	£59 18s.	£2 19s. 10d.	
Oldphers		3000 Meiboroughe deals – £120.	£120	£6; £1 10s.	
Bankes		18 cwt hops – £18; 3 cwt rice – £2 110s.; 5 cwt 40 lbs prunes – £2 13s. 6d.; 4 pcs Malaga raisins – £2; 104 lbs raisins of the sun – 16s. 8d.; 6 cwt 102 lbs currants – £10 7s. 3d.; 20 lbs cloves – £2; 10 lbs mace – £2 10s.; 62 lbs pepper – £5 3s. 4d.; 12 lbs cinnamon – £2; 100 lbs grains – £3 6s. 8d.; 1 cwt 77 lbs aniseeds – £2 10s. 7d.; 2 cwt 104 lbs liquorice – £1 9s. 3d.; 2 cwt 61 lbs white starch – £10 10s. 10d.; 6 lbs outnall thread – 10s.; 4 framed chairs – 6s. 8d.; 10 framed stools – 13s. 4d.; 6 half pcs cambric – £7 10s.; 106 ells holland – £7 1s. 4d.; 33 lbs blue starch – 16s. 6d.; 1 cwt 78 lbs alum – £1 13s. 11d.; 5 cellars with bottles – £1 13s. 4d.; 1 pc kersey – 2s. 2d.; 20 tons coal – £5.	£91 3s. 2d.	£4 11s. 2d.	
Cockran		4 tons coal – £1; 40 English gallons aquavite – £3 6s. 8d.; 40 lbs aniseeds	£5 13s.	5s. 7 1/2d.; 1s. 4 3/4d.	

Number	Folio	Date	Ship	Captain – Forename	Captain – Surname	Place – From	Place – To	Merchant Forename
321	f	4 Sep. 1615	Small boat of Scotland – 8 tons	James	Lyon		Londonderry	James
322		26 Sep. 1615	Small boat of Scotland – 12 tons	William	Gaulte		Londonderry	William
Outgates								
323		25 Mar. 1615	*Margaret* of Renfrew – 8 tons	James	Eury	Londonderry	Renfrew	James
		25 Mar. 1615	*Margaret* of Renfrew – 8 tons	James	Eury	Londonderry	Renfrew	John
324		27 Mar. 1615	*Swallow* of Dumbarton – 20 tons	Peter	Williamson	Londonderry	Dumbarton	Sir John
325		1 Apr. 1615	*John* of Dumbarton – 16 tons	Peter	Donnell	Londonderry	Glasgow	James
		1 Apr. 1615	*John* of Dumbarton – 16 tons	Peter	Donnell	Londonderry	Glasgow	William
		1 Apr. 1615	*John* of Dumbarton – 16 tons	Peter	Donnell	Londonderry	Glasgow	Ringing
		1 Apr. 1615	*John* of Dumbarton – 16 tons	Peter	Donnell	Londonderry	Glasgow	James
		1 Apr. 1615	*John* of Dumbarton – 16 tons	Peter	Donnell	Londonderry	Glasgow	David
		1 Apr. 1615	*John* of Dumbarton – 16 tons	Peter	Donnell	Londonderry	Glasgow	Hugh
		1 Apr. 1615	*John* of Dumbarton – 16 tons	Peter	Donnell	Londonderry	Glasgow	William
326	f	1 Apr. 1615	*Blessing* of Burntisland	David	Barran	Londonderry	Scotland	William
327		8 Apr. 1615	*William* of Dumbarton – 6 tons	Alan	Allison	Londonderry		Alan
		8 Apr. 1615	*William* of Dumbarton – 6 tons	Alan	Allison	Londonderry		William
328		8 Apr. 1615	*Guifie of God* of Strabane	Robert	Linsey	Londonderry	Scotland	Earl of
329		10 Apr. 1615	*Hopwell* of Dumbarton	Saunder	Euen	Londonderry	Dumbarton	Saunder
330	f	17 Apr. 1615	*Bride* of Londonderry – 30 tons	George	Woodroofe	Londonderry	Chester	John
		17 Apr. 1615	*Bride* of Londonderry – 30 tons	George	Woodroofe	Londonderry	Chester	John
		17 Apr. 1615	*Bride* of Londonderry – 30 tons	George	Woodroofe	Londonderry	Chester	William
		17 Apr. 1615	*Bride* of Londonderry – 30 tons	George	Woodroofe	Londonderry	Chester	Brute

Merchant Surname	Where Merchant is from	Goods	Total Value	Tax	Notes
		and grains – 19s.; 2 bal Spanish salt – 5s. 4d.; 1 bal French salt – 2s.			
Lion		6 tons coal – £1 10s.	£1 10s.	1s. 6d.; 4 1/2d.	Surnames as given.
Gaulte		7 tons coal – £1 15s.	£1 15s.	1s. 9d.; 5 1/4d.	RJH wrote the following note in the margin beside these values – 'Put these in to indicate that only one man paid the petty subsidy'.
Eury		15 dicker hides – £75; 8 bal oats – £5 6s. 8d.			
Strong		18 dicker hides – £90; 4 bal beef – £8.	£178 6s. 8d.	£8 18s. 4d.; £2 4s. 7d.	
Steward		60 hhd oats – £80; 10 hhd beef – £40.	£120	£6; £1 10s.	
Kile		4 dicker hides – £20; 3 hhd oatmeal – £3.			
Hamelton		10 dicker hides – £50; 1 cwt tallow – £1; 100 goatskins – 13s. 4d.; 3 bal beef – £6.			
Grave		5 dicker hides – £25.			
Watson		5 hhd oatmeal – £5; 2 bal beef – £4; 1 doz. calfskins – 6s. 8d.			
Wemes		6 cwt rough tallow – £6.			
McKenny		150 sheepskins – £1 2s. 6d.; 27 hides – £13 10s.	£214 12s. 6d.	£10 14s. 7 1/2d.; £2 13s. 7 3/4d.	
Keningham		15 dicker hides – £75; 4 cwt tallow – £4.			
Rogers		35 hides – £17 10s.	£17 10s.	17s. 6d.; 4s. 4 1/2d.	
Allison		3 dicker hides – £15; 10 bal oats – £6 13s. 4d.			
Keningham		12 dkr hides – £60; 40 goatskins 4s. 6d.; 60 sheepskins – 7s. 6d.; 100 lambskins – £1; 27 fox skins – £2 5s.; 1 other skin – 2s. 6d.; 2 fkn butter – 13s. 4d.	£86 6s. 2d.	£4 6s. 3 1/2d.; £1 1s. 6 3/4d.	
Abercorn		260 bal oats – £173 6s. 8d.; 480 lbs tallow – £4 5s.; 1 last pork and beef – £24; 6 dkr hides – £30.	£231 12s. 4d.	£11 11s. 7d.; £2 17s. 10 3/4d.	
Euen		30 hhd oats – £40; 128 hides – £64; 3 doz. goatskins – 4s.; 3 doz. sheepskins – 4s. 6d.	£104 8s. 4d.	£5 4s. 5d.; £1 6s. 1 1/4d.	
Leach		28 hhd beef – £112; 3 cwt tallow – £3.			
Andrew		1 pack yarn – £13 6s. 8d.			
Parry		1 tun train oil – £4; 3 hhd beef – £12; 3 cwt iron – £1 10s.; 24 sheepskins – 3s.; 2 packs yarn – £26 13s. 4d.; 3 dkr hides – £15.			
Hamonde		1/2 pack yarn – £6 13s. 4d.			

Number	Folio	Date	Ship	Captain – Forename	Captain – Surname	Place – From	Place – To	Merchant Forename
		17 Apr. 1615	*Bride* of Londonderry – 30 tons	George	Woodroofe	Londonderry	Chester	Richard
331		27 Apr. 1615	*John* of Renfrew – 10 tons	Adam	Moderwell	Londonderry	Scotland	William
332		29 Apr. 1615	*Peeter* of Londonderry	Wibrand	Oldphers	Londonderry	Norway	Wibrand
333		3 May 1615	*Grace of God* of Greenock – 6 tons	Thomas	Stobone	Londonderry	Greenock	Sir James
334	f	5 May 1615	*Thomas* of Clyde – 6 tons	Thomas	Lon	Londonderry	Clyde	Thomas
335		5 May 1615	*Trinitie* of Chester – 30 tons	Robert	Gill	Londonderry	Chester	Robert
		5 May 1615	*Trinitie* of Chester – 30 tons	Robert	Gill	Londonderry	Chester	George
		5 May 1615	*Trinitie* of Chester – 30 tons	Robert	Gill	Londonderry	Chester	Alexander
336		6 May 1615	Small boat of Scotland	Edward	Wilson	Londonderry	Scotland	Sir James
		6 May 1615	Small boat of Scotland	Edward	Wilson	Londonderry	Scotland	James
337		6 May 1615	*Robarte* of Renfrew – 8 tons	Robert	Landles	Londonderry	Renfrew	Sir George
338	f	12 May 1615	*Guifte of God* of Clyde – 5 tons	Patrick	Cobereth	Londonderry	Scotland	John
339		12 May 1615	*Guifte of God* of Irvine	William	Gaulte	Londonderry	Irvine	William
340		13 May 1615	*Robarte* of Renfrew – 5 tons	Robert	Robinson	Londonderry	Renfrew	John
341		13 May 1615	*Jennet* of Greenock (small boat)	James	Warden	Londonderry	Scotland	John
342		15 May 1615	*John* of Dumbarton – 6 tons	John	Hunter	Londonderry	Dumbarton	John
		15 May 1615	*John* of Dumbarton – 6 tons	John	Hunter	Londonderry	Dumbarton	Patrick
		15 May 1615	*John* of Dumbarton – 6 tons	John	Hunter	Londonderry	Dumbarton	Robert
343	f	18 May 1615	*William* of Renfrew	Andrew	Cokran	Londonderry	Renfrew	Andrew
		18 May 1615	*William* of Renfrew	Andrew	Cokran	Londonderry	Renfrew	George
344		26 May 1615	*Grace of God* of Largs – 7 tons	William	Fleming	Londonderry	Scotland	Hugh
345		26 May 1615	*Jennet* of Ayr	John	Browne	Londonderry	Ayr	John
346		27 May 1615	*Hopewell* of Renfrew	John	Boide	Londonderry	Renfrew	John
347		1 June 1615	*Margaret* of Renfrew – 6 tons	John	Robinson	Londonderry	Renfrew	John
	f	1 June 1615	*Margaret* of Renfrew – 6 tons	John	Robinson	Londonderry	Renfrew	Thomas
348	f	1 June 1615	Small boat of Scotland	John	Scott	Londonderry	Scotland	William
349		5 June 1615	*Jennet* of Renfrew	Adam	Knoxe	Londonderry	Scotland	Adam
350		5 June 1615	*Margret* of Renfrew	James	Eury	Londonderry	Renfrew	James

Merchant Surname	Where Merchant is from	Goods	Total Value	Tax	Notes
Sadler		3 dkr hides – £15; 1 pack yarn – £13 6s. 8d.	£222 13s.	£11 2s. 7 3/4d.	
Watt		4 1/2 tons beef – £72; 6 dkr hides – £30; 12 bal oatmeal – £8.	£110	£5 10s.; £1 7s. 6d.	
Oldphers		3 bal butter – £4.	£4	4s.; 1s.	
Keningham		16 hhd oats – £21 6s. 8d.	£21 6s. 8d.	£1 1s. 4d.; 5s. 4d.	
Lan		40 bal oats – £26 13s. 4d.	£26 13s. 4d.	£1 6s. 4d.; 6s. 8d.	Surnames as given.
Tomson		1 pack yarn – £13 6s. 8d.; 32 hides – £16.	£29 6s. 8d.	£1 9s. 4d.; 7s. 4d.	
Hamond		3 1/2 packs yarn – £46 13s. 4d.			
Steward		1 pack 1 cwt 60 lbs yarn – £17 15s. 6d.; 6 dkr hides – £30.	£47 15s. 6d. Overall total – £123 15s. 6d.	£2 7s. 9d.; 11s. 11 1/4d. £6 3s. 9d.; 19s. 3 1/2d.	
Keningham		6 hhd barley – £8.			
Stewarde		200 sheepskins – £1 10s.; 100 lambskins, 10 calfskins – 5s. 6d.; 4 horsehides – 6s.	£10 11s. 6d.	10s. 7d.; 2s. 7 1/2d.	
Hamilton		100 bal oats – £66 13s. 4d.; 33 hhd oatmeal – £44; 40 bal barley – £26 13s. 4d.	£137 6s. 8d.	£6 17s. 4d.; £1 14s. 4d.	
Cambell		74 bal oats – £49 6s. 8d.	£49 6s. 8d.	£2 9s. 4d.; 12s. 4d.	
Gaulte		2 dkr hides – £10.	£10	10s.; 2s. 6d.	
Loggie		14 dkr hides – £70; 4 bal oatmeal – £2 13s. 4d.; 100 sheepskins – 15s.	£73 8s. 4d.	£3 13s. 5d.; 18s. 4 1/4d.	
Strong		9 dkr hides – £45; 60 sheepskins – 7s. 6d.; 20 bal barley – £13 6s. 8d.; 2 doz. calf skins – 13s. 4d.; 800 lambskins – £4.	£63 7s. 6d.	£3 3s. 4 1/2d.; 15s. 10d.	
[Blank]		15 dkr hides – £75.			
Forsithe		Sheep and lamb skins – £6.			
Woolle		9 bal malt – £6.	£87	£4 7s.; £1 1s. 9d.	
Cokran		14 bal oats – £9 6s. 8d.; 5 dkr hides – £25.			
Orre		3 dkr hides – £15.	£49 6s. 8d.	£2 9s. 4d.; 12s. 4d.	
Tomson		70 bal oats – £46 13s. 4d.	£46 13s. 4d.	£2 6s. 8d.; 11s. 8d.	
Keningham		80 bal oats – £53 6s. 8d.	£53 6s. 8d.	£2 13s. 4d.; 13s. 4d.	
Boid		1 dkr hides – £5.	£5	5s.; 1s. 3d.	Surnames as given.
Strong		5 cwt tallow – £5; 7 dkr hides – £35; 100 lambskins – 10s.; 50 sheepskins – 7s. 6d.; 15 bal oats – £10.			
McBourney		300 lambskins – £1 10s.; 80 sheepskins – 10s.; 20 goatskins – 2s. 2d.; 1 doz. calf skins – 6s. 8d.	£53 6s. 8d.	£2 13s. 3 1/2d.; 13s. 3 3/4d.	
Steward		48 hhd oats – £64.	£64	£3 4s.; 16s.	
Knox		50 bal oats – £33 6s. 8d.; 7 dkr hides – £35.	£68 6s. 8d.	£3 8s. 4d.; 17s. 1d.	Surnames as given.
Eury		60 bal oats – £40; 4 dkr hides – £20.	£60	£3; 15s.	

Number	Folio	Date	Ship	Captain – Forename	Captain – Surname	Place – From	Place – To	Merchant Forename
351		5 June 1615	*Roberte* of Dumbarton	Robert	Cohone	Londonderry	Dumbarton	Archibald
352	f	9 June 1615	*Roberte* of Greenock	James	Wraye	Londonderry	Scotland	James
353		13 June 1615	*Harry* of Ayr – 12 tons	James	Mallon	Londonderry	Ayr	Henry
354		13 June 1615	*Thomas* of Greenock	Thomas	Long	Londonderry	Scotland	Thomas
355		13 June 1615	*Michaell* of Parton	Thomas	Saunderson	Londonderry	Workington	John
356		15 June 1615	Small boat of Scotland	Gabriell	Homes	Londonderry	Scotland	Gabriell
357	f	19 June 1615	*Daniell* of Leith	James	Lucoppe	Londonderry	La Rochelle	James
	f	8 July 1615	*Daniell* of Leith	James	Lucoppe	Londonderry	La Rochelle	James
358		19 June 1615	Small boat of Greenock	William	Simson	Londonderry	Scotland	William
359		19 June 1615	*William* of Renfrew	William	Somerell	Londonderry	Renfrew	William
		19 June 1615	*William* of Renfrew	William	Somerell	Londonderry	Renfrew	Thomas
360		20 June 1615	Small boat of Clyde	James	Wraye	Londonderry	Clyde	James
361		20 June 1615	*Bride* of Londonderry	John	Hamlett	Londonderry	Chester	George
		20 June 1615	*Bride* of Londonderry	John	Hamlett	Londonderry	Chester	Giles
		20 June 1615	*Bride* of Londonderry	John	Hamlett	Londonderry	Chester	Brute
362	f	3 July 1615	*Unicorne* of Chester	William	Smithe	Londonderry	Chester	William
		3 July 1615	*Unicorne* of Chester	William	Smithe	Londonderry	Chester	Laurence
363		11 July 1615	Small boat of Scotland	William	Glasse	Londonderry	Scotland	William
364		13 July 1615	Small boat of Scotland	Alan	Allison	Londonderry	Scotland	Alan
365		13 July 1615	Small boat of Scotland	John	McKenny	Londonderry	Scotland	John
366		21 July 1615	*William* of Renfrew	John Andrew	Cokran	Londonderry	Renfrew	John Andrew
367	f	21 July 1615	Small boat of Scotland	Ringen	Hunter	Londonderry	Scotland	Ringen
		21 July 1615	Small boat of Scotland	Ringen	Hunter	Londonderry	Scotland	William
368		22 July 1615	*Swallow* of Dumbarton	Peter	Williamson	Londonderry	Chester	William
		22 July 1615	*Swallow* of Dumbarton	Peter	Williamson	Londonderry	Chester	Nicholas
		22 July 1615	*Swallow* of Dumbarton	Peter	Williamson	Londonderry	Chester	Hugh
369		25 July 1615	Small boat of Scotland	John	Love	Londonderry	Scotland	John

Merchant Surname	Where Merchant is from	Goods	Total Value	Tax	Notes
Harbinson		20 dkr hides – £100; 4 bal oats – £2 13s. 4d.; 50 lambskins – 5s.	£102 18s. 4d.	£5 2s. 11d.; £1 5s. 8 3/4d.	
Wray		30 bal oats – £20; 30 bal barley – £20.	£40	£2; 10s.	Surnames as given.
Osbone		80 bal oats – £53 6s. 8d.	£53 6s. 8d.	£2 13s. 4d.; 13s. 4d.	
Long		20 bal oats – £13 6s. 8d.	£13 6s. 8d.	13s. 4d.; 3s. 4d.	
Banckes		8 cwt 109 lbs iron – £4 9s. 8d.; 6 cwt 62 lbs tallow – £6 11s.; 88 lbs pewter – £2 7s.; 1 hhd 1 bal beef – £6; 1 bal honey – £1 2s. 6d.; 2 cwt Meiboroughe – £8; 30 boulls black and brown thread – £15; 32 yds linsey–wolsey – £1 12s.; 60 lbs Guinea pepper – £3; 1 fkn train oil – 1s. 3d.; 1 small iron anchor (1 cwt) – 10s.; 1 horse vocat a garron – £1 10s.	£50 3s. 5d.	£2 10s. 2d.	
Homes		5 dkr hides – £25; 5 hhd barley – £6 13s. 4d.	£31 13s. 4d.	£1 11s. 8d.; 7s. 11d.	
Lucuppe		20 dkr hides – £100.			Surnames as given.
Lucuppe		34 dkr tanned hides – £170; 20 dkr salt hides – £100; 6 bal salmon – £6 15s.	£376 15s.	£18 16s. 9d.; £4 14s. 2 1/4d.	
Simson		60 bal oats – £40; 2 dkr hides – £10; 20 sheepskins – 2s. 6d.	£50 2s. 6d.	£2 10s. 1 1/2d.; 12s. 6 1/4d.	
Somerell		20 bal wheat – £20.			
Browne		22 hides – £11.	£31	£1 11s.; 7s. 9d.	
Mason		40 bal oats – £26 13s. 4d.; 5 bal barley – £3 6s. 8d.; 2 dkr hides – £10.	£40	£2; 10s.	
Hamond		3 cwt yarn – £10.			
Baker		1/2 pack yarn – £6 13s. 4d.			
Hamond		1 pack yarn – £13 6s. 8d.; 40 sheepskins – 5s.	£30 5s.	£1 10s. 3d.	
Boulton		1 pack yarn – £13 6s. 8d.			
Holland		5 nags vocat garrons – £7 10s.	£20 16s. 8d.	£1 10d.	
Glasse		9 hhd barley – £12; 1 hhd oats – £1 6s. 8d.	£13 6s. 8d.	13s. 4d.; 3s. 4d.	
Allison		5 cwt hoop staves – 5s.; 6 dkr hides – £30.	£30 5s.	£1 10s. 3d.; 7s. 6 3/4d.	
McKenny		3 bal oatmeal; 3 bal malt – £6.	£6	6s.; 1s. 6d.	
Cokran		6 bal beef – £12; 2 dkr hides – £10; 4 bal malt – £2 13s. 4d.; 150 sheepskins – £1 2s. 6d.	£25 15s. 10d.	£1 5s. 9 1/2d.; 6s. 5d.	
Hunter		10 dkr hides – £50; 6 bal malt – £4; 6 cwt hoop staves – 6s.; 2 bal salmon – £2 5s.			
Hamelton		2 dkr hides – £10.	£66 11s.	£3 6s. 6d.; 16s. 7 1/2d.	
Denall		4 bal salmon – £4 10s.; 3 1/2 cwt tallow – £3 10s.; 4 1/2 dkr hides – £22 10s.; 450 sheepskins – £3 7s. 6d.; 15 doz. calf skins – £5; 3 cwt yarn – £10.			
Tiling		5 packs yarn – £66 13s. 4d.			
Tomson		6 packs yarn – £80; 2 cwt tallow – £2.	£82 Overall total: £197 10s. 10d.	£4 2s.; £1 6d. £9 17s. 6 1/2d.; £1 6d.	
Dunkenson		12 dkr hides – £60.	£60	£3; 15s.	

Number	Folio	Date	Ship	Captain – Forename	Captain – Surname	Place – From	Place – To	Merchant Forename
370		29 July 1615	Small boat of Scotland	William	Snape	Londonderry	Scotland	William
371	f	2 Aug. 1615	*Hopwell* of Ayr	Saunder	Euen	Londonderry	Ayr	Saunder
372		2 Aug. 1615	Small boat of Scotland	John	Gland	Londonderry	Scotland	John
373		4 Aug. 1615	*John* of Dumbarton	Peter	Donnell	Londonderry	Dumbarton	Peter
		4 Aug. 1615	*John* of Dumbarton	Peter	Donnell	Londonderry	Dumbarton	William
		4 Aug. 1615	*John* of Dumbarton	Peter	Donnell	Londonderry	Dumbarton	John
374		8 Aug. 1615	*Guifte of God* of Glasgow	John	Wilson	Londonderry	Glasgow	Ninian
375	f	8 Aug. 1615	*Trinitie* of Chester	Robert	Gill	Londonderry	Chester	William
		8 Aug. 1615	*Trinitie* of Chester	Robert	Gill	Londonderry	Chester	Jesse
		8 Aug. 1615	*Trinitie* of Chester	Robert	Gill	Londonderry	Chester	Michael
376		12 Aug. 1615	*Blessing* of Glasgow	Duncan	Simple	Londonderry	Diepe	Richard
		12 Aug. 1615	*Blessing* of Glasgow	Duncan	Simple	Londonderry	Diepe	John
377		12 Aug. 1615	*Guifte of God* of Burntisland	Robert	Gardner	Londonderry	Diepe	Richard
		12 Aug. 1615	*Guifte of God* of Burntisland	Robert	Gardner	Londonderry	Diepe	John
378		14 Aug. 1615	*Seaflower* of London	John	Zachary	Londonderry	Chester & London	George
		14 Aug. 1615	*Seaflower* of London	John	Zachary	Londonderry	Chester & London	John
379	f	18 Aug. 1615	Small boat of Scotland	David	Morrison	Londonderry	Scotland	David
		18 Aug. 1615	Small boat of Scotland	David	Morrison	Londonderry	Scotland	William
380		21 Aug. 1615	*Grace of God* of Ayr	William	Fleming	Londonderry	Ayr	William
381		21 Aug. 1615	*Mary Grace* of Burntisland	John	Browne	Londonderry	Bilbao	Martin
		21 Aug. 1615	*Mary Grace* of Burntisland	John	Browne	Londonderry	Bilbao	John
382		28 Aug. 1615	Small boat of Scotland	John	Wilson	Londonderry	Scotland	John
383		30 Aug. 1615	*John* of Glasgow	John	Smithe	Londonderry	Glasgow	John
384	f	31 Aug. 1615	Small boat of Scotland	Adam	Moderell	Londonderry	Scotland	Adam
385		4 Sep. 1615	*Bride* of Londonderry	John	Hamlett	Londonderry	Chester	John
		4 Sep. 1615	*Bride* of Londonderry	John	Hamlett	Londonderry	Chester	Richard
		4 Sep. 1615	*Bride* of Londonderry	John	Hamlett	Londonderry	Chester	Jesse

Merchant Surname	Where Merchant is from	Goods	Total Value	Tax	Notes
Snape		3 dkr hides – £15; 4 garrons – £4.	£19	19s.; 4s. 9d.	
Euen		6 hhd barley – £8; 2 dkr hides – £10; 60 sheepskins – 7s. 6d.; 64 lbs cheese – 3s. 2d.; 7 garrons – £7.	£25 10s. 8d.	£1 5s. 6d.; 6s. 4 1/2d.	
Glande		4 dkr hides – £20; 100 sheepskins – 15s.; hoop staves – 10s.; 4 bal malt – £2 13s. 4d.; 1 cwt 28 lbs cheese – 6s. 4d.	£24 4s. 8d.	£1 4s. 2 3/4d.; 6s. 0 1/2d.	
Donnell		10 dkr hides – £50.			
Cuningham		24 dkr hides – £120; 3 cwt tallow – £3; 2 bal butter – £2 13s. 4d.; 3 doz. goat skins – 4s.; 3 doz. sheepskins – 4s. 6d.			
Graisie		200 sheepskins – £1 10s.; 1 dkr hides – £5.	£182 11s. 10d.	£9 2s. 7d.; £2 5s. 7 3/4d.	
Englishe		10 dkr hides – £50.	£50	£2 10s.; 12s. 6d.	
Boulton		1 pack yarn – £13 6s. 8d.			
Smithe		4 1/2 tons salmon – £40 10s.; 3 dkr hides – £15; 2 bal beef – £4.			
Graves		1 pack yarn – £13 6s. 8d.	£86 3s. 4d.	£4 6s. 2d.	
Fittzimons		18 tons salmon – £162.			John Poore seems to have paid a separate tax on his goods, unlike Richard Fittzimons.
Poore		18 tons salmon – £162.	£162 Overall total – £324	£8 1s.; £2 6d. £16 4s.; £2 6d.	
Fitzimons		15 tons salmon – £135.			
Poore		15 tons salmon – £135; 50 cwt tallow – £50; 50 dkr hides – £250; 3 cwt wool – £8 8s.	£443 8s. Overall total – £578 8s.	£22 3s. 4d.; £5 10s. 10d. £28 18s. 4d.; £5 10s. 10d.	
Swetenham		70 cwt panele – £116 13s. 4d.; 12 cwt tallow – £12; 70 hides – £35.			
Bettson		30 salt hides – £15; 1 bal beef – £2; 2 cwt tallow – £2.	£222 13s. 4d.	£11 2s. 8d.	
Morrison		80 sheepskins – 10s.; 3 dkr hides – £15; 23 calf skins – 12s. 10d.			
Cunningham		8 dkr hides – £40; 6 goat skins – 8d.; 2 stag skins – 6s. 8d.	£57 10s. 2d.	£2 17s. 6d.; 14s. 4 1/2d.	
Fleming		60 bal oats – £40.	£40	£2; 10s.	
Fleming		12 tons 1 hhd salmon – £110 5s.			
Poore		6 tons 3 hhd salmon – £60 15s.	£60 15s. Overall total – £171	£3 9d.; 15s. 2 1/4d. £8 11s.; 15s. 2 1/4d.	
Wilson		15 cwt hoop staves – 15s.; 24 hides – £12; 2 garrons – £2	£14 15s.	14s. 9d.; 3s. 8 1/4d.	
Bartley		6 garrons – £6; 6 cows – £4; 8 doz. sheepskins – 12s.; 1 dkr hides – £5.	£15 12s.	15s. 7d.; 3s. 10 3/4d.	
Moderell		8 beeves – £5 6s. 8d.	£5 6s. 8d.	5s. 4d.; 1s. 4d.	
Davis		1/2 pack yarn – £6 13s. 4d.; 1 bal beef – £2; 1 garron – £1.			
Stanton		4 dkr hides – £20; 10 cwt tallow – £10; 1/2 pack yarn – £6 13s. 4d.			
Smithe		8 dkr hides – £40; 1 hhd beef – £4; 8 cwt tallow – £8.	£98 6s. 8d.	£4 18s. 4d.	

The Port Books
of Coleraine

Number	Folio	Date	Ship	Captain – Forename	Captain – Surname	Place – From	Place – To	Merchant Forename
1	f.	15 Mar. 1613	*Enere* of Resa			Scotland	Coleraine	
2		20 Mar. 1613	*Kathrine* of Glasgow – 8 tons	John	Longhe	Scotland	Coleraine	
3		3 April 1613	*Elizabeth* of Derry – 12 tons	Robert	Shen	Scotland	Coleraine	
4	f.	13 May 1613	*Seaflower* of Dover – 100 tons	John	Zacarie	London	Coleraine	Edmond
5		14 May 1615	*Sundoay* of Scotland	Patrick	Harton	Scotland	Coleraine	
6		10 June 1613	*Bride* of Hibre – 25 tons	Henry	Sadler	Chester	Coleraine	John

Merchant Surname	Where Merchant is from	Goods	Total Value	Tax	Notes
		4 hhd white herrings – £6; 7 Scotch gals aquavite – 11s. 8d.; 23 stones iron – £1 12s. 10d.	£8 4s. 6d.	8s. 3d.; 2s.	There is no named captain or merchant, just a space and then the words 'in his boat'.
		7 Scotch gals aquavite – £2 6s. 8d.; 1/2 cwt brass kettles – £2 16s; 4 stones iron – 5s. 8d.; 2 1/2 bal small wares – £8.	£13 8s. 4d.	13s. 5d.; 3s. 4d.	
		9 tons coal – £3 12s; 7 Scotch gals aquavite – £2 6s. 8d.; 40 ells Scotch cloth – £2 10s.; 7 hhd bag salt – £1 8s.	£9 16s. 8d.	9s. 10d.; 2s. 3d.	
Haward	Coleraine	3 bal soap – £6; 4 cwt prunes – £2; 4 cwt currants – £6; 12 doz. drinking glasses – £3; 6 doz. men's wool–knit stockings – £7 4s.; 14 lbs almonds – 5s.; 6 1/2 ells lawn – £1; 6 1/2 ells cambric – £1 5s.	£26 14s.	£1 6s. 9d.	
		80 bal wheat – £13 6s. 8d.; 1 tun High Country wine – £6; 10 cwt iron – £5.	£24 6s. 8d.	£1 4s. 4d.; 6s.	
Hatton	Coleraine	12 doz. men's stockings – £14 8s.; 10 lbs coloured silk lace – £13 6s. 8d.; 2 lbs coloured silk £2 13s. 4d.; 2 pcs velvet lace – £1 18s. 6d.; 1 1/2 grs 2d. ribbon – £1 7s.; 2 lbs black spanish silk – £2; 1 1/2 grs 3d. ribbon – £2 6d.; 3 grs cales lace – £2 9s. 6d.; 2 grs silk erom points – £1; 19 doz. silk butts and loops – £4 8s. 6d.; 2 1/2 doz. [?] garters – £2 10s; [f] 4 grs silk and silver butts – £1 10s.; 1 grs 4 doz. silk ribbons – £2 14s.; 6 pair ruffs – 10s.; 2 doz. box lace – £1 7s.; 18 grs silk buttons – 15s.; 3 pcs perpetuana – £9 5s.; 2 pcs navaretto – £1 19s. 9d.; 1 double pc red silk philosell – £3 6s.; 2 double pcs mixed says – £5 16s.; 1 white Milan fustian – £2; 30 ells taffeta – £14 18s.; 15 yds silk cyprus – 17s. 6d.; 1 pc philosell – £2 12s.; 2 1/2 pcs broad buffines – £2 10s.; 1 pc Flanders serge – £3; 1 pc black silk rashe – £2 12s. 6d.; 1 fine calico – 10s.; 3 pcs cambric – £7 10s.; 3 pcs lawn – £6; 9 1/2 ells coloured canvas – £1 11s. 8d.; 69 ells holland – £4 12s.; 1 pc striped canvas – 16s. 8d.; 1 pc fine shag – £2 2s.; 30 ells browne canvas – £1 10s.; 2 pcs white holmes – £1 16s.; 5 pcs Jenes – £3 15s.; 1 English fustian – £1; 4 lbs 12 oz. wrought inkle – 7s.; tape and filleting – 8s. 6d.; 6 yds crimson calico – 10s.; 12 doz. crewel garters – £2 10s. 8d.; 3 lbs sisters thread – £1 10s.; 48 yds cotton – £1 5s. 8d.; 2 pcs English says – £2 13s. 4d.; 27 yds wadmoll – £1 3d.; 2 muffs – 9s.; 4 1/2 doz. pins – 18s. [f]; 2 3/4 doz. pairs gloves – 9s. 2d.; 1 doz. steel glasses – 13s. 4d.; 12 doz. chequer glasses – 10s.; 3 1/2 doz. loomwork – £1 9s. 6d.; 8 lbs			No total or tax noted.

Number	Folio	Date	Ship	Captain – Forename	Captain – Surname	Place – From	Place – To	Merchant Forename
7		22 June 1613	*William* of Renfrew – 10 tons	Andrew	Cockerryn	Scotland	Coleraine	
8	f.	6 July 1613	*Spedewell* of Liverpool – 25 tons	George	Farrall	Liverpool	Coleraine	
9		24 July 1613	*Bride* of Hibre – 25 tons	Henry	Sadler	Chester	Coleraine	Edmond
10		25 July 1613	*Sea Flower* of Dover – 100 tons	John	Zacary	London	Coleraine	John
	f.	26 July 1613	*Sea Flower* of Dover – 100 tons	John	Zacary	London	Coleraine	Paul
11	f.	26 July 1613	Boat of Scotland	Richard	Fyar	Scotland	Coleraine	
12		1 Sep. 1613	*Margery* of Hilbre – 30 tons	Robert	Ormesonn	Chester	Coleraine	John
	f.	2 Sep. 1613	*Margery* of Hilbre – 30 tons	Robert	Ormesonn	Chester	Coleraine	John

Merchant Surname	Where Merchant is from	Goods	Total Value	Tax	Notes
		cloves – £1 12s.; 5 lbs large cinnamon – 16s. 8d.; 3 lbs mace – 15s. [page damaged]; 12 lbs indigo – £2 8s.; 2 1/2 lbs wine – £1; 12 doz. girdles – £2 8s.; 15 pairs hangers – £1 12s.; 6 lbs nutmeg – 15s.; 1 1/4 cwt sugar – £4 3s. 4d.; 4 doz. pennars and inkhorns – 3s. 4d.; 15 lbs tobacco – £7 10s.; 3 cwt hops – £3; 2 northern dozens – £6 13s. 4d.; 36 yds broad cloth – £10; 4 pcs kerseys – £8 17s. 10d.; 8 yds kersey – £1 9s. 8d.; 12 lbs pepper – £1; 14 lbs white candy – 12s. 6d.; 1 grs whalebone – £1; 1 doz. scythes – £1 3s.; 1 doz. knit stockings – £1 4s.; 1 silver buttons – 10s.; 3 lbs 13 oz. blue Spanish silk laces – £5.			
		3 hhd malt – 15s.; 3 Scotch gals aquavite – £1; 3 bal wheat – 10s.; 3 hhd salt – 16s. 8d.; 5 stones hemp – £1 8s. 8d.	£4 10s. 4d.	4s. 6d.; 1s.	
		10 tons coal – £4; 3 hhd bay salt – 12s.; 1 hhd vinegar – 11s. 8d.; 1/2 tun French wine – £3; 7 1/4 cwt (2 cakes) Rosin – £1 16s. 3d.; 3 doz. shod spades – £2 5s.; 2 saddles and 3 doz. girths – £1.	£13 4s. 11d.	13s. 3d.	
Haward	Coleraine	260 yds wrought penistones – £27 1s. 8d.; 144 yds cottons £3 14s. 3d.; 12 pcs kerseys – £26 13s. 4d.; 2 grs silk points – £1; 3 doz. hats – £3; 2 doz. hats – £4; 3 doz. gloves bands and other trifles – £6.	£71 9s. 3d.	£3 11s. 6d.	
Hatton	Coleraine	32 fkn soap – £16; 2 hhd aquavite – £8; 3 cwt white starch – £3; 3 cwt raisins – £2; 2 cwt currants – £3.			
Brasiar	Coleraine	4 cwt 5lbs sugar – £13 9s. 3d.; 3 cwt steel hemps – £6; 6 bal soap – £12; 4 hhd aquavite – £16.	£79 9s. 3d.	£3 19s. 6d.	
		50 bal wheat – £8 6s. 8d.; 10 cwt Spanish iron – £5.	£13 6s. 8d.	13s. 4d.; 3s. 4d.	
Walton	Coleraine	6 cwt white sugar – £20; 40 grs silk buttons – £1 13s. 4d.; 4 grs thrum silk points – £2; 100 yds silk curl – £20; 32 yds natural camlet £4; 2 cwt white starch – £2; 84 lbs blue starch £3 10s.; 12 pcs kerseys – £26 13s. 4d.; 100 yds bays – £5; 13 1/2 cwt hops – £13 10s.; 2 hhd aquavite – £8; 3 bal soap – £6; 3 bal pitch – 16s. 8d.; 14 doz. fine hats – £28; 3 1/2 tuns French wine – £10 10s.; 2 tuns beer – £4.			
Hatton	Coleraine	4 Yorkshire dozens – £13 6s. 8d.; 25 yds broad cloth – £7; 10 pcs kerseys – £22 4s. 6d.; 72 yds Manchester friezes – £3 12s.; 6 pcs bays – £12; 4 yds white cottons – £2; 12 doz.	£268 13s. 9d.	£13 8s. 8d.	

Number	Folio	Date	Ship	Captain – Forename	Captain – Surname	Place – From	Place – To	Merchant Forename
13	f.	24 Sep. 1613	*Dove* of London – 30 tons	Richard	Pett	London	Coleraine	Paul
14	f.	9 Oct. 1613	*Cathren* of Ayr – 20 tons	Robert	Holeston	Low Countries	Coleraine	William
15		20 Oct. 1613	*Pellican* of Coleraine – 10 tons	James	Wise	Chester	Coleraine	Edmond
	f.	6 Nov. 1613	*Pellican* of Coleraine – 10 tons	James	Wise	Chester	Coleraine	John
16		13 Nov. 1613	*Bride* of Hilbre – 25 tons	Henry	Sadler	Chester	Coleraine	Edmond
17	f.	10 Mar. 1614	*Genett* of Greenock (?) – 8 tons	Robert & John	Willstone	Scotland	Coleraine	Robert & Joh
18		11 Mar. 1614		John	Kile	Scotland	Coleraine	

Merchant Surname	Where Merchant is from	Goods	Total Value	Tax	Notes
		knives – £2 8s. 8d.; 1 pc buckram – 5s.; 6 yds loom work – 5s.; 9 yds cobweb lawn – 10s. 6d.; 2 pair bodyes – £1 11s. 10d.; 7 reams pott paper – £1 8s; 1 1/2 grs playing cards – £1 10s.; 2 1/2 doz. women's hose – £3; 1 doz. knit stockings – £1 4s.; bone lace – £3 7s. 4d.; 3 doz. leas [?] weak yarn – £1 4s.; 1 great grs silk buttons – 10s.; 40 quarts honey – 10s.; 98 lbs sugar – £2 18s. 4d.; 4 cwt 100 lbs madder – £6 10s.; 200 horsehoes – £1 8s.; 1/2 cwt shot – 19s. 5d.; 1 hhd aquavite – £4; 5 doz. hats – £5; 1 doz. hats – £2; 5 doz. bands – 10s.; 6 bundles brown paper – 6s.; 30 lbs gunpowder – 7s.; 3 doz. long reins – £1 1s.; 1 grs girth web – 9s. 6d.; 6 doz. spurs – 18s.; 3 doz. snaffles 9s.; 5 cwt hops – £5; 1 Yorkshire dozen – £3 6s. 8d.			
Brasiar	Coleraine	37 3/4 cwt hops – £37 15s.; 9 hhd aquavite – £36; 3 cwt white sugar – £10; 4 cwt currants – £6; 3 bal soap – £6.	£95 15s.	£4 15s. 9d.	
Perrie	Coleraine	2000 tilestones – 8s.; 1 bal tar – 5s. 6d.; 3 bal pitch – 16s. 8d.; 5 cwt 70 lbs hops – £5 12s. 6d.; 5 maunds earthen pots – £2; 1 doz. iron pots – £1; 50 bushels white salt – £1 13s. 4d.; 4 hhd vinegar – £2 6s. 8d.; 12 fkn soap – £6; 1 bal spice and sugar – £3; 1 barrel small wares – £4.	£27 2s. 8d.	£1 7s. 2d.	
Haward	Coleraine	16 half pcs Milan fustians – £16; 8 doz. hats – £8; 6 doz. fine hats – £12; 10 doz. woollen knit stockings – £12; 6 doz. kersey stockings – £12; 120 yds peniston – £12 10s.	£72 10s.	£3 12s. 6d.	
Hatton	Coleraine	13 cwt 75 lbs hops – £13 13s. 6d.; 2 fine felts with treble Cyprus bands – £1 16s.; 2 pcs white Genoa – £1 10s.; 2 1/2 doz. loomwork – £1 9s.; 5 doz. stockings – £6; 1 1/2 doz. hats – £1 10s.; 1 grs whalebone – £1; 20 lbs steel hemp – 7s. 6d.; 1 doz. fine hats – £2.	£101 16s.	£5 1s. 9d.	
Haward	Coleraine	14 pcs Kerseys – £31 2s. 3d.; 143 yds cottons – £3 16s.; 103 yds peniston cottoned – £10 15s.; 14 doz. hats – £14; 4 doz. fine hats – £8; 4 great grs silk buttons – £2; 3 lbs coloured silk – £4; 6 doz. gloves – £1 10s.; 2 grs silk thrum points – £1; 5 doz. falling bands – £3 6s. 8d.	£79 9s. 11d.	£3 19s. 6d.	
Willstone		10 doz. salt cod – £2; 10 Scotch gals aquavite – £3 6s. 8d.; 12 pair shoes – 18s.; 2 lbs garden seeds – 5s.; 8 lbs blue starch – 6s. 8d.; 1 doz. knives – 5s.; 8 stones iron – 11s. 5d.	£7 12s. 9d.	7s. 8d.; 1s. 10d.	
		13 tons coal – £5 6d.	£5 6d.	5s. 3d.; 1s. 3d.	Name of boat not given, just noted 'John Kile in his boat'.

Number	Folio	Date	Ship	Captain – Forename	Captain – Surname	Place – From	Place – To	Merchant Forename
19		14 Mar. 1614		John	Larkmor	Scotland	Coleraine	
20		16 Mar. 1614	*Pellican* of Coleraine – 10 tons	James	Wise	Chester	Coleraine	John
21	f.	16 Mar. 1614		James	Howe	Scotland	Coleraine	
22		16 Mar. 1614		William	Grege	Scotland	Coleraine	
23		27 Mar. 1614		Alan	Allson	Scotland	Coleraine	
Outgates								
24	f	20 Apr. 1613	*William* of Renfrew – 8 tons	Andrew	Cougharen	Coleraine	Scotland	
25		16 May 1613	*Bride* of Hilbre – 25 tons	Henry	Sadler	Coleraine	Chester	Edmond
26		10 June 1613	*Mathew Margerett* of Coleraine – 10 tons	James	Wise	Coleraine	Chester	
27		13 June 1613	*Pellican* of Coleraine – 10 tons	James	Wise	Coleraine	Chester	Edmond
28	f	15 July 1613	Boat of Andrew Michell	Andrew	Michell	Coleraine	Scotland	
29		5 Sep. 1613	*Pellican* of Coleraine – 10 tons	James	Wise	Coleraine	Chester	Edmond
30	f	5 Oct. 1613	*Grace of God* of Burntisland – 50 tons	Thomas	Suntar	Coleraine	Spain	Richard
31		11 Nov. 1613	*Cathren* of Glasgow	John	Longe	Coleraine	Scotland	
32		23 Dec. 1613	*Dove* of London – 60 tons	Thomas	Johnson	Coleraine	London	Paul
	f	23 Dec. 1613	*Dove* of London – 60 tons	Thomas	Johnson	Coleraine	London	Edmond
		23 Dec. 1613	*Dove* of London – 60 tons	Thomas	Johnson	Coleraine	London	Nicholas
		23 Dec. 1613	*Dove* of London – 60 tons	Thomas	Johnson	Coleraine	London	Tr[istram]
		23 Dec. 1613	*Dove* of London – 60 tons	Thomas	Johnson	Coleraine	London	Thomas
		23 Dec. 1613	*Dove* of London – 60 tons	Thomas	Johnson	Coleraine	London	George
		23 Dec. 1613	*Dove* of London – 60 tons	Thomas	Johnson	Coleraine	London	Thomas
33		27 Feb. 1614	*Poote* of Londonderry – 70 tons	Robert	Berres	Coleraine	France	

Merchant Surname	Where Merchant is from	Goods	Total Value	Tax	Notes
		5 1/2 tons coal – £2 4s.	£2 4s.	2s. 3d.; 6d.	RJH unsure of spelling of captain's surname.
Hatton	Coleraine	3 doz. hats – £3; 1000 ft. glass – £11; 2 bal figs – £1 5s; 1 cwt raisins of the sun – 9s.; 4 lbs nutmeg – 10s.; 3 lbs cinnamon – 10s.; 1 doz. brushes – 10s.; 3 lbs cloves – 12s.	£17 16s.	17s. 9d.	
		3 tons coal – £1 4s.	£1 4s.	1s. 3d.; 3d.	Name of boat not given – just noted 'James Howe in his boat'.
		4 tons 3 bal coal – £1 15s.	£1 15s.	1s. 9d.; 5d.	Name of boat not given, just noted 'William Grege in his boat'.
		3 tons coal – £1 4s.; 6 Scotch gals aquavite – £2; 12 yds woollen cloth – £1 4s.; 6 iron pots – 10s.; 1 bal white herrings – 15s.; 2 doz. salt cod – 8s.; 20 yds Scotch canvas – 6s. 8d.	£6 7s. 8d.	6s. 2d.; 1s. 6d.	
		100 sheepskins – 15s.; 12 salt hides – £6; butter – 13s. 4d.; 6 hides – £3.	£10 8s. 4d.	10s. 5d.; 2s. 7d.	
Haward	Coleraine	7 1/2 cwt tallow – £7 10s.; 40 hides – £20; 4 cwt yarn – £13 6s. 8d.	£40 16s. 8d.	£2 10d.	
		5 1/4 cwt yarn – £17 10s.; 2 cwt (42 lbs) tallow – £2 7s. 6d.	£19 17s. 6d.	19s. 10d.	
Haward	Coleraine	16 cwt tallow – £16.	£16	16s.	
		4 doz. calf skins – £1 6s. 8d.; 100 lamb skins – 10s.; 15 sheepskins – 2s. 5d.	£1 19s. 1d.	2s.; 6d.	
Haward	Coleraine	24 cwt tallow – £24; 200 salt hides – £100; 8 bal beef – £16.	£140	£7	
Fitchsimons	Drogheda	36 tons salmon – £324.	£324	£16 4s.	
		20 salt hides – £10; 3 sheepskins – 6d.	£10 6d.	10s.; 2s. 6d.	
Brasiar	Coleraine	2000 hogshead staves – £4; 30 bal small eels – £30; 5 bal great eels – £7 10s.; 1/2 ton 3 kits salmon – £7 17s.; 39 1/2 cwt tallow £39 10s.; 100 hides – £50; 1 bal beef – £2.			
Haward	Coleraine	63 cwt tallow – £63; 6 cwt hog's grease – £6; 60 hides – £30; 2 cwt sumacke – £1; 1 cwt 10 lbs bell metal – £1 16s. 8d.			
Grill	Coleraine	28 bal beef – £56.			
Beresford		2 hhd 2 bal salmon – £6 15s.			
Casie		2 bal beef – £4.			
Robinson		2 bal beef – £4.			
Egerton		2 bal beef – £4.		£317 8s. 8d.	£15 17s. 5d.
		12 hhd beef – £24; 2301 lbs candles – £38 7s.; 12 3/4 cwt tallow – £12 15s.; 106 salt hides – £53.			

Number	Folio	Date	Ship	Captain – Forename	Captain – Surname	Place – From	Place – To	Merchant Forename
		27 Feb. 1614	*Poote* of Londonderry – 70 tons	Robert	Berres	Coleraine	France	Thomas
34		22 Mar. 1614	*Guifte of God* of Irvine – 12 tons	William	Gawlton	Coleraine	Chester	William
		26 Mar. 1614	*Guifte of God* of Irvine – 12 tons	William	Gawlton	Coleraine	Chester	Henry
35	f	30 Mar. 1614	*Pellican* of Coleraine – 10 tons	James	Wise	Coleraine	Chester	Alexander
		30 Mar. 1614	*Pellican* of Coleraine – 10 tons	James	Wise	Coleraine	Chester	William
		30 Mar. 1614	*Pellican* of Coleraine – 10 tons	James	Wise	Coleraine	Chester	John

The account of Coleraine for custom of such goods as have been exported and brought into the port of Coleraine from 1 April 1614 until 30 September 1614 according to Mr Richard Barsiar's book of entries kept by him for the city of London (TN/PO7/1/1b)

Number	Folio	Date	Ship	Captain – Forename	Captain – Surname	Place – From	Place – To	Merchant Forename
36	f	6 Apr. 1614	Boat of Duncan Alche of Scotland	Duncan	Alche	Scotland	Coleraine	
37		10 Apr. 1614	Boat of Andrew Allises	Andrew	Allises	Scotland	Coleraine	
38		10 Apr. 1614	Boat used by James Fusher of Coleraine	James	Fusher	Isles of Scotland	Coleraine	
39		15 Apr. 1614	Boat of Duncan Leche	Duncan	Leche	Scotland	Coleraine	
40		16 Apr. 1614	Boat of John Morrishe	John	Morrishe	Scotland	Coleraine	
41	f	19 Apr. 1614	Boat of Walter Stente	Walter	Stente	Scotland	Coleraine	
42		20 Apr. 1614	Boat of John Taylor	John	Taylor	Scotland	Coleraine	
43		23 Apr. 1614	Boat of Davie Mellen	Davie	Mellen	Scotland	Coleraine	
44		30 Apr. 1614	Boat of William Somson	William	Somson	Scotland	Coleraine	
45		30 Apr. 1614	Boat of William Gaulte	William	Gaulte	Scotland	Coleraine	
46	f	6 May 1614	Boat of Robert Borne	Robert	Borne	Scotland	Coleraine	
47		7 May 1614	*Seaflower* of Dover – 100 tons	John	Zacary	London	Coleraine	Henry
	f	13 May 1614	*Seaflower* of Dover – 100 tons	John	Zacary	London	Coleraine	Phillip

Merchant Surname	Where Merchant is from	Goods	Total Value	Tax	Notes
Hillman	Coleraine	70 salt hides – £35; 2 cwt 44 lbs tallow – £2 7s. 10d.	£165 9s. 10d.	£8 5s. 6d.	
Ingman	Coleraine	4 cwt yarn – £13 6s. 8d.; 1 hhd beef – £4; 9 1/2 cwt tallow – £9 10s.; 560 lbs candles – £9 6s. 8d.; 43 flitches bacon – £5 6s. 8d.			
Catar	Chester	2 cwt yarn – £6 13s. 4d.; 60 salt hides – £30; 20 bal wheat – £20.	£98 3s. 5d.	£4 18s. 2d.	
Steward	Scotland	3 1/4 cwt yarn – £10 16s. 8d.; 2 bal salmon – £2 5s.; 2 cwt 14 lbs tallow – £2 5s.; 22 salt hides – £11.			
Ingman	Coleraine	30 hides – £15; 2 cwt tallow – £2; 2 cwt yarn – £6 13s. 4d.; 4 bal rye – 10s.			
Walton		6 bal beef – £12.			No total given for this entry.
		4 tons coal – £1 12s.; 30 gals aquavite – £2 10s.	£4 2s.	4s. 2d.; 1s.	
		3 tons 3 bal coal – £1 7s.	£1 7s.	1s. 4d.; 4d.	
		6 tuns French wine – £36.	£36	£1 16s.; 9s.	
		2 1/2 tons coal – £1 16s.	£1 16s.	1s. 10d.; 4d.	
		4 1/2 tons coal – £1 16s.	£1 16s.	1s. 10d.; 4d.	
		8 tons coal – £3 4s.	£3 4s.	3s. 3d.; 9d.	
		5 1/2 tons coal – £2 4s.	£2 4s.	2s. 3d.; 6d.	RJH has question mark at Scotland as place of origin. Page torn.
		8 tons coal – £3 4s.; 84 lbs brass kettles – £2 5s.; 3 bal pitch and tar – 16s. 8d.; 16 pair shoes – £1 4s.	£7 9s. 8d.	7s. 6d.; 1s. 10d.	
		5 tons coal – £2.	£2	2s.; 6d.	
		7 tons coal – £2 16s.; 1 cwt hops £1; 12 yds broad cloth – £7 5s.; 1 doz. horse locks – 10s.; 1 doz. chest locks – 18s.; 2 doz. fine hats – £4.	£16 9s.	16s. 6d.; 4s. 1d.	
		6 tons coal – £2 8s.; 16 gals aquavite – £1 6s. 8d.; 40 lbs madder 9s. 6d.; 16 lbs alum – 2s. 10d.; 86 lbs iron – 7s. 11d.	£[page damaged]	4s. 9d.; 1s. 2d.	
Jackson	London (Vintner)	Divers several sorts of nails, iron and iron tools – £15.			
Taylor	Coleraine	4 hhd aquavite – £16; 7 cwt hops – £7; 2 cwt prunes – £1; 2 pcs raisins – £1; 2 cwt white starch – £2; 2 cwt madder – £2 13s. 4d.; 3 cwt alum – £3; 1 cwt currants – £1 10s.; 1 cwt raisins of the sun – 18s.; 12 fkn soap – £6; 24 yds broad cloth – £6 13s. 4d.; 4 Devonshire dozens – £6 13s. 4d.; 6 doz. men's woollen stockings – £7 4s.; 30 pair men's worsted stockings – £7 10s; 4 doz. gloves – £2 8s. [page damaged]; 60 yds bays – £3; 1 pc Milan fustian – £2; 3 pcs serge deboyse – £15; 1 pc			

Number	Folio	Date	Ship	Captain – Forename	Captain – Surname	Place – From	Place – To	Merchant Forename
	f	14 May 1614	*Seaflower* of Dover – 100 tons	John	Zacary	London	Coleraine	Paul
48		17 May 1614	*William* of Northam – 10 tons	William	Jeffery	Barnstaple	Coleraine	Fulke
49	f	17 May 1614	Boat of William Somerll	William	Somerll	Scotland	Coleraine	
50		29 May 1614	Boat of John Renkeyn	John	Renkeyn	Scotland	Coleraine	
51		30 May 1614	Boat of William Browne	William	Browne	Scotland	Coleraine	
52		30 May 1614	Boat of John Lawramor	John	Lawramor	Scotland	Coleraine	
53		30 May 1614	Boat of John Taylor	John	Taylor	Scotland	Coleraine	
54		30 May 1614		James	Brocher	Scotland	Coleraine	
55		3 June 1614	*Bride* of Londonderry – 15 tons	Henry	Sadler	Chester	Coleraine	William
	f	5 June 1614	*Bride* of Londonderry – 15 tons	Henry	Sadler	Chester	Coleraine	John

Merchant Surname	Where Merchant is from	Goods	Total Value	Tax	Notes
		satin cypress – £3; 1 pc proropus – £5 10s.; 52 yds tammet – £6; 6 doz. garters – £1 10s.; 4 grs girdling – £3 4s.; 4 great grs thread points – £2; 1 great grs silk points – £6.			
Brasiar	Coleraine	4 hhd aquavite – £16; 24 fkn soap – £12; 2 cwt 68 lbs prunes – £5 14s. 8d.; 4 3/4 cwt powder sugar – £15 16s. 8d.; 3 cwt 14 lbs refined sugar – £10 8s. 4d.; 11 cwt 91 lbs raisins of the sun – £10 12s. 8d.; 138 pair men's worsted stockings – £34 10s.; 24 pair women's worsted stockings – £3 4s.; 96 pair men's woollen stockings – £9 12s.; 24 pair women's woollen stockings – £2 8s.; 36 pair children's stockings – £1 10s.; 1 bal drugs & 1 box oils – £12 11s. 7d.	£304 1s. 2d.	£15 4s.	
Downe	Barnstaple	10 Devonshire dozens – £16 13s. 4d.; 1 1/2 cwt hops – £1 10s.; 1 kilderkin soap – £1; 2 tons spanish iron – £20; 64 bushels spanish salt – £1 12s.; 1 cwt 101 lbs Spanish soap – £4 15s.; 2 cwt 4 lbs prunes – £1 5d.; 2 cwt 4 lbs currants – £3 1s.; 12 lbs tobacco – £6; 1 cwt 15 lbs white starch – £1 2s. 8d.; 75 lbs white sugar – £2 4s. 8d.; 169 lbs powder sugar – £5 7d.; 132 yds dowlas – £3 6s. 8d.; divers small wares – £27 17s.	£95 3s. 4d.	£4 15s. 2d.	
		5 tons coal – £2.	£2	2s.; 6d.	
		3 tuns French wine – £18.	£18	18s.; 4s. 6d.	
		6 tons coal – £2 8s.	£2 8s.	2s. 5d.; 7d.	
		8 tons coal – £3 4s.			
		7 tons coal – £2 16s.			
		9 tons coal – £3 12s.	£9 12s.	9s. 7d.; 2s. 5d.	Total given is for entries 52–4. No boat named.
Parry	Londonderry	3 cwt hops; 1 hhd salt; 4 doz. gloves and other things – £12 17s. 4d.			
Hatton	Coleraine	54 yds broad cloth – £15; 5 pcs kerseys – £11 2s.; 7 pcs mixed serges – £10 10s.; 6 pcs Genoa fustian – £4 10s.; 8 doz. (3 pcs) silk cyprus – £5 12s.; 4 pcs buffins – £4; 2 pcs silk rash – £5; 48 yds Flanders serge – £9 12s.; 11 ells coloured taffeta – £4 11s. 8d.; 2 pcs buckham – 10s.; 3 pcs ulm fustiam – £2 14s.; 7 lbs coloured silk lace – £9 6s. 8d.; 3 great grs silk buttons – £1 10s.; 1 paper Spanish silk – £2; 4 lbs coloured silk – £5 6s. 8d.; 1 pc shag – £1 10s.; 1 pc tuft canvas – 16s. 8d.; 46 ells holland – £3 1s. 4d.; 3 doz. men's worsted stockings – £9; 2 doz. men's woollen stockings – £2 8s.; 3 doz. women's woollen stockings – £3 12s.; 2 pcs says	£156 17s. 8d.	£7 16s. 10d.	RJH believes pott paper may have been cancelled.

Number	Folio	Date	Ship	Captain – Forename	Captain – Surname	Place – From	Place – To	Merchant Forename
56	f	4 June 1614	Boat of John Gouse	John	Gouse	Scotland	Coleraine	
57		5 June 1614	Boat of Thomas Gove	Thomas	Gove	Scotland	Coleraine	
58	f	19 June 1614	*Elizabeth* of London – 70 tons	Thomas	Parsonn	Chester	Coleraine	Ralph
		20 June 1614	*Elizabeth* of London – 70 tons	Thomas	Parsonn	Chester	Coleraine	William
59	f	12 July 1614	Boat of John Maddrell	John	Maddrell	Scotland	Coleraine	
60		21 July 1614	Boat of Davy Corphed	Davy	Corphed	Scotland	Coleraine	
61		28 July 1614	Boat of William Gaulte	William	Gaulte	Scotland	Coleraine	
62		28 July 1614	Boat of Robert Borne	Robert	Borne	Scotland	Coleraine	
63	f	24 Sep. 1614	*Consent* of London – 50 tons	Thomas	Evans	Chester	Coleraine	John
Outgates								
64	f	21 Apr. 1614	Boat of Andrew Allenson	Andrew	Allenson	Coleraine	Scotland	
65		21 Apr. 1614	Boat of Alan Allson	Alan	Allson	Coleraine	Scotland	
66		27 May 1614	*John Dumbart* of Scotland – 10 tons	John	Sempell	Coleraine	Chester	John
67		28 May 1614	*Seaflower* of Dover – 100 tons	John	Zacary	Coleraine	Spain	Paul
68	f	29 May 1614	Boat of Thomas Jackson	Thomas	Jackson	Coleraine	Scotland	
69		3 June 1614	Boat of Duncan Lecth	Duncan	Lecth	Coleraine	Scotland	
70		3 June 1614	Boat of William Norton	William	Norton	Coleraine	Scotland	

Merchant Surname	Where Merchant is from	Goods	Total Value	Tax	Notes
		– £2 13s. 4d.; 30 lbs fine indigo – £6; 2 cwt white sugar – £6 13s. 4d.; 12 lbs white candy – 11s.; 1 doz. women's bodices – £1 10s.; 1 hhd aquavite – £4; 1 doz. fine hats – £2; 2 reams pott paper – 13s.; 6 grs thread points – 13s.; 3 doz. fine knives 1 pc sackcloth – £3; 1 cwt gunpowder, 3 doz. men's hats – £4 6s. 8d.; 2 pcs calico – £1.			
		7 tons coal – £2 16s.			
Rowley	Coleraine	8 tons coal – £3 4s.	£6	6s.; 1s. 6d.	Total given is for entries 56–7.
		2 doz. men's hats – £4; 2 pcs kersey – £4 8s.; 1 fkn soap – 10s.; 2 doz. horse locks – £1; 6 saddles – £2 10s.; 2 doz. bridles – £1 4s.; 1 pc Milan fustian – £2; 3 pcs stuffs – £5; 1 Yorkshire dozen – £3 6s. 8d.			
Ingman	Coleraine	3 doz. men's hats; 3 doz. bridles; 12 doz. spurs and other wares – £14.	£37 18s. 8d.	£1 17s. 11d.	
		1 tun French wine – £6; 12 gals aquavite – £1; 2 hhd bay salt – 8s.	£7 8s.	7s. 5d.; 1s. 10d.	
		6 tons coal – £2 8s.	£2 8s.	2s. 5d.; 7d.	
		7 tons coal – £2 16s.; 12 pcs broad cloth – £7 5s.; horse locks, files and other iron tools – 18s.	£10 19s.	10s. 11d.; 2s. 9d.	
		40 yds Scotch cloth – £1 10s.; 2 cwt iron – £1; 16 gals aquavite – £1 6s. 8d.	£3 16s. 8d.	3s. 10d.; 11d.	
Hatton	Coleraine	7 doz. broad cloth – £23 6s. 8d.; 10 pcs kerseys – £22 5s.; 80 yds bays – £4; 44 yds cotton – £1 2s.; 4 1/2 cwt hops – £4 10s.; 5 reams pott paper – £1; 6 bal soap – £12; 2 cwt shot – £1 4s.; 3 hhd aquavite – £12; 2 cwt alum – £2; 3 pcs raisins – £1 10s.; 8 doz. knives – £2 10s.; 1 1/2 grs paste boards – £1.	£88 7s. 8d.	£4 8s. 5d.	
		30 bal oats – £20.			
		1000 hogshead staves – £2; 700 barrel staves – £1 1s.; 8 hides – £4; 4 doz. lamb skins – 4s. 6d.	£27 5s. 6d.	£1 7s. 3d.; 6s. 10d.	Total given is for entries 64–5.
Flud	Denbigh	59 bal wheat – £59; 40 bal oats – £26 13s. 4d.; 6 bal malt – £4; 5 bal barley – £3 6s. 8d.; 15 hides – £7 10s.	£100 10s.	£5 6d.	RJH notes that a John Lloyd was mentioned in the Chester port book.
Brasiar	Coleraine	1300 pipe staves – £5 4s.	£5 4s.	5s. 3d.	
		6 doz. cleft boards 16s.; 1 bal butter – £1 6s. 8d.; 2 doz. lamb skins – 2s.	£2 4s. 8d.	2s. 3d.; 6d.	
		40 tanned hides – £20; 1 doz. sheepskins – 1s. 7d.; 2 doz. lamb skins – 2s.; 1 doz. calf skins – 6s. 8d.; 4 goat skins – 1s.	£20 11s. 3d.	£1 7d.; 5s. 1d.	
		19 hides – £9 10s.; 100 calf skins – £2 15s. 6d.; 50 sheepskins – 7s. 6d.; 400 lamb skins – £2.	£14 13s.	14s. 8d.; 3s. 8d.	

Number	Folio	Date	Ship	Captain – Forename	Captain – Surname	Place – From	Place – To	Merchant Forename
71		24 June 1614	*William* of Northam – 10 tons	William	Gefferey	Coleraine	Barnstaple	Fulke
72		29 June 1614	*Hopewell* of Scotland – 14 tons	Davi	Mullen	Coleraine	Neston	Thomas
73	f	13 July 1614	*Blessing* of Coleraine – 60 tons	John	Betsonn	Coleraine	Chester	Nicholas
		14 July 1614	*Blessing* of Coleraine – 60 tons	John	Betsonn	Coleraine	Chester	John
		15 July 1614	*Blessing* of Coleraine – 60 tons	John	Betsonn	Coleraine	Chester	Thomas
		15 July 1614	*Blessing* of Coleraine – 60 tons	John	Betsonn	Coleraine	Chester	Davie
		15 July 1614	*Blessing* of Coleraine – 60 tons	John	Betsonn	Coleraine	Chester	Edward
		15 July 1614	*Blessing* of Coleraine – 60 tons	John	Betsonn	Coleraine	Chester	William
		15 July 1614	*Blessing* of Coleraine – 60 tons	John	Betsonn	Coleraine	Chester	George
		15 July 1614	*Blessing* of Coleraine – 60 tons	John	Betsonn	Coleraine	Chester	Edmond
		15 July 1614	*Blessing* of Coleraine – 60 tons	John	Betsonn	Coleraine	Chester	William
74	f	17 Aug. 1614	*Grace of God* of Burntisland – 40 tons	John	Hunter	Coleraine	Bilbao	Richard
75		16 Sep. 1614	*Hopewell* of Largs – 14 tons	John	Mellenton	Coleraine	Scotland	John
76		19 Sep. 1614	*Consent* of London – 50 tons	Thomas	Evans	Coleraine	London	William
		20 Sep. 1614	*Consent* of London – 50 tons	Thomas	Evans	Coleraine	London	John
	f	20 Sep. 1614	*Consent* of London – 50 tons	Thomas	Evans	Coleraine	London	Thomas
		20 Sep. 1614	*Consent* of London – 50 tons	Thomas	Evans	Coleraine	London	John
Ingates								
77	f	16 Oct. 1614	*Gifte of God* of Irvine – 15 tons	William	Gawlt	Irvine	Coleraine	William
78		23 Nov. 1614	*William* of Barnstaple – 10 tons	William	Jeffery	Barnstaple	Coleraine	John

Merchant Surname	Where Merchant is from	Goods	Total Value	Tax	Notes
Downe	Barnstaple	23 bal grotes – £15 6s. 8d.; 6 bal wheat – £6; 10 bal oatmeal – £4; 14 bal beef – £28; 5 bal pork – £10; 3 tons 1/2 bal salmon – £23 1s. 3d.; 80 salt hides – £40; 100 white leather – £1; 80 yds Irish canvas – £2; 5 cwt hog's grease – £5; 187 lbs Irish wool – £4 13s. 6d.; 2 doz. sheepskins – 3s. 2d.; 257 lbs Irish yarn – £7 2s. 6d.	£146 7s. 1d.	£7 6s. 4d.	
Hellman	Coleraine	20 hhd oatmeal – £16; 60 bal oats – £40; 6 bal rye – £4; 3 bal wheat – £3.	£63	£3 3s.	
Tirlaigh	Drogheda	4 packs Irish yarn – £53 6s. 8d.			
Aldersey	London-derry	80 bal oats – £53 6s. 8d.			
Helman	Coleraine	11 hhd oatmeal – £8 16s.; 120 bal oats – £80.			
Townesend	Coleraine	180 bal malt – £120; 60 bal oats – £40; 6 bal oatmeal – £2 8s.			
Watson	Coleraine	46 bal malt – £30 13s. 4d.			
Boulton	London	1 pack yarn – £13 6s. 8d.			
Hamond	London-derry	1 pack yarn – £13 6s. 8d.			
Haward	Coleraine	24 bal wheat – £24; 20 bal oats – £13 6s. 8d.			
Ingman	Coleraine	1/2 pack yarn – £6 13s. 4d.; 8 bal wheat – £8.	£467 4s.	£23 7s. 2d.	
Fitsimons	Drogheda	9 tons 1 bal salmon – £82 2s. 2d.	£82 2s. 2d.	£4 2s. 2d.	
Mellenton		30 bal barley, 30 bal oats – £40.	£40	£2 10s.	
Boulton	London	1 pack yarn – £13 6s. 8d.; 3 bal beef – £6; 16 cwt tallow – £16.			
Goodchild	Coleraine	6 1/2 cwt tallow – £8 10s.			
Welles	Wappinge	12 bal beef – £24; 3 cwt tallow – £3; 2 bal pork – £4; 7 hides – £3 10s.; 1 fkn salmon – 10s.			
Wallton	Coleraine	1 pack yarn – £13 6s. 8d.; 3 bal beef – £6.	£98 3s. 4d.	£4 18s. 2d.	
Gawlt		7 tons coal – £2 9s.; 4 bal bay salt – 8s.; 2 bal white herrings – £1 10s.; 40 gals aquavite – £3 6s. 8d.; 60 yds broadcloth – £36 5s.; 40 yds linen cloth – £1 6s. 8d.; 2 hhd apples – 4s.	£45 9s. 4d.	£2 5s. 6d.; 11s. 4d.	
Sparrow	Barnstaple	487 yds dowlas – £12 5s.; 40 ells holland – £2 13s. 4d.; 2 pcs says – £2 13s. 4d.; 12 yds calico – 12s.; 3 doz. pins, 1 doz. yds inkle; 3 bunches inkle rolls; 2 [missing]; 2 caps; 1 3/4 yds stoolwork – £2; 5 pcs Hamburg linin cloth – £3; 5 half pcs lawn – £5; 3 half pcs cambric – £3 15s.; 7 doz. girdles; 1 roll caddis; 1 boult blue thread;	£217 12s. 4d.	£10 17s. 7d.	

Number	Folio	Date	Ship	Captain – Forename	Captain – Surname	Place – From	Place – To	Merchant Forename
79	f	5 Dec. 1614	*Thomas* of Glasgow – 8 tons	Thomas	Jackson	Scotland	Coleraine	Thomas
80		29 Jan. 1615	Boat of Duncan Leach	Duncan	Leach	Scotland	Coleraine	
81		31 Jan. 1615	Boat of James [blank]	James	Blaick	Scotland	Coleraine	
82		31 Jan. 1615	*Salamander* of Irvine – 40 tons	Steven	White	Scotland	Coleraine	Archebell
83	f	15 Feb. 1615	*Gifte of God* of Irvine – 15 tons	William	Gawlt	Irvine	Coleraine	William
		15 Feb. 1615	*Gifte of God* of Irvine – 15 tons	William	Gawlt	Irvine	Coleraine	Robert
84		16 Mar. 1615	*Edward* of Hilbre – 24 tons	Henry	Androse	Chester	Coleraine	Edmond
85	f	13 Nov. 1614	*Blessing of God* of Shoreham – 30 tons	John	Mane	Coleraine	London	Humphrey

Merchant Surname	Where Merchant is from	Goods	Total Value	Tax	Notes
		12 grs thread points – £1 4s.; pepper, prunes, ginger, mace – £1; 2 1/4 cwt currants – £3 7s. 6d.; 12 lbs smalts; 4 lbs nutmeg – £1; 14 lbs aniseeds – 3s. 9d.; files scissors and compasses – £1 5s.; tailor's shears and glover's knives – £1 10s. (f) 4 masks – 10s.; 27 doz. knives – £3 10s.; 3 doz. and spurs – £1; 6 reams pott paper – £1 4s.; 2 cwt white sugar – £6 13s. 4d.; 2 1/4 cwt powder sugar – £7 10s.; 1 pc linen cloth – £1 2s.; axes hatchets and locks – £1 3s.; 2 doz. men's worsted stockings – £6; 1 doz. women's worsted stockings – £1 12s.; hard soap – £4; 2 pcs raisins – £1; 6 shovels 1 doz. woolcards – £1; 64 1/2 cwt Spanish iron – £32 5s.; 71 lbs pewter with plates candlesticks beakers and spoons, 17 [bra]ss kettles; i[ron] fry[ing pans]; dripping pans, saws locks and other wares – £17; 45 yds sackcloth and ropes – £1 4s.; 1 pc poldavis – £1; 6 doz. weak yarn; 10 doz. pasteboards – £3 16s.; 10 pcs mixed kerseys – £22 4s. 6d.; 1 1/2 cwt hops – £1 10s.; 23 bal bay salt – £2 6s.; 1 hhd vinegar – 11s. 8d.; 4 fkn soap – £2; 46 doz. earthen pots – £3; 3000 nails – 10s; 51 lbs tobacco – £25 10s.; silk ribbon, falling bands and gloves – £6; 4 pcs bays – £8; 6 1/2 grs tobacco pipes – £1.			
Jackson		44 hhd salt – 16s. 6d.; 3 hhd white herrings – £4 10s.; 21 quarts aquavite – 8s. 9d.	£5 14s. 9d.	5s. 9d.; 1s. 5d.	
		6 bal bay salt – 12s.; 2 gals aquavite – 3s. 4d.			No total or tax noted.
		24 gals aquavite – £2; 12 yds frieze – [12s.]	£3 7s. 4d.	3s. 4d.; 10d.	Page damaged where price of frieze is noted, but RJH believes it to be 12s. Total given for entries 80–81.
George	Irvine	136 bal bay salt – £13 12s.; 3 hhd Rochelle wine – £4 10s.; 60 lbs lead 3s. 6d.; 2 cwt iron – £1.	£19 5s. 6d.	19s. 3d.; 4s. 10d.	
Gawlt		10 tons coal – £2 10s.; 8 Scotch gals aquavite – £1 6s. 8d.; 60 yds frieze – £3; 12 pcs broadcloth – £7 5s.; 7 bal bay salt – 14s.; 1 brass kettle – £4.			
Stevensonn		1 brass kettle – £2; 5 pcs Scotch cloth – £7 10s.; 10 grs thread points – 8s. 4d.; 40 yds canvas – £1.	£29 14s.	£1 9s. 8d.; 7s. 6d.	
Haiward	Coleraine	114 yds broadcloth – £65; 14 1/2 pcs kerseys – £32 5s.; 100 yds coloured bays – £5; 10 doz. fine knives – £3 10s.; 24 grs silk buttons – £1; 6 lbs 8 oz. coloured silk lace – £8 13s. 4d.; 6 lbs cinnamon, 4 lbs cloves, 4 lbs mace – £2 16s.	£118 4s. 4d.	£5 18s. 3d.	
Lee	London	40 cwt tallow – £40; 5 1/2 tons beef – £88.			

Number	Folio	Date	Ship	Captain – Forename	Captain – Surname	Place – From	Place – To	Merchant Forename
		17 Nov. 1614	*Blessing of God* of Shoreham – 30 tons	John	Mane	Coleraine	London	Davy
		21 Nov. 1614	*Blessing of God* of Shoreham – 30 tons	John	Mane	Coleraine	London	Robert; Henry; Robert
		21 Nov. 1614	*Blessing of God* of Shoreham – 30 tons	John	Mane	Coleraine	London	Nicholas
		21 Nov. 1614	*Blessing of God* of Shoreham – 30 tons	John	Mane	Coleraine	London	Davy
86		5 Dec. 1614	*Thomas* of Glasgow – 8 tons	Thomas	Jackson	Coleraine	Scotland	Thomas
87	f	7 Dec. 1614	*William* of Barnstaple – 10 tons	William	Jeffery	Coleraine	Barnstaple	John
88		29 Jan. 1615	Scotch Boat			Coleraine	Islay	Davy
89		27 Feb. 1615	*Mary Grace* of Burntisland – 50 tons	John	Brene	Coleraine	France	Licktower
		27 Feb. 1615	*Mary Grace* of Burntisland – 50 tons	John	Brene	Coleraine	France	James
Ingates								
90	f	6 Apr. 1615	Boat of Duncan Leach	Duncan	Leach	Scotland	Coleraine	
91		6 Apr. 1615	Boat of William Sampsonn	William	Sampsonn	Scotland	Coleraine	
92		6 Apr. 1615	Boat of John Maccon	John	Maccon	Scotland	Coleraine	
93		6 Apr. 1615	*Perdew* of Scotland – 6 tons	Ringin	Andersonn	Scotland	Coleraine	Ringin
94		7 Apr. 1615	Boat of John White	John	White	Scotland	Coleraine	
		8 Apr. 1615	Boat of John White	John	White	Scotland	Coleraine	
95		7 Apr. 1615	*Bride* of Hilbre – 30 tons	Henry	Sadler	Chester	Coleraine	Henry
96	f	8 Apr. 1615	*Grace of God* of Scotland – 12 tons	John	Blage	Scotland	Coleraine	John
97		8 Apr. 1615	Boat of James Raye	James	Raye	Scotland	Coleraine	
98		8 Apr. 1615	Boat of Humphrey Warden	Humphrey	Warden	Scotland	Coleraine	

Merchant Surname	Where Merchant is from	Goods	Total Value	Tax	Notes
Townsend	Coleraine	8 dkr hides – £40; 19 cwt tallow – £19; 7 tons 1 hhd beef – £116.			
Rixon; Jackson; Wright	Coleraine	11 tons 3 bal beef – £182.			Three merchants named here.
Gill	London	1 1/2 tons beef – £24.			
Brenson	Coleraine	2 1/2 tons beef – £40.	£549	£27 9s.	
Jackson	Glasgow	10 bal oats – £6 13s. 4d.; 45 salt hides – £22 10s.; 4 horses – £80; 150 sheepskins – 18s. 9d.	£110 2s. 1d.	£5 10s. 1d.; £1 7s. 6d.	Not stated definitely that Jackson is captain. Jackson is referred to in the entry as a 'stranger'.
Sparrow	Barnstaple	41 bal beef – £82; 17 1/2 cwt tallow – £17 10s.; 7 bal pork – £14; 2 fkn eels – 15s.; 1 bal salmon – £1 2s. 6d.; 32 salt hides – £16; 16 flitches bacon – £2.	£133 7s. 6d.	£6 13s. 5d.	
Townesend	Coleraine	5 tuns beer [page damaged]; 1 hhd 1/2 bal aquavite [page damaged] 6s. 8d.; 2 cwt cheese – 13s. 4d.; 4 doz. cloth stockings – £8.	£24	£1 4s.	No captain named.
Markemack		28 hhd beef – £112.			
Fusher	Coleraine	8 tons beef – £128; 120 salt hides – £60; 8 1/2 cwt candles – £16; 12 1/4 curt tallow – £12 5s.	£328 5s.	£16 8s. 3d.; £4 2s.	
		4 tons coal – £1.			
		5 tons coal – £1 5s.			
		6 tons coal – £1 10s.			
Andersonn		12 yds blue cloth – £1 16s.; 3 1/2 doz. woolcards – £2 5s.; 16 yds lawn – £2; 5 grs horn spoons – 15s.; 40 yds Scotch cloth – £3; 1 doz. Scotch daggers – £2 8s.; 2 doz. stirrup leathers with bridles and spurs – £2; 6 yds bone lace – £1 4s.; 1 doz. Scotch caps – 14s.; 2 chequer carpets – £1 6s.; 14 yds fine white cloth – £2 12s.; 3 lbs blue starch – 2s. 6d.; 48 yds white cloth – £3 12s.; 19 pair gloves – 11s. 4d.			
		4 tons coal – £1.			
		3 Scotch gals aquavite – 10s.; 9 tons coal – £2 5s.	£29 10d.	£1 9s.; 7s. 3d.	Total given for entries 90–94.
Wright	Coleraine	1/2 cwt aniseeds; 1/2 cwt grains – £2 12s. 4d.; 1 cwt liquorice; 27 lbs pepper – £2 10s.; 6 lbs nutmeg, 4 oz. saffron – £1; 1 cwt ginger, 2000 pins – £1 15s.	£7 17s. 4d.	7s. 10d.	
Blage		12 tons coal – £3; 10 Scotch gals aquavite – £1 13s. 4d.; 1 bal herrings – 15s; 3 bal bay salt – 6s.			
		4 tons coal – £1; 2 Scotch gals aquavite – 6s. 8d.			
		4 tons coal – £1; 2 Scotch gals aquavite – 6s. 8d.			

Number	Folio	Date	Ship	Captain – Forename	Captain – Surname	Place – From	Place – To	Merchant Forename
99		8 Apr. 1615	Boat of William Snape	William	Snape	Scotland	Coleraine	
100		8 May 1615	Boat of John Wiatt	John	Wiatt	Scotland	Coleraine	
101		8 May 1615	*Robert*	John	Robarsonn	Scotland	Coleraine	
102		8 May 1615	*John* of Scotland – 6 tons	John	Robarsonn	Scotland	Coleraine	
103	f	8 May 1615	Boat of William Gragke	William	Gragke	Scotland	Coleraine	
104		8 May 1615	Boat of James Howe	James	Howe	Scotland	Coleraine	
105		16 May 1615	*Saray* of Hilbre – 25 tons	John	Howe	Chester	Coleraine	Davie
		16 May 1615	*Saray* of Hilbre – 25 tons	John	Howe	Chester	Coleraine	Brute
		17 May 1615	*Saray* of Hilbre – 25 tons	John	Howe	Chester	Coleraine	John
	f	18 May 1615	*Saray* of Hilbre – 25 tons	John	Howe	Chester	Coleraine	John
106	f	19 May 1615	*Mary* of Barnstaple – 24 tons	John	Bepell	Barnstaple	Coleraine	Peter

Merchant Surname	Where Merchant is from	Goods	Total Value	Tax	Notes
		6 tons coal – £1 10s.; 7 iron pots – £3 10s.; 40 yds linen cloth – £5; 2 yds woollen cloth – 4s.			
		4 tons coal – £1.			
		6 tons coal – £1 10s.; 1 hhd white salt – 5s. 4d.; 12 Scotch gals aquavite – £2.			
		12 gals aquavite – £1; 6 tons coal – £1 10s.	£28 12s.	£1 8s. 7d.; 7s. 2d.	Total given for entries 96–102.
		4 tons coal – £1; 3 Scotch gals aquavite – 10s.			
		3 1/2 tons coal – 17s. 6d.; 4 gals aquavite – 6s. 8d.	£2 14s. 2d.	2s. 9d.; 7d.	Total given for entries 103–4.
Townesend	Coleraine	5 Northern dozens – £16 13s. 4d.; 36 yds Kentish cloth – £10; 16 pcs of Devonshire dozens – £22 3s.; 1 pc cotton – 18s.; fustians and other wares – £33.			
Hammond	London-derry	4 pcs Milan fustian; 3 pcs Spanish rashes and other wares – £30; 4 Northern dozens – £10 6s. 8d.; 5 pcs Devonshire kerseys – £11 1s. 8d.; 3 pcs Manchester stuffs – £4 4s.			
Goodchild	Coleraine	112 yds broadcloth – £31 3s. 4d.; 6 lbs tobacco – £3; 7 doz. fine hats – £14; 7 doz. hatbands – £8 8s.; 4 doz. saddle-trees – £2 16s.			
Hatton	Coleraine	72 yds broadcloth – £20; 10 doz. fine knives – £4; 1000 foot glass – £12; 29 fine hats – £4 16s. 8d.; 50 lbs comfits – £2 10s.; 6 pcs kerseys – £13 6s. 8d.; 40 yds bays – £2; 18 ells holland – £1 4s.; 2 pcs says – £2 13s. 4d.; 6 pcs Genoa fustian – £4 10s.; 4 pcs ulm fustian – £3 12s.; 1 pc Milan fustian – £2; 1 pc white shag – £2 8s.; 8 ells coloured taffita – £3 6s. 8d.; 12 doz. men's woollen stockings – £14 8s.; 2 pcs mixed broad says – £3; 2 pcs Spanish rash – £9; 2 pcs Flanders say – £4 16s.; 1 pc lisle grogham – £1 16s.; 1 pc silk rash – £2 8s.; 12 lbs nutmeg – £1 10s.; 6 lbs mace – £1 10s.; 6 lbs coloquintida – 12s.; 12 lbs senna – 18s.; 3 doz. gloves – £1 16s.; 1 doz. girdles and hangers – £1 10s.; 3 doz. bottles covered with leather – 18s.; 2 doz. scythes – £2 8s.; 3 lbs coloured silk – £4; 2 1/2 lbs silk lace – £3 6s. 8d.; 1 doz. collars – 18s.; 1 grs gartering – 13s.; 4 doz. sweet bales – £1; 2 doz. bodices – £3; 2 doz. pins, 4 doz. – 4d.; silk ribons – £1.	£339 3s.	£16 19s. 2d.	
Cogan	Coleraine	181 yds dowlas, points pins, inkle and other small wares – £16 10s.; 162 yds dowlas, pins, gartering and other wares – £18 2s.; 4 pcs fustians, sackcloth, holland and other wares – £24 4s. 4d.; 68 lbs weak yarn – £3 7s.;	£208 18s. 8d.	£10 8s. 11d.	

Number	Folio	Date	Ship	Captain – Forename	Captain – Surname	Place – From	Place – To	Merchant Forename
107	f	19 May 1615	Boat of John Tenkell	John	Tenkell	Scotland	Coleraine	
108		22 May 1615	Boat of John Longe	John	Longe		Coleraine	
109		3 June 1615	Boat of Robert Forrest	Robert	Forrest		Coleraine	
110		3 June 1615	Boat of John Millar	John	Millar		Coleraine	
111		5 June 1615	Boat of John Overry	John	Overry		Coleraine	
112		5 June 1615	Boat of John Tenkoll	John	Tenkoll		Coleraine	
113		5 June 1615	Boat of John Longe	John	Longe		Coleraine	
114		15 June 1615	*Seaflower* of London – 60 tons	John	Zacary	London	Coleraine	Henry
		15 June 1615	*Seaflower* of London – 60 tons	John	Zacary	London	Coleraine	George
		15 June 1615	*Seaflower* of London – 60 tons	John	Zacary	London	Coleraine	John
	f	6 July 1615	*Seaflower* of London – 60 tons	John	Zacary	London	Coleraine	William
		6 July 1615	*Seaflower* of London – 60 tons	John	Zacary	London	Coleraine	William
		6 July 1615	*Seaflower* of London – 60 tons	John	Zacary	London	Coleraine	Davie

Merchant Surname	Where Merchant is from	Goods	Total Value	Tax	Notes
		134 pairs shoes boots and slippers – £13 10s. 6d.; 12 chamber pots, 6 lbs arsenic, 1 doz. quart pots, onion seeds and other wares – £3 18s. 4d.; 4 hhd 3 bal apples – 11s.; 28 lbs cinnamon and other spices, 6 pcs raisins, aniseeds and other wares – £18 8s. 6d.; 4 bal peas – 8s.; 2 bal fine meal – £2 16s.; 62 lbs succade marmalade and Genoa treacle – £4 16s.; 2 tons iron – £20; 3 pcs raisins – £1 10s.; 4 doz. hemp halters – 12s.; 112 lbs white sugar – £3 6s. 8d.; 3 pcs harfords 1/2 cwt madder, 18 lbs comfits and other small wares – £30 5s.; 1 hhd green copperas – £2; 55 yds dowlas and other small wares – £10 14s. 1d.; 2 maundes earthen pots – £3 19s. 3d.; 100 bushels bay salt – £2 10s.; 2 cwt prunes – £1; divers sorts of small wares – £20; 5 lbs leaf tobacco – £2 10s.; ropes and cords – £4.			
		6 tons coal – £1 10s.			
		5 tons coal – £1 5s.			
		5 tons coal – £1 5s.			
		12 1/2 tons coal – £3 2s. 6d.			
		4 tons coal – £1.			
		6 tons coal.			No price noted.
		5 tons coal – £1 5s.	£10 17s. 6d.	10s. 10d.; 2s. 8d.	Total given is for entries 107–13.
Jackson		3 sums – 2d.; nails, spades, chisels and other iron tools, 12 calivers, 6 bills, shot, powder and other things – £13 6s. 8d.			Henry Jackson, acting on behalf of the Vintners' Company.
Canning		5 fkn nails, 5 cwt iron, shovels, locks, crows, pickaxes and other things – £20.			George Canning, acting on behalf of the Ironmongers' Company.
Hatton	Coleraine	1 tun aquavite – £16; 2 cwt currants, 2 doz. pepper – £5, 1 cwt liquorice, 1 cwt gunpowder – £1 16s. 8d.; 2 cwt raisins of the sun, 6 lbs quicksilver – £2 6s.; 4 bal soap – £8; 5 cwt shot, 1 chest glasses – £6; 6 reams pott paper – £1 4s.; 1 grs box combs, 3 doz. pins – 17s.; 6 doz. primers, 2 grs cards – £2 18s.; 1 doz. crystal glasses – £1 4s.; 12 buckets, 2 pcs boulter – £2 10s.			
Bowlton	London	2 tuns aquavite – £32; 6 cwt hops – £6; Norwich stuffs and gartering – £40; 10 doz. London knives – £3; 3 cwt madder – £2 13s. 4d.; 2 cwt alum – £2; 28 lbs indigo – £5 12s.; 2 pcs raisins, 1 cwt raisins of the sun – £1 18s.			
Barrow		40 gals aquavite – £3 6s. 8d.; 1 fkn soap – 10s.			
Townesend	Coleraine	6 cwt hops – £6; 2 cwt shot – £1 4s.			

Number	Folio	Date	Ship	Captain – Forename	Captain – Surname	Place – From	Place – To	Merchant Forename
	f	29 July 1615	*Seaflower* of London – 60 tons	John	Zacary	London	Coleraine	George
		29 July 1615	*Seaflower* of London – 60 tons	John	Zacary	London	Coleraine	Richard

Merchant Surname	Where Merchant is from	Goods	Total Value	Tax	Notes
Swetnam	Coleraine	60 lbs indigo – £12; 4 3/4 cwt prunes – £2 7s. 6d.; Norwich stuffs – £56; [page damaged] pcs cambric – £2 10s.; 3 pcs lawn – £3; 198 ells holland – £13 4s.; 7 1/4 cwt hops – £7 5s.; 4 doz. children's stockings – £2; 4 doz. women's stockings – £4 16s.; 3 doz. men's woollen stockings – £3 12s.; 8 1/2 doz. men's worsted stockings – £25 10s.; 10 doz. gloves – £3 10s.; 40 yds blue and coloured satin – £18; 84 ells blue and coloured taffita – £35; 12 lbs 13 oz. coloured silk lace – £17 1s. 8d.; 8 lbs 8 oz. blue silk lace – £11 6s. 8d.; 3 1/2 grs silk points – £1 15s.; 1 lb silver parchment – £4; 12 yds blue velvet – £9; 80 fine hats – £13 6s. 8d.; 40 taffita bands – £10; haberdashery wares – £24; girdles, whalebone, bodices – £13; 2 lbs Spanish silk – £2; 33 yds [?] Cyprus – £1 2s. 6d. [f] 32 yds London dye Cyprus – £1 17s. 4d.; 31 yds coloured French velvet – £23 5s.; Grayier's wares – £8; 6 cwt raisins of the sun – £5 8s.; 8 cwt currants – £12; 4 1/2 cwt white starch – £4 10s.; 2 1/4 cwt Castile soap – £4 10s.; 2 1/2 cwt liquorice – £2 5s.; 70 lbs smalts – £4 13s. 4d.; 8 pcs raisins – £4; 25 lbs cloves – £5; 50 lbs nutmeg – £6 5s.; 27 lbs mace – £6 15s.; 3 lbs wormseed – 12s.; 3 cwt pepper – £28; 3 cwt treacle – £1 10s.; 2 cwt gunpowder – £2 13s. 4d.; 6 cwt madder – £8; 53 grs silk buttons – £2 4s. 2d.; 8 pcs Genoa fustian – £6; 74 pcs ulm fustian – £3 12s.; 1 pc green say – £1 6s. 8d.; 6 bal soap – £12; 30 cwt iron – £15; 2 1/2 cwt steel – £1 17s. 6d.; 93 lbs white candy – £4 13s.; iron wares – £16; [?] cotton yarn – £8 8s.; 2 bal salad oil – £5; sweetmeats – £24; 1 cwt brown candy – £3 6s. 8d.; 47 yds tabby silk grogham – £11 15s.; 560 lbs white sugar – £16 13s. 4d.; 80 lbs fine indigo – £16; 3 hhd aquavite – £12; pewter – £50; 20 reams capp paper, 10 reams pott paper – £4 10s.			
Pitt	London	8 doz. men's woollen stockings – £9 12s.; 8 doz. men's worsted stockings – £24; 6 grs gartering; 2 1/2 doz. coloured inkles – £4 12s.; 3 doz. loom work, 3 doz. pickadellies – £3 1s. 6d.; 4 lbs sisters thread – 16s.; 2 pcs Osborrow fustians – £2; 8 pcs Milan fustians – £16; 2 pcs tufted sackcloth – £1; 6 doz. blue coifs – £1; tobacco pipes and points – 12s.; 1 pc Spanish satin – £1 3s. 4d.			

Number	Folio	Date	Ship	Captain – Forename	Captain – Surname	Place – From	Place – To	Merchant Forename
		29 July 1615	*Seaflower* of London – 60 tons	John	Zacary	London	Coleraine	George
115	f	22 June 1615	Boat of John Morrison	John	Morrison	Scotland	Coleraine	
116		23 June 1615	*Grace of God* of Saltcoats – 24 tons	John	Blage	Scotland	Coleraine	John
117		23 June 1615	*Gifte of God* of Irvine – 15 tons	William	Gawlte	Scotland	Coleraine	William
118		23 June 1615	*Good Fortune* of Irvine – 15 tons	William	Hambleton	Scotland	Coleraine	William
119		23 June 1615	Boat of Andrew Garvan	Andrew	Garvan	Scotland	Coleraine	
120		23 June 1615	Boat of Robert Forrest	Robert	Forrest		Coleraine	
121		22 June 1615	*Cathren* of Carlingford – 15 tons	James	Booth	France	Coleraine	James
122	f	30 June 1615	*Elizabeth* of Glasgow – 6 tons	Duncan	Leech	Scotland	Coleraine	Duncan
123		10 July 1615	Boat of John Jackson	John	Jackson	Scotland	Coleraine	
124		15 July 1615	*Salamander* of Irvine – 40 tons	Steeven	Wheett	France	Coleraine	Archibald
125	f	22 July 1615	*Robert* of Irvine – 12 tons	James	Blare	Scotland	Coleraine	James
126	f	29 July 1615	*John* of Scotland – 6 tons	Robert	Forrest	Scotland	Coleraine	
		29 July 1615	*John* of Scotland – 6 tons	Robert	Forrest	Scotland	Coleraine	John
		29 July 1615	*John* of Scotland – 6 tons	Robert	Forrest	Scotland	Coleraine	John
		29 July 1615	*John* of Scotland – 6 tons	Robert	Forrest	Scotland	Coleraine	William
		29 July 1615	*John* of Scotland – 6 tons	Robert	Forrest	Scotland	Coleraine	Peter

Merchant Surname	Where Merchant is from	Goods	Total Value	Tax	Notes
Costardyne		4 1/2 bal nails – £60; crows, sledges and other wrought iron – £8; 1 crane and 1 coil, shovels and spades – £2 4s.	£959 4s.	£47 17s. 1d.	George Costardyne, acting on behalf of the Merchant Taylors' Company.
		5 tons coal – £1 5s.			
Blage		24 tons coal – £24.			
Gawlte		28 Scotch gals aquavite – £4 13s. 4d.; 12 yds Scotch cloth – 14s.; 30 yds linen cloth – £1; 8 yds linen cloth – £1; 34 knives – 9s. 5d.; 15 tons coal – £3 15s.			
Gawlte		15 tons coal – £3 15s.; 12 yds grey cloth – £1 6s.; 48 Scotch gals aquavite – £8.			
		6 tons coal – £1 10s.			
		5 tons coal – £1 5s.	£34 12s. 9d.	£1 14s. 7d.; 8s. 8d.	Total given is for entries 115–20.
Booth		80 bal bay salt – £8; 4 tun French wine – £12; 1 ton French nuts – £1 6s. 8d.; 1/2 ton prunes – £5; 1 1/2 tuns vinegar – £3 10s.	£29 16s. 8d.	£1 9s. 8d.	
Leech		8 hhd bay salt – £1 12s.; 1 brass pan (70 lbs), 1 brass pot (56 lbs) – £3 17s.; 32 Scotch gals aquavite – £5 6s. 8d.; 20 spades – 10s.; 3 yds cloth – 7s. 6d.; 70 yds linen cloth – £4 1s. 8d.; 4 doz. horseshoes, 6 forks, 4 baking irons – 15s.; fustian madder, alum – 19s. 2d.; 2 1/2 grs knives – £1 16s.	£19 5s.	19s. 3d.; 4s. 9d.	
		4 tons 2 bal coal – £1 1s.			
George		120 bal bay salt – £12; 6 tuns Rochell wine – £18.	£31 1s.	£1 11s.; 7s. 9d.	Total given is for entries 123–4.
Blare		8 tons coal – £2; 1 cwt madder – £1 6s. 8d.; 40 lbs alum – 7s. 6d.; 26 lbs aniseeds – 7s.; 14 lbs grains – 9s. 4d.; 12 yds grey cloth – £1 4s.; 500 yds linen cloth – £25; 1 brass kettle (40 lbs) – £1 1s. 4d.	£31 15s. 10d.	£1 11s. 9d.; 8s.	
		5 tons coal – £1 5s.			Robert Forrest probably the merchant also.
Sommaran		12 iron pots – £1; 100 yds linen cloth – £6 13s. 4d.; 20 yds cloth – £2 10s; 6 yds broad cloth – £3 12s.; 8 doz. reaping hooks – £2; 1 cwt madder – £1 6s. 8d.; 5 doz. knives – £1.			
Breddy		6 Scotch gals aquavite – £1; 40 yds linen cloth – £4; 50 lbs madder – 13s. 4d.; 6 doz. knives – £1 4s.			
Breddy		50 ells Scotch cloth – £3 2s. 6d.; 2 doz. woolcards – £1; 10 Scotch hats – 16s. 8d.; 12 blue bonnets – 12s.; 4 iron pots – 6s. 8d.; 12 doz. knives – £2 8s.; 12 lbs madder – 3s.			
Som'er		16 yds grey cloth – £1 1s. 4d.; 12 Scotch gals aquavite – £2; 60 yds linen cloth – £3; 2 doz. bridles – £1 4s.; 2 doz. brass spurs – £1; 30 lbs aniseeds – 8s.; 50 horseshoes – 12s. 6d.			

Number	Folio	Date	Ship	Captain – Forename	Captain – Surname	Place – From	Place – To	Merchant Forename
127		20 Aug. 1615	*John* of Scotland – 6 tons	John	Harvie	Scotland	Coleraine	John
128		12 Sep. 1615	*Grace of God* of Scotland – 10 tons	Walter	Steven	Scotland	Coleraine	Walter
Outgates								
129	f	5 Apr. 1615	*John* of Scotland – 6 tons	Renninge	Andiose	Coleraine	Scotland	Renninge
130		5 Apr. 1615	*John* of Saltcoats – 5 tons	John	White	Coleraine	Scotland	James
131		12 Apr. 1615	*Bride* of Londonderry – 30 tons	Henry	Sadler	Coleraine	Chester	Henry
132		13 Apr. 1615	*Grace of God* of Scotland – 12 tons	John	Blage	Coleraine	Chester	Lawrence
133		26 Apr. 1615	*Fyall* of Scotland – 6 tons	William	Helpe	Coleraine	Scotland	William
134		27 Apr. 1615	Boat of William Greeson	William	Gresson	Coleraine	Scotland	
135	f	2 May 1615	*Clemott* of Scotland – 6 tons	Robert	Bockes	Coleraine	Scotland	Robert
136		9 May 1615	Boat of Steven Robinson	Steven	Robinson	Coleraine	Scotland	
137		9 May 1615	Boat of John Hunter	John	Hunter	Coleraine	Scotland	
138		17 May 1615	Boat of John Marsonn	John	Marsonn	Coleraine	Scotland	
139		27 May 1615	Boat of Thomas Blacke	Thomas	Blacke	Coleraine	Scotland	
140		28 May 1615	Boat of John Robartsonn	John	Robartsonn	Coleraine	Scotland	
141		28 May 1615	Boat of Andrew Mellar	Andrew	Mellar	Coleraine	Scotland	
142		28 May 1615	*Genett* of Scotland – 5 tons	John	Wilson	Coleraine	Scotland	John
143	f	28 May 1615	Scotch Boat			Coleraine	Scotland	Thomas
144		28 May 1615	Boat of Robert Forrest	Robert	Forrest	Coleraine	Scotland	
145		28 May 1615	Boat of John Robinson	John	Robinson	Coleraine	Scotland	
146		28 May 1615	Boat of Scotland – 5 tons	Robert	Portar	Coleraine	Scotland	Robert
147		5 June 1615	Boat of Adam Follarton	Adam	Follarton	Coleraine	Scotland	
148		16 June 1615	*Griffin* of Drogheda – 50 tons	Patrick	Creeley	Coleraine	Spain	Richard
		23 June 1615	*Griffin* of Drogheda – 50 tons	Patrick	Creeley	Coleraine	Spain	Richard
149		21 June 1615	*Unicorne* of Chester – 30 tons	Davie	Hill	Coleraine	Chester	Steven

Merchant Surname	Where Merchant is from	Goods	Total Value	Tax	Notes
Harvie		100 yds Scotch cloth – £7 10s.; 40 lbs aniseeds – 12s.; 20 lbs grains – 13s. 4d.; 4 doz. girths – 12s.; 8 grs leather points – 10s. 8d.; 1 doz. spurs – 7s.; 2 doz. pins – 8s.; 2000 needles – 2s. 8d.; 3 doz. bridle bits – 10s. 6d.			
Steven		9 tons coal – £2 5s.; 8 stone iron – 8s.; 4 Scotch gals aquavite – 13s. 4d.	£58 11s. 7d.	£2 18s. 8d.; 14. 6d.	Total given is for entries 126–8.
Andiose		130 hides – £65.			
Blaier		50 hides – £25; 1 bal beef – £2.	£92	£4 12s.; £1 3s.	Total given is for entries 129–30.
Sadler		22 dkr hides – £110; 7 hhd beef – £28; 4 1/2 cwt tallow – £4 10s.			
Rabon	Coleraine	4 dkr salt hides – £20; 2 dkr tanned hides – £10.	£172 10s.	£8 12s. 6d.	Total given is for entries 131–2.
Helpe		1 1/2 dkr salt hides – £7 10s.; 200 sheepskins – £1 10s.; 1 doz. calf skins, 6 doz. lamb skins – 14s. 4d.	£53 4s. 9d.	£2 13s. 3d.; 13s. 3d.	Total given is for entries 133–4.
Bockes		80 salt hides – £40; 30 sheepskins, 5 bal oats – £3 10s. 5d.			
		15 dkr salt hides – £75; 600 coney skins – £1; 200 sheepskins, 200 lamb skins – £2 10s.; 40 bal oats – £26 13s. 4d.; 8 doz. inch boards – £3 4s.			
		16 stone iron – £1 11s. 9d.			
		80 bal oats – £53 6s. 8d.; 100 clove boards – £1.			
		20 hides – £10; 200 clove boards – £2.			
		700 ft planks – £3 10s.; 3 tons timber – £3; 4 beams – £1; 6 doz. clove boards – 14s.			
		40 doz. clove boards – £3 13s. 4d.; 400 clove boards – £4; 15 hides – £7 10s.; 1 timber beam – 5s.			
		2 1/2 dkr hides – £12 10s.; 200 lamb skins – £1.	£214 8s. 1d.	£2 13s. 7d.	Total given is for entries 135–41.
Halton	Coleraine	80 bal oats – £53 6s. 8d.	£53 6s. 8d.	£2 13s. 4d.	
Helman	Coleraine	100 bal oats – £66 13s. 4d.	£66 13s. 4d.	£3 6s. 8d.	
Forrest		100 hides – £50; 200 sheepskins – £1 10s.			
		40 hides – £20.			
		20 hides – £10; 200 sheepskins – £1 10s.			
		80 bal oats – £53 6s. 8d.; 35 hides – £17 10s.	£153 16s. 8d.	£7 13s. 9d.; £1 18s. 5d.	Total given is for entries 144–7.
Fitesimons	Drogheda	12 dkr tanned hides – £60.			
Fitesimons	Drogheda	10 dkr tanned hides – £50; 68 salt hides – £34.			
Smith	Chard	1 1/2 packs Irish linen yarn – £20; 30 ells Scotch cloth – £4.	£168	£8 8s.	Total given is for entries 148–9.

Number	Folio	Date	Ship	Captain – Forename	Captain – Surname	Place – From	Place – To	Merchant Forename
150	f	24 June 1615	Boat of William Semson	William	Semson	Coleraine	Scotland	
151		27 June 1615	*Grace of God* of Saltcoats – 24 tons	John	Blage	Coleraine	Scotland	Edward
152		27 June 1615	*Margett* of Dumbarton – 12 tons	James	Rooe	Coleraine	Scotland	Edward
153		28 June 1615	*John* of Renfrew – 7 tons	John	Reede	Coleraine	Scotland	John
154		28 June 1615	Boat of Duncan Leech	Duncan	Leech	Coleraine	Glasgow	
155		28 June 1615	Boat of William Gage	William	Gage	Coleraine	Scotland	
156		28 June 1615	*Bride* of Hilbre – 30 tons	Richard	Sadlar	Coleraine	Chester	William
157	f	29 July 1615	*Mary* of Barnstaple – 20 tons	John	Beple	Coleraine	Barnstaple	Peter
158		29 July 1615	*Seaflower* of London – 60 tons	John	Zacary	Coleraine	London and Chester	John
		29 July 1615	*Seaflower* of London – 60 tons	John	Zacary	Coleraine	London and Chester	George
		29 July 1615	*Seaflower* of London – 60 tons	John	Zacary	Coleraine	London and Chester	William
	f	10 Aug. 1615	*Seaflower* of London – 60 tons	John	Zacary	Coleraine	London and Chester	Richard
		17 Aug. 1615	*Seaflower* of London – 60 tons	John	Zacary	Coleraine	London and Chester	George
159		29 July 1615	Boat of William Snape	William	Snape	Coleraine	Scotland	
160		29 July 1615	*Gift of God* of Burntisland – 40 tons	Robert	Garnere	Coleraine	France	John
161	f	3 Aug. 1615	*Grace of God* of Burntisland – 34 tons	Thomas	Sunter	Coleraine	Spain	Richard
162		3 Aug. 1615	*Blessing of God* of Burntisland – 39 tons	Davie	Barraine	Coleraine	Spain	Richard
163		17 Aug. 1615	*Elizabeth* of Scotland – 9 tons	Duncan	Leach	Coleraine	Glasgow	Duncan
164	f	28 Aug. 1615	*John* of Renfrew – 20 tons	Adam	Modwill	Coleraine	Chester	John
165		29 Aug. 1615	*Bride* of Londonderry – 20 tons	Richard	Sadler	Coleraine	Chester	John
		4 Sep. 1615	*Bride* of Londonderry – 20 tons	Richard	Sadler	Coleraine	Chester	Richard
166		27 Sep. 1615	*Trenyty* of Chester – 20 tons	Richard	Sadler	Coleraine	Chester	William
		27 Sep. 1615	*Trenyty* of Chester – 20 tons	Richard	Sadler	Coleraine	Chester	Raph

Merchant Surname	Where Merchant is from	Goods	Total Value	Tax	Notes
		3 doz. lamb skins – 3s. 6d.; 20 goat skins – 2s. 8d.; 8 doz. calf skins – £2 13s. 4d.	£2 18s. 6d.	3s. 9d.	
Wattsonn	Coleraine	20 horses – £400.			
Wattson	Coleraine	10 horses – £200.	£600	£30	Total given is for entries 151–2.
Samreste		8 dkr dry hides – £40; 3 horses – £60.			
		8 dkr hides – £40; 3 horses – £60.			
		36 bal oats – £24; 3 bal barley – £1 6s. 8d.	£225 6s. 8d.	£11 5s. 4d.; £2 16s. 3d.	Total given is for entries 153–5.
Boulton	London	7 cwt Irish linen yarn – £23 6s. 8d.	£23 6s. 8d.	£1 3s. 4d.	
Cogan	Coleraine	5 tons timber – £5; 46 doz. clove boards – £5 15s.; 500 hogshead staves – £1; 20 dkr salt hides – £100; 4 cwt Irish linen yarn – £13 6s. 8d.; 10 cwt tallow – £10; 60 lbs tallow – 10s.; 1 hhd 1 bal 1 fkn salmon – £3 13s. 1d.; 3 cwt 52 lbs wool – £12 10s.; 30 doz. sheepskins – £2 14s.; 8 hides – £4.			
Rowley	Coleraine	20 dkr tanned hides – £100.			
Swetnam	Coleraine	10 cwt tallow – £10; 30 salt hides – £15.			
Boulton	London	3 bal salmon – £3 7s. 6d.			
Pitt	London	4 dkr tanned hides – £20; 3 fkn salmon – £1; 1 cwt Irish linen yarn – £3 6s. 8d.; 5 horses – £66 13s. 4d.; 12 cows – £12; 5 flitches bacon – 12s. 6d.; 1 small bal neats' tongues – £1.			
Swetnam	Coleraine	8 cwt tallow – £8; 4 bal salmon – £4 10s.; 90 lbs Irish linen yarn – £2 10s.	£406 8s. 9d.	£20 6s. 5d.	
		6 dkr raw hides – £30; 1 horse – £20; 600 hogshead – 6s.			
Power		50 dkr hides – £250.	£300 6s.	£15 3d.; £3 15s.	Total given is for entries 159–60.
Fitesimons	Drogheda	34 tons salmon – £306.			
Fitesimons	Drogheda	39 tons salmon – £351.	£657	£32 17s.	Total given is for entries 161–2.
Leach		7 dkr hides – £35; 1000 barrel staves – £1 10s.; 200 sheepskins – £1 10s.; 1 hhd salmon – £2 5s.	£40 5s.	£2 3s.; 10s.	
Aldersey	London-derry	20 tons timber – £20; 1 cwt linen yarn – £3 6s. 8d.			
Rowley	Coleraine	5 dkr tanned hides – £25.			
Stanton	Shrewsbury	60 salt hides – £30; 20 cwt tallow – £20.			
P[arry]	Chester	4 1/2 tons beef – £72; 9 hides – £4 10s.			
Hilton	Chester	1 ton 6 bal beef – £28; 30 salt hides – £15; 9 cwt tallow – £9.	£226 16s. 8d.	£11 6s. 10d.	Total given is for entries 164–6.

The Port Books
of Carrickfergus

Number	Folio	Date	Ship	Captain – Forename	Captain – Surname	Place – From	Place – To	Merchant Forename
1		23 Oct. 1614	*Guifte of God* of Isle of Man – 14 tons	Silvester	Stephenson		Carrickfergus	Silvester
2		14 Oct. 1614	*Trynnitie* of Parton	Richard	Griffen	Parton	Carrickfergus	
3		25 Oct. 1614	*Sara* of Chester	Richard	Ryman	Chester	Carrickfergus	Laurence
4		25 Oct. 1614	*Anne* of Parton	Thomas	Beande		Carrickfergus	Thomas
5		30 Oct. 1614	*Jennett* of Ayr	Henry	Steward	Ayr	Carrickfergus	Thomas
6	f.	2 Nov. 1614	*Daniell* of Leith – 50 tons	James	Lookeuppe		Carrickfergus	James
7		6 Nov. 1614	*Speedwell* of Beaumaris	Richard	Gryffen		Carrickfergus	Mathew
8		9 Nov. 1614	*Martyn* of Chester	Thomas	Dawson	Chester	Carrickfergus	Richard
9		6 Dec. 1614	*Guifte of God* of Glasgow	John	Smythe		Carrickfergus	John
10		7 Dec. 1614	*Sarah* of Weymouth	Gregory	Wattson		Carrickfergus	William
11	f.	7 Dec. 1614	*Fortune* of London – 20 tons	William	Armoulde		Carrickfergus	George
12		10 Dec. 1614	*Faullkon* of Liverpool	Edward	Nichollsone		Carrickfergus	Edward
13	f.	27 Jan. 1615	*Guift of God* of Glasgow	John	Murdoe		Carrickfergus	Mathew

Merchant Surname	Where Merchant is from	Goods	Total Value	Tax	Notes
Stephenson		12 tons coal – 4s.	4s.		RJH queries whether the date should read 13 October instead of 23 October.
		12 tons coal – 4s.	4s.		
Holland		1 cwt raisins of the sun – 18s.; 4 fkn soap – £2; 2 hhd vinegar – £1 3s. 4d.; 20 gals aquavite – £1 6s. 8d.; 2 pcs coarse lawn – £2; 6 lbs pepper – 10s.; 14 lbs aniseeds – 3s. 3d.; 5 lbs sugar candy – 4s. 6d.; 6 tons coal – £2.	£10 5s. 9d.	10s. 3d.	
Beande		3 tons coal – 1s.	1s.		
Gylpatricke	Carrick-fergus	1 hhd aquavite – £4; 80 deal boards – £3 13s. 4d.; 4 tons coal – £1 6s. 8d.; 2 copper pans (2 cwt) – £6; 40 lbs loaf sugar – £1; 2 bal soap – £4; 30 lbs powder – £1; 11 bal salt – £1 2s.	£22 2s.	£1 2s. 1d.	
Lookeuppe		15 gals aquavite – £1; 2 hhd wine – 3s.	1s.; 3d.		
Marshe		4 bal salt 2s.; 30 yds broadcloth – £9 6s. 8d.; 35 ells coarse linen cloth – £1 15s.; 3 bal pitch – 15s.; 30 lbs loaf sugar – 15s.; 8 lbs tobacco – £4; 12000 slates – £3; 1 cwt Brazil – £1 13s. 4d.; 1 boult black thread – 10s.; 1 pc white inkle – 13s. 4d.; 1 grs red inkle – 13s. 4d.; 4 doz. narrow silk ribbon – 6s. 8d.; 12 pair silk garters – £1 4s.; 40 parcel–lined men's hats – £6; 4 doz. tobacco pipes – 8s.; 10 ells coarse holland – £1.	£31 2s. 4d.	£1 11s. 1d.	
Barwicke		4 Yorkshire dozens – £13 6s. 8d.; 2 broadcloths – £13 6s. 8d.; 4 Devonshire dozens – £8 17s. 8d.; 3 hhd aquavite – £12; 5 doz. coarse unlined men's hats – £10; 3 cwt hops – £3; 3 bal soap – £6; 1/2 cwt logwood – £1; 3 pcs Genoa fustian – £2 5s.; 1 cwt starch – £1; other small wares – £10.	£80 16s.	£4 10s.	
Smythe		3 iron pots – 12s.; 18 gals aquavite – £1 10s.; 3 tons coal – £1.	£3 2s.	3s. 2d.; 9d.	
Harris		20 bal salt – £2; 2 hhd vinegar – £1 3s. 4d.; 4 cwt poor Johns – £1 6s. 8d.; 1 cwt hops – £1; 1 bal soap – £1; 1 cwt prunes – 10s.	£7	7s.	The following item is placed after the total value – 2 hhd French wine – 1s. 6d.
Randall		3 hhd aquavite – £12; 2 bal soap – £2; 10 cwt hops – 10; 2 cwt loaf sugar – £6 13s. 4d.; 4 tuns English beer – £8.	£38 13s. 4d.	£1 18s. 8d.	The following item is placed after the total value: 2 tons sack – 6s.
Nichollsone		1 cwt madder – £1 6s. 8d.; 2 hhd beer – £1; 2 cwt wrought iron – £1; 1 hhd vinegar – £1; 2 fkn soap – £1; 2 bal wheat – 13s. 4d.; 2 bal peas – 8s.	£6 8s.	6s. 5d.	The following item is included after the total value: 1 hhd French wine – 9d.
Wyldes		20 bal salt – £2; 100 gals aquavite – £6 13s. 4d.; 2 fkn soap – £1; 3 cwt madder – £4; 30 yds coarse linen cloth – £2; 3 pcs cambric – £6; 10 iron pots – £2.	£23 13s. 4d.	£1 3s. 8d.; 5s. 11 1/2d.	

Number	Folio	Date	Ship	Captain – Forename	Captain – Surname	Place – From	Place – To	Merchant Forename
14		28 Jan. 1615	*Sarah* of Chester – 20 tons	Richard	Rayman		Carrickfergus	Laurence
15	f.	30 Jan. 1615	*Margett* of Glasgow	Jacob	Anderson		Carrickfergus	William
16		30 Jan. 1615	*Anne* of Parton	Thomas	Beane		Carrickfergus	Thomas
17		6 Mar. 1615	*Anne* of Parton	William	Cooplande		Carrickfergus	William
18	f.	1 April 1615	*Elizabeth* of Liverpool	Thomas	Lawrenson		Carrickfergus	Edward
19		1 April 1615	*John* of Carrickfergus	John	Pike		Carrickfergus	Sir Fowcke
		1 April 1615	*John* of Carrickfergus	John	Pike		Carrickfergus	Edward
20	f.	5 Apr. 1615	*Blessing* [of] Ayr	Adam	Willy		Carrickfergus	Bartholemew
21		12 April 1615	*Guifte of God* of Carrickfergus	John	Smythe		Carrickfergus	Bartholemew
22	f.	24 Apr. 1615	*Guifte of God* of Glasgow	Mathew	Wildes		Carrickfergus	William
23		24 Apr. 1615	*Margett* of Glasgow	John	Keale		Carrickfergus	John
24		25 Apr. 1615	*Jennett* of Largs	Adam	Loddener		Carrickfergus	Adam
25	f.	10 May 1615	*Speedwell* of Beaumaris	Richard	Griffen		Carrickfergus	Mathew
26		22 May 1615	*Jennitt* of Saltcoats	Adam	Lodener		Carrickfergus	Adam
27	f.	7 June 1615	*John* of Carrickfergus	John	Pike	La Rochelle	Carrickfergus	Edward
28		12 June 1615	*William* of Northam	Samuel	Stribbell	Barnstaple	Carrickfergus	Michael
	f.	12 June 1615	*William* of Northam	Samuel	Stribbell	Barnstaple	Carrickfergus	William
29		14 June 1615	*Robert*	Rowland	Sum'erwell		Carrickfergus	Rowland
30		17 June 1615	*John* of Renfrew	Adam	Madrell		Carrickfergus	Adam
31	f.	18 June 1615	*Margett* of Saltcoats	John	Keele		Carrickfergus	James
32		21 June 1615	*Cuthberde* of R. Alt	John	Browne	Chester	Carrickfergus	Richard

Merchant Surname	Where Merchant is from	Goods	Total Value	Tax	Notes
Holland		1 hhd aquavite – £4; 4 hhd vinegar – £2 6s. 8d.; 2 cwt hops – £2; 12 yds broadcloth – £3 6s. 8d.; 12 yds coarse holland – £1 10s.; 56 lbs iron – 10s.; 15 yds coloured fustian – £1; 2 fkn soap – £1.	£15 13s. 4d.	15s. 8d.	The following item is included after the total value: 2 hhd French wine – 1s. 6d.
Dobbine		20 gals aquavite – £1 5s.; 2 cwt iron – £1; 1 hhd vinegar – 11s. 8d.	£2 16s. 8d.	2s. 10d.	The following item is included after the total value: 3 hhd French wine – 2s. 3d.
Beane		3 tons coal – £1.	£1	1s.	
Fletcher		6 half pcs Northern cloth – £20; 6 tons coal – £2.	£22	£1 2s. 1d.	
Nicollsone		2 tuns beer – £4; 12 bal peas – £2 8s.	£6 8s.	6s. 5d.	
Conway		5 cwt prunes – £2 10s.; 5 pcs raisins – £2 6s. 8d.; 1 bal raisins of the sun – £1 6s. 8d.; 1 bal currants – £3; 1 bal powder sugar – £3 6s. 8d.	£12 10s.	12s. 6d.	The following item is inserted following this total value: 6 butts [piece missing] – 9s.
Willkinsine		4 broad cloths – £26 13s. 4d.; 5 cwt prunes – £2 10s.; 2 cwt raisins – £1 6s. 8d.; spices – £10; 1 cwt figs – 16s. 8d.	£41 6s. 8d.	£2 1s. 8d.	
Johnsone		22 tuns French wine – £3 6d.	£3 6s.		No tax noted.
Johnson		80 gals aquavite – £5 6s. 8d.; 5 iron pots – 13s. 4d.	£6	6s.	The following item is noted after the total value: 10 hhd French wine – 7s. 6d.
Dobbine	Carrick-fergus	40 gals aquavite – £2 13s. 4d.; 1 doz. deal boards – 10s.; 56 lbs figs – 8s. 4d.; 56 lbs raisins of the sun – 9s.; 56 lbs prunes – 5s.; 4 tons coal – £1 6s. 8d.; 8 gals honey – 6s. 8d.	£5 19s.	5s. 11 1/2d.	
Gardner		5 tons coal – £1 13s. 4d.	£1 13s. 4d.	1s. 8d.	
Loddener		9 tons coal – £3	£3	3s.; 9d.	
Marshe		8 doz. hats – £8; 24 yds broadcloth – £6 13s. 4d.; 256 lbs prunes – £1 5s.; 4 half pcs coarse holland – £4; 16 yds bays £1 10s.	£21 8s. 4d.	£1 1s. 5d.	
Lodener		3 tons coal – £1.	£1	1s.; 3d.	
Hall		2 tuns aquavite – £32; 3 hhd vinegar – £1 5s.; 96 bal bay salt – £9 12s.	£42 17s.	£2 2s. 10d.	The following is noted after the total value: 2 tons French wine – 6s.
Louerance		59 lbs wet succade – £1 10s.; 63 lbs green ginger – £1 11s. 6d.; 67 lbs loaf sugar – £2; 47 lbs treacle – £1 3s. 6d.; 12 lbs dry succade – 12s.; 25 lbs nutmeg – £1 17s. 6d.; 4 grs tobacco pipes – £4 16s.	£13 10s. 6d.	13s. 6d.	The following is noted after the total value: 1 pipe canary wine – 1s. 6d.
Predis		5 cwt rosin – £1 5s.; 1 cwt liquorice – 10s.; 1 cwt powder sugar – £3 6s. 8d.; 2 cwt prunes – £1.			No total or tax for these items.
Sum'erwell		8 tons coal – £2 13s. 4d.	£2 13s. 4d.	2s. 8d.; 8d.	
Madrell		12 tons coal – £4.	£4	4s.; 1s.	
Murphy		3 tons coal – £1.	£1	1s.	
Barwicke		2 long cloths – £13 6s. 8d.; 4 Yorkshire dozens – £13 6s. 8d.; 3 kerseys – £6; 60 yds bays – £5; 3 doz. coarse black hats – £3; 2 doz. coarse coloured hats for children – £1; 3 small grs coarse	£49 14s.	£2 9s. 9d.	

Number	Folio	Date	Ship	Captain – Forename	Captain – Surname	Place – From	Place – To	Merchant Forename
33	f.	26 June 1615	*Guifte of God* of Parton	John	Burton		Carrickfergus	John
34		26 June 1615	*Margett* of Parton	Thomas	Bowllton		Carrickfergus	Thomas
35		29 June 1615	*George* of Douglas	John	Care		Carrickfergus	John
36		25 July 1615	*Sunday* of Ardglass	John	Fane		Carrickfergus	Michael
37	f.	25 July 1615	*Fortune* of London	John	Wallche	Flanders	Carrickfergus	George
38	f.	29 July 1615	*Haucke of Muscoovia* of Amsterdam	Francis	Nicholls		Carrickfergus	Andrew
39		1 Aug. 1615	*Guifte of God* of Parton	Edward	Murto		Carrickfergus	Hercules
40		14 Aug. 1615	*Goulden Gray* of Liverpool	William	Davis		Carrickfergus	William
41	f.	15 Aug. 1615	*Creason* of Le Croisic	John	White	Le Croisic	Carrickfergus	John
42		20 Aug. 1615	*Guifte of God* of Glasgow	John	Hunter		Carrickfergus	James
43		25 Sep. 1615	*John* of Saltcoats	John	Gravan		Carrickfergus	John
44	f.	25 Sep. 1615	*Robert* of Saltcoats	Robert	Wattsone		Carrickfergus	Robert
Outgates								
45	f.	3 Oct. 1614	*God before Maste*	John	Robbynson	Carrickfergus		Anthony
46		6 Oct. 1614	*Trynitie* of Liverpool – 20 tons	George	Farrer	Carrickfergus		Richard
47	f.	8 Oct. 1614	*Anne* of Workington – 26 tons	William	Copland	Carrickfergus	Workington	William
48		27 Oct. 1614	*Faulken* of Liverpool – 20 tons	Edward	Nicholson	Carrickfergus	Chester	Laurence
49	f.	2 Nov. 1614	*Peeter* of Ayr – 6 tons	John	Murfyn	Carrickfergus	Chester	Michael
50		4 Nov. 1614				Carrickfergus		Bartholemew
51		5 Nov. 1614	*Gifte of God* of Carrickfergus	Arte	Makan	Carrickfergus		Bartholemew
52	f.	12 Nov. 1614	*Sara* of Chester – 20 tons	Richard	Ryman	Carrickfergus	Chester	Laurence
53		16 Nov. 1614	*Guifte of God* of Isle of Man	Silvester	Stephenson	Carrickfergus		Henry
54	f.	21 Nov. 1614	*Martin* of Chester	Thomas	Dawson	Carrickfergus		William
		21 Nov. 1614	*Martin* of Chester	Thomas	Dawson	Carrickfergus		Richard

Merchant Surname	Where Merchant is from	Goods	Total Value	Tax	Notes
		knives – £3; 3 doz. spurs – 12s.; 2 1/2 doz. headstalls and reins – 16s. 8d.; 2 doz. snaffles – 10s.; frail raisins – 10s.; 2 cwt hops – £2; 1 hhd white salt – 5s. 4d.; 6 doz. shoemaker's lasts – 6s. 8d.			
Burton		6 tons coal – £2.	£2	2s.	
Bowllton		3 tons coal – £1.	£1	1s.	
Care		12 bal malt – £4.	£4	4s.	
White	Carrick-fergus	8 tons coal – £2 13s. 4d.; 6 hhd French wine – 4s. 4d.		13s. 4d.	Tax appears to have been paid on the coal only, no tax given for wine, nor any total noted.
Randall		10 bal soap – £20; 8 cwt loaf sugar – £40; 5 cwt aniseeds – £7 10s.; 4 cwt liquorice – £2; 1 cwt rice – 16s. 8d.; 1 cwt raisins of the sun – 16s.; 6 cwt prunes – £3; 5 cwt currants – £7 10s.; 12 cwt white starch – £12; 1 cwt pepper – £9 6s. 8d.; 40 frying pans – 10s.; 20 lbs nutmeg – £2 10s.; 40 lbs wormseed – 8s.; 5 cwt cording – £2 10s.; 2 hhd vinegar – £1 3s. 4d.	£110 8d.	£5 10s.	The following entry is noted following the total and tax: 4 1/2 tons French wine and sack – 13s. 6d.
Lucas		3000 deal boards – £144; 3 cwt hops – £3; grocery wares – £50.	£197	£9 17s.; £2 9s. 3d.	Francis Nicholls and Andrew Lucas are both named together with no indication as to who is captain and who is merchant.
Lanckeforder		8 tons coal – £2 13s. 4d.	£2 13s. 4d.	2s. 8d.	Merchant identified as Mayor of Carrickfergus.
Davis		12 tons coal – £4	£4	4s.	
White		200 bal French salt – £20	£20	£1; 5s.	
Wattson		8 tons coal – £2 13s. 4d.	£2 13s. 4d.	2s. 8d.; 8d.	
Gravan		4 tons coal – £1 6s. 8d.	£1 6s. 8d.	1s. 4d.; 4d.	
Wattsone		4 tons coal – £1 6s. 8d.	£1 6s. 8d.	1s. 4d.; 4d.	
Bowche		20 cows – £20; 2 bal beef – £4; 1 cwt tallow – £1.	£25	£1 5s.	
Brookes		7 bal beef – £14; 4 hides – £2; 9 cattle – £10.	£26	£1 6s.	
Fletcher		27 cows – £27.	£27	£1 7s.	
Holland		24 bal beef – £48; 24 salt hides – £12; 10 cwt tallow – £10; 2 bal butter – £2 13s. 4d.; 2000 barrel staves – £3; 1000 hogshead staves – £2.	£77 13s. 4d.	£3 17s. 8d.	
White	Carrick-fergus	8 dkr salt hides – £40; 4 hhd beef – £16; 7 bal tallow – £14.	£80	£4	
Johnsone		8 cows – £8.	£8	8s.	Only details given are date, one name and cargo. No ship name.
Johnsone		12 cows – £12.	£12	12s.	
Holland		24 bal beef – £48; 20 salt hides – £10; 12 cows – £12; 2 cwt tallow – £2.	£72	£3 12s.	
Howlecott		21 cows – £21.	£21	£1 1s.	
Denwell		4 bal beef – £8; 5 salt hides – £2 10s.			
Barwicke		8 bal beef – £16; 2 dkr salt hides – £10; 3 dkr kips – £7 10s.			

Number	Folio	Date	Ship	Captain – Forename	Captain – Surname	Place – From	Place – To	Merchant Forename
		21 Nov. 1614	*Martin* of Chester	Thomas	Dawson	Carrickfergus		Thomas
		21 Nov. 1614	*Martin* of Chester	Thomas	Dawson	Carrickfergus		Henry
	f.	21 Nov. 1614	*Martin* of Chester	Thomas	Dawson	Carrickfergus		Thomas
		21 Nov. 1614	*Martin* of Chester	Thomas	Dawson	Carrickfergus		Edward
55	f.	22 Nov. 1614	*Daniel* of Leith	James	Lookeuppe	Carrickfergus		James
56		22 Nov. 1614	*Speedwell* of Beaumaris	Richard	Gryffen	Carrickfergus		Mathew
57		24 Jan. 1615	*Fortune* of London	William	Arnowld	Carrickfergus		Thomas
		24 Jan. 1615	*Fortune* of London	William	Arnowld	Carrickfergus		Henry
58	f.	25 Jan. 1615	*Sarah* of Weymouth	Gregory	Wattson	Carrickfergus		William
		25 Jan. 1615	*Sarah* of Weymouth	Gregory	Wattson	Carrickfergus		Henry
59		26 Jan. 1615	*John* of Plymouth	John	Picke	Carrickfergus		John
	f.	26 Jan. 1615	*John* of Plymouth	John	Picke	Carrickfergus		Edward
60		4 Feb. 1615	*Guifte of God* of Glasgow	John	Murden	Carrickfergus		Mathew
61		10 Feb. 1615	*Guifte of God* of Carrickfergus	John	Smythe	Carrickfergus		Bartholemew
62	f.	25 Feb. 1615	*Joseph* of [blank]	Aunsell	Wells	Carrickfergus		Richard
		25 Feb. 1615	*Joseph* of [blank]	Aunsell	Wells	Carrickfergus		Richard
63		1 Mar. 1615	*Sarah* of Chester	Richard	Ryman	Carrickfergus		Laurence
64	f.	2 Mar. 1615	*Margett* of Glasgow	Jacob	Anderson	Carrickfergus		Jacob
65		16 Mar. 1615	*Trynitie* of Liverpool	George	Farrell	Carrickfergus		John
		16 Mar. 1615	*Trynitie* of Liverpool	George	Farrell	Carrickfergus		Richard
66	f.	11 Apr. 1615	*Blessing* of Ayr	Adam	Willes	Carrickfergus		Bartholemew
67		18 Apr. 1615	*Elizabeth* of Liverpool	Thomas	Lawrenson	Carrickfergus		Edward
		18 Apr. 1615	*Elizabeth* of Liverpool	Thomas	Lawrenson	Carrickfergus		George
68	f.	18 Apr. 1615	*John* of Carrickfergus	John	Pike	Carrickfergus		Edward
69		22 May 1615	*George* of Carrickfergus	Arctt	McCan	Carrickfergus		Michael
70		23 May 1615	*Speedewell* of Beaumaris	Richard	Griffen	Carrickfergus		Mathew
71	f.	28 May 1615	*Speedwell* of Liverpool	Thomas	Farry	Carrickfergus		John
72		4 June 1615	*Anne* of Workington	William	Copland	Carrickfergus		Bartholemew

Merchant Surname	Where Merchant is from	Goods	Total Value	Tax	Notes
Cooper		6 bal beef – £12.			
Cater		12 bal beef – £24; 1 dkr salt hides – £5; 2 dkr kips – £5.			
Cooper	Chester	1 bal beef – £2; 2 cwt tallow – £2; 5 salt hides – £2 10s.			
Hall		4 bal beef – £8; 2 cwt tallow – £2; 5 salt hides – £2 10s.	£109	£5 9s.	
Lookeuppe		15000 pipestaves – £60.	£60	£3; 15s.	
Marshe		22 bal beef – £44; 8 cwt tallow – £8.	£52	£2 12s.	
Oxwicke		30 dkr salt hides – £150; 10 bal butter – £13 6s. 8d.; 16 cwt tallow – £16; 20 flitches bacon – £2 10s.			
Spenser		11 tons beef – £176; 1 ton pork – £16.	£371 16s. 8d.	£18 11s. 10d.	
Harris		6 bal beef – £12; 1 dkr salt hides – £5; 4000 barrel staves – £10; 3 bal pork – £6.			
Spenser		5 tons beef – £80; 16 cwt tallow – £16.	£129	£6 9s.	
Picke		12 bal beef – £24; 60 flitches bacon – £7 10s.			
Willkenson		3 tons beef – £48; 4 bal pork – £8.	£87 10s.	£4 7s. 6d.	
Wildes		10 dkr green hides – £50.	£50	£2 10s.; 12s. 6d.	
Johnson		6 dkr green hides – £30; 6 cwt tallow – £6.	£36	£1 16s.	
Barwicke		10 tons beef and pork – £160; 3 dkr green hides – £15; 140 flitches bacon – £17 10s.			RJH has a question mark above the captain's surname.
Brooke		7 hhd beef and pork – £28; 4 cwt tallow – £4.	£224 10s.	£11 4s. 6d.	
Holland		4 tons beef – £64; 6 dkr green hides – £30; 20 flitches bacon – £2 10s.	£96 10s.	£4 16s. 6d.	
Anderson		3 dkr green hides – £15; 2 cwt tallow – £2.	£17	17s.; 4s. 3d.	
Brookes		2 tons beef – £32; 6 dkr hides – £30.	£107 6s. 8d.	£5 7s. 4d.	
Barwicke		1 ton beef – £16; 16 cwt tallow – £16; 1 dkr green hides – £5; 40 flitches bacon – £5; 1 cwt yarn – 6s. 8d.			
Johnson	Carrick-fergus	26 dkr green hides – £130.	£130	£6 10s.	
Nicollsone		1000 barrel staves – £2.			
Mase		8 cows – £8.	£10	10s.	
Hall		12 dkr green hides – £60.	£60	£3	
White		2 packs Irish yarn – £26 13s. 4d.; 2 dkr green hides – £10.	£36 13s. 4d.	£1 16s. 8d.	
Marshe		5 dkr – green hides – £25; 3 dkr kips – £7 10s.; 1 pack Irish yarn – £13 6s. 8d.; 56 lbs tallow – 10s.; 8 bal salt – 16s.; 2 fkn soap – £1.	£48 2s. 8d.	£2 8s. 1 1/2d.	
Freaue		6 cattle – £6; 2 horses – £4; 1 dkr green hides – £1; 1 1/2 packs Irish yarn – £19 10s.	£34 10s.	£1 14s. 6d.	
Johnsone		10 cows – £10.	£10	10s.	

Number	Folio	Date	Ship	Captain – Forename	Captain – Surname	Place – From	Place – To	Merchant Forename
73		27 June 1615	*Elizabeth* of Liverpool	Thomas	Lawrenson	Carrickfergus		Sir Fowlke
74	f.	28 June 1615	*John* of Carrickfergus	John	Pyke	Carrickfergus		Edward
75		4 July 1615	*William* of Northam	Samuel	Stribble	Carrickfergus		Nicholas
		4 July 1615	*William* of Northam	Samuel	Stribble	Carrickfergus		Richard
76	f.	5 July 1615	*Guifte of God* of Croston	John	Jurdayne	Carrickfergus		Edward
77		10 July 1615	*Cuttbert* of R. Alt	John	Browne	Carrickfergus		Richard
78		18 July 1615	*Peter* of Ayr	John	Murfey	Carrickfergus		Henry
79	f.	26 July 1615	*Unicorne* of Chester	William	Smyth	Carrickfergus		Stephen
80		5 Aug. 1615	*Guyfie of God* of Parton	Edward	Slater	Carrickfergus		John
81		8 Aug. 1615	*Sarah* of Chester	Richard	Ryman	Carrickfergus		Simon
82	f.	17 Aug. 1615	*Peter* of [blank]	Peter	Leamon	Carrickfergus		Bartholemew
83		19 Aug. 1615	*George* of [blank]	Murtha	Crofer	Carrickfergus		Bartholemew
84		22 Aug. 1615	*Golden Grey* of Liverpool	William	Davis	Carrickfergus		Richard
85	f.	26 Aug. 1615	*Fortune* of London	John	Welche	Carrickfergus		George
86		29 Aug. 1615	*Trinitie* of Ardglass	Christopher	Cowlty	Carrickfergus		Christopher
87		6 Sep. 1615	*Haucke of Muscovye* of Amsterdam	Debut	Peterson	Carrickfergus		Francis & Andrew
88	f.	6 Sep. 1615	*Moises* of Carrickfergus	Robert	Goste	Carrickfergus		Ingram
89		9 Sep. 1615	*Fortune* of Chester	John	a Conlon	Carrickfergus		Laurence
90		16 Sep. 1615	*Elizabeth* of Liverpool	John Thomas	Lawrenson	Carrickfergus		William

Merchant Surname	Where Merchant is from	Goods	Total Value	Tax	Notes
Conwaye		10 tons iron – £100.	£100	£5	
Hall		1000 pipestaves – £4.	£4	4s.	
Lauerance		3 dkr green hides – £15.			
Brasier		2 cwt tallow – £2; 12 green hides – £6; 4 cwt wool – £11 4s.	£34 4s.	£1 14s. 2 1/2d.	
Hall		15 cows – £15; 2 horses – £3 10s.	£19 10s.	19s. 6d.	
Barwicke		1 pack Irish yarn – £13 6s. 8d.; 5 green hides – £2 10s.; 4 garrownes – £5.	£20 16s. 8d.	£1 10d.	
Hollcott		10 cows – £10.	£10	10s.	
Smythe		8 cows and oxen – £10.	£10	10s.	
a Conlon		7 cows – £7.	£7	7s.	
Richardson		17 cows – £18; 2 horses – £4.	£22	£1 2s.	
Johnson		6 dkr hides – £30; 16 cows and oxen – £20.	£50	£2 10s.	
Johnson		8 cows – £8; 2 horses – £4.	£12	12s.	
Barwicke		1 1/2 packs Irish yarn – £19 10s.; 15 garrownes – £16 10s.	£36	£1 16s.	
Randall		20 dkr green hides – £100; 3 dkr kips – £7 10s.	£107 10s.	£5 7s. 6d.	
Cowlty		10 cows – £11.	£11	11s.	
Lucas		17000 pipe staves – £68.	£68	£3 8s.; 17s.	Two merchants named.
Horseman		20 garrownes – £30; 120 lbs Irish yarn – £3 3s. 8d.	£33 3s. 8d.	£1 13s. 4d.	
Hollande		14 cows – £15.	£15	15s.	
Hill		4 cows – £4 10s.	£4 10s.	4s. 6d.	

The Port Books
of the Lecale Ports

Number	Folio	Date	Ship	Captain – Forename	Captain – Surname	Place – From	Place – To	Merchant Forename
1	f	3 Oct. 1614	*Jelleflower* of Fairlie – 16 tons	John	Boyde	Strangford	Workington	John
2		10 Oct. 1614	*Sondaye* of R. Wyre – 18 tons	Richard	Jackson	Dundrum	R. Wyre	Richard
3		17 Oct. 1614	*George* of R. Wyre – 20 tons	Thomas	Dawson	Ardglass	R. Wyre	Thomas
4		1 Nov. 1614	*Jelleflower* of Irvine – 15 tons	John	Boyde	Portaferry	Wyre	John
5		13 Nov. 1614	*Sondaye* of Ardglass – 12 tons	John	Flynne	Dundrum	Wyre	John
6		18 Nov. 1614	*Henry* of Wyre – 10 tons	Thomas	Lawtham	Ballintogher	Lancaster	Thomas
7		18 Nov. 1614	*Stephen* of Wyre – 10 tons	John	Smythe	Strangford	Wyre	John
8		23 Nov. 1614	*Peeter* of Irvine – 20 tons	John	Hamelton	Portaferry	Wyre	John
9		26 Nov. 1614	*Blessinge* of London – 20 tons	John	Browne	Ardglass	Wales	John
10		29 Nov. 1614	*Speedwell* of Strangford – 16 tons	Robert	Speeres	Portaferry	Wyre	Robert
11		12 Dec. 1614	*George* of Lancaster – 12 tons	George	Brafforde	Ballintogher	Lancaster	George
12	f.	12 Dec. 1614	*Trynitie* of Wyre – 20 tons	Gowyn	Dawson	Ballintogher	Workington	Robert
13		29 Dec. 1614	*Sondaye* of Ardglass – 12 tons	John	Flynne	Strangford	Beaumaris	John
14		[blank] Jan. 1615	*Sondaye* of Ardglass – 20 tons	Thomas	Blealicke	Ardglass	Beaumaris	Thomas
15		19 Jan. 1615	*Katherine* of Whithorn – 4 tons	Robert	Nicholson	Ardglass	Whithorn	Robert
16		3 Feb. 1615	*Katherine* of Ardglass – 7 tons	Christopher	Coulter	Strangford	Ayr	James
17		4 Feb. 1615	*Henry* of Ayr – 7 tons	Henry	Osborne	Downpatrick	Ayr	Peter
18		10 Feb. 1615	*Jelliflower* of Irvine – 15 tons	John	Boyde	Strangford	Workington	William
19		16 Feb. 1615	*George* of Lancaster – 12 tons	George	Brafford	Ballintogher	Lancaster	George
20		16 Feb. 1615	*Trynitie* of Wyre – 20 tons	Gowyn	Daunson	Ballintogher	Wyre	Robert
21	f	26 Feb. 1615	*Speedwell* of Wyre – 20 tons	Richard	Jackson	Ardglass	Wyre	Richard
		26 Feb. 1615	*Swyfte sure* of Wyre – 20 tons	Henry	Johnson	Ardglass	Lancaster	Henry
		12 Mar. 1615	*Speedewell* of Strangford – 16 tons	Robert	Speeres	Strangford	Irvine	Thomas
		18 Mar. 1615	*Anne* of Parton – 6 tons	Michael	Allyson	Strangford	Parton	Robert
		18 Mar. 1615	*Swifte sure* of Wyre – 16 tons	Henry	Johnson	Strangford	Wyre	Henry
		23 Mar. 1615	*Katherine* of Ardglass – 10 tons	Edmund	Mackeniste	Ardglass	Ayr	Patrick
		23 Mar. 1615	*George* of Isle of Man – 10 tons	Henry	Younge	Dundrum & Portaferry	Workington	Alexander
		23 Mar. 1615	*George* of Isle of Man – 10 tons	Henry	Younge	Dundrum & Portaferry	Workington	Alexander

Merchant Surname	Where Merchant is from	Goods	Total Value	Tax	Notes
Boyde		25 cows – £25.	£25	£1 5s.	
Jackson		26 cows – £26.	£26	£1 5s.	
Dawson		30 cows – £30; 3 cwt tallow – £3.	£33	£1 13s.	
Boyde		60 bal oats – £40.	£40	£2; 10s.	
Flynne		20 bullocks – £16.	£16	16s.	
Lawtham		16 bullocks – £10.	£10	10s.	
Smythe		60 bal wheat – £60.	£60	£3	
Hamelton		120 bal oats – £80.	£80	£4; £1	
Browne		6 dkr hides and 3 bal pork – £36.	£36	£1 16s.	
Braye		16 cows – £16.	£16	16s.	
Brafforde		24 bullocks – £20.	£20	£1	
Nicholson		20 bal barley – £13 6s. 8d.; 10 bullocks – £6 13s. 4d.	£20	£1	
Smythe		2 1/2 dkr hides – £12 10s.	£12 10s.	12s. 6d.	
Blealicke		40 bal barley – £26 13s. 4d.; 10 bal wheat – £10.	£36 13s. 4d.	£1 16s. 8d.	Full date not given.
Nicholson		16 bal wheat – £16.	£16	16s.	
Hewston		60 bal barley and oats – £40.	£40	£2; 10s.	
Moresey		5 dkr salt hides – £25.	£25	£1 5s.	
Gunnell		6 bal beef – £12; 3 cwt tallow – £3;	£51 13s. 4d.	£2 11s. 8d.	
Brafforde		30 bal wheat – £30; 10 bal oats – £6 13s. 4d. 20 bal wheat – £20; 20 bal oats – £13 6s. 8d.	£33 6s. 8d.	£1 13s. 4d.	
Nicholson		26 bal wheat – £26; 31 bal barley – £20.	£46	£2 6s.	
Jackson		80 bal oats and 40 bal barley – £80.	£80	£4	No more numbers are provided from here on.
Johnson		15 bal barley and 20 bal oats – £23 6s. 8d.	£23 6s. 8d.	£1 3s. 4d.	
Dungelson		80 bal barley – £53 6s. 8d.	£53 6s. 8d.	£2 13s. 4d.; 13s. 4d.	
Hewstone		40 bal oats – £26 13s. 4d.	£26 13s. 4d.	£1 6s. 8d.; 6s. 8d.	
Johnson		60 bal oats – £40.	£40	£2	
Meaughe		60 bal barley – £40.	£40	£2	
Goyne	Dundrum	20 bal barley – £13 6s. 8d.			
Goyne	Portaferry	60 bal oats and barley – £40.	£53 6s. 8d.	£2 13s. 4d.	

Number	Folio	Date	Ship	Captain – Forename	Captain – Surname	Place – From	Place – To	Merchant Forename
Ingates								
	f	26 Nov. 1614	*Blessinge of God* of London – 30 tons	John	Browne	London	Ardglass	John
	f	15 Jan. 1615	*Henery* of Carlingford – 8 tons	William	Wilson	Carlingford	Downpatrick	Walter

Merchant Surname	Where Merchant is from	Goods	Total Value	Tax	Notes
Browne		2 hhd huscubaughe, 1 cwt sugar – £11 6s. 8d.	£11 6s. 8d.	11s. 4d.	
Thomas	Down-patrick	Certain small parcels – £9.	£9	9s.	

Number	Folio	Date	Ship	Captain – Forename	Captain – Surname	Place – From	Place – To	Merchant Forename
1	f. 2	29 Jan. 1614	*Gufte* of Strangford – 30 tons	Robert	Speres	Strangford	Whithorn	Robert
2		5 Feb. 1614	*Jonas* of Largs – 20 tons	Saunder	Clarke	Killough	Largs	Saunder
3		8 Feb. 1614	*Trynitye* of Ardglass – 7 tons	John Boye	a Felyn	Ardglass	Whithorn	John Boye
4		11 Feb. 1614	*Mariegould* of Strangford – 20 tons	John	Mackeienkyn	Strangford	Whithorn	John
5		7 Mar. 1615	*Grase* of Strangford – 25 tons	Edmond	Mackeneiskey	Strangford	Whithorn	Edmond
6		10 Mar. 1614	*Jonas* of Ayr – 25 tons	John	Maxwell	Strangford	Ayr	John
7		10 Mar. 1614	*George* of Ribble Water (?) – 26 tons	John	Boomer	Ardglass	Bristol	John
	f. 2v	26 Mar. 1614	*George* of Ribble Water (?) – 26 tons	John	Boomer	Dundrum	Bristol	John
8		14 Mar. 1614	*Hope* of Kinghorn – 14 tons	John Boye	a Felyn	Strangford	Ayr	John Boye
9		15 Mar. 1614	*Katherine* of Strangford – 28 tons	John	Hughestone	Strangford	Ayr	Richard & William
		15 Mar. 1614	*Katherine* of Strangford – 28 tons	John	Hughestone	Strangford	Ayr	Robert & John
10		21 Mar. 1614	*Henery* of Ayr – 10 tons	Robert	Hughson	Dundrum	Ayr	Robert
11		28 Mar. 1614	*Jonas* of Largs – 18 tons	Saunder	Clarke	Strangford	Largs	Saunder
12		6 Apr. 1614	*Jonas* of Ardglass – 10 tons	Patrick	Mage	Dundrum	Ayr	Patrick
13		18 Apr. 1614	*Jonas* of Ayr – 25 tons	John	Maxwell	Ardglass	Ayr	John
14		19 Apr. 1614	*Peeter* of Kirkcudbright – 10 tons	John	Hamblett	Ardglass	Kirkcudbright	John
15	f. 3	25 Apr. 1614	*Thomas* of Kirkcudbright – 12 tons	Herbert	Maxwell	Dundrum	Ayr	Herbert
16		6 May 1614	*Katherine* of Strangford – 20 tons	William	Hunter	Strangford	Ayr	William
17		6 May 1614	*Trynitye* of Ardglass – 6 tons	John Boye	a Felyn	Ardglass	Tenby	John Boye
18		12 May 1614	*Julian* of Strangford – 10 tons	William	Hughson	Strangford	Liverpool	William
19		16 May 1614	*Katherine* of Ardglass – 10 tons	Mack	Aniskey	Ardglass	Kirkcudbright	Macke
20		19 May 1614	*Jonas* of Rosses – 18 tons	John	Maxwell	Ardglass	Rosses	John
21	f. 3v	6 June 1614	*Jonas* of Ayr – 7 tons	William	Hewston	Strangford	Whithorn	William
22		6 June 1614	*Henery* of Kirkcudbright – 3 tons	James	Moore	Dundrum	Kirkcudbright	James
23		9 June 1614	*George* of Ardglass – 10 tons	William	Mc Aniske	Ardglass	Kirkcudbright	Thomas
24		16 June 1614	*James* of Ayr – 7 tons	Robert	Hewston	Ardglass	Ayr	Robert
25		2 July 1614	*Speedwell* of Ardglass – 8 tons	Rowland	Mc Aniske	Ardglass	Workington	Thomas
26		15 July 1614	*Jonas* of Largs – 5 tons	Herbert	Maxewell	Ardglass	Whithorn	Herbert
27		20 July 1614	*Peeter* of Largs – 5 tons	Thomas	Blealicke	Ardglass	Kirkcudbright	Thomas
28		24 July 1614	*William* of Ardglass – 9 tons	Peter	Roney	Ardglass	Workington	Patrick

Merchant Surname	Where Merchant is from	Goods	Total Value	Tax	Notes
Speres		70 bal seed oats – £46 13s. 4d.	£46 13s. 4d.	£2 6s. 8d.; 11s. 8d.	
Clarke		60 bal oats – £40; 70 bal barley – £46 13s. 4d.	£86 13s. 4d.	£4 6s. 8d.; £1 1s. 8d.	
a Felyn		60 bal oats – £40.	£40	£2; 10s.	
Mackeienkyn		56 bal oats – £37 6s. 8d.	£37 6s. 8d.	£1 17s. 4d.	
Mackeniskey		110 bal barley and 20 bal oats – £86 13s. 4d.	£86 13s. 4d.	£4 6s. 8d.; £1 1s. 8d.	
Maxwell		180 bal wheat – £180.	£180	£9; £2 5s.	
Boomer		40 bal barley – £26 13s. 4d.; 20 bal wheat – £20.			
Boomer		80 bal barley – £53 6s. 8d.	£100	£5	
a Felyn		40 bal barley – £26 13s. 4d.	£26 13s. 4d.	£1 6s. 8d.; 6s. 8d.	
Dobb		50 bal oats and 60 bal barley – £73 6s. 8d.			
Nicholson & Boomer		120 bal barley – £100.	£173 6s. 8d.	£8 13s. 4d.; £2 3s. 4d.	Richard & William Dobb are joint merchants as are Robert Nicholson & John Boomer.
Hughson		20 bal barley – £13 6s. 8d.	£13 6s. 8d.	13s. 4d.; 3s. 4d.	
Clarke		20 bal barley – £13 6s. 8d.	£13 6s. 8d.	13s. 4d.; 3s. 4d.	
Mage		40 bal oats – £26 13s. 4d.	£26 13s. 4d.	£1 6s. 8d.; 6s. 8d.	
Maxwell		60 bal barley – £40.	£40	£2	
Hamblett		25 bal barley – £16 13s. 4d.	£16 13s. 4d.	16s. 8d.; 4s. 2d.	
Maxwell		40 bal barley – £23 13s. 4d.	£23 13s. 4d.	£1 6s. 8d.; 6s. 8d.	
Hunter		20 bal oats – £13 6s. 8d.	£13 6s. 8d.	13s. 4d.; 3s. 4d.	
a Felyn		160 bal barley – £106 13s. 4d.; 40 bal wheat – £40.	£146 13s. 4d.	£7 6s. 8d.; £1 16s. 8d.	
Hughson		25 bal barley – £16 13s. 4d.	£16 13s. 4d.	16s. 8d.	
Aniskye		100 bal barley – £66 13s. 4d.; 20 bal wheat – £20.	£86 13s. 4d.	£4 6s. 8d.; £1 1s. 8d.	
Maxwell		30 bal oats – £20.	£20	£1	
Hewstone		110 bal barley –£73 6s. 8d.; 40 bal oats – £26 13s. 4d.	£100	£5; £1 5s.	
Moore		40 bal oats – £26 13s. 4d.	£26 13s. 4d.	£1 6s. 8d.; 6s. 8d.	
Blealike		12 bal oats – £8.	£8	8s.	
Hewston		40 bal oats – £26 13s. 4d.	£26 13s. 4d.	£1 6s. 8d.	
Haughton		30 bal barley – £20.	£20	£1; 5s.	
Maxewell		12 cows – £12.	£12	12s.	
Blealicke		40 bal barley – £26 13s. 4d.	£26 13s. 8d.	£1 6s. 8d.; 6s. 8d.	
Meagh		12 bal wheat – £12.	£12	12s.	

Number	Folio	Date	Ship	Captain – Forename	Captain – Surname	Place – From	Place – To	Merchant Forename
29		25 July 1614	*Gifte of God* of Strangford – 16 tons	Robert	Speres	Strangford	Workington	Robert
30	f. 4	26 July 1614	*Marygould* of Ballintogher – 20 tons	Robert	Nicholson	Strangford	Wyre	Robert
31		26 July 1614	*Speedewell* of Ardglass – 8 tons	Rowland	Mc Aniske	Ardglass	Workington	Rowland
32		27 July 1614	*Blesseinge of God* of Wyre – 7 tons	John	Thomas	Ardglass	Wyre	John
33		27 July 1614	*Jonas* of Ayr – 20 tons	Robert	Nicholson	Strangford	Wyre	Robert
34		27 July 1614	*Violett* of Liverpool – 18 tons	William	Thomas	Strangford	Chester	William
35		28 July 1614	*Peeter* of Kirkcudbright – 6 tons	John	Hunter	Ardglass	Kirkcudbright	John
36		28 July 1614	*Trynity* of Ardglass – 10 tons	John	Flynne	Ardglass	Wyre	John
37		8 Aug. 1614	*Blesseinge of God* of Killough – 6 tons	Patrick	Done	Killough	Kirkcudbright	Patrick
38		9 Aug. 1614	*Peeter* of Largs – 5 tons	Thomas	Blealike	Ardglass	Ayr	Thomas
39		16 Aug. 1614	*Speedewell* of Ardglass – 8 tons	Rowland	Mc Aniske	Ardglass	Workington	Rowland
40	f. 4v	19 Aug. 1614	*Jonas* of Largs	Saunder	Mc Cullin	Strangford	Largs	Saunder
41		22 Aug. 1614	*Katherine* of Ardglass – 12 tons	Edmund	Mc Aniske	Ardglass	Wyre	Roger
42		22 Aug. 1614	*Jelleflower* of Ayr	William	Pemberton	Ardglass	Wyre	William
43		1 Sep. 1614	*Henery* of Kirkcudbright – 6 tons	John	Boyd	Ardglass	Kirkcudbright	John
44		1 Sep. 1614	*Marygould* of Strangford – 16 tons	James	Hueston	Strangford	Kirkcudbright	James
45		2 Sep. 1614	*Michaell* of Largs – 5 tons	Thomas	Blealicke	Ardglass	Workington	Thomas
46		6 Sep. 1614	*Katherine* of Ardglass – 12 tons	Edmund	Mc Aniske	Ardglass	Chester	Walter
47		6 Sep. 1614	*Gifte of God* of Strangford – 18 tons	Robert	Speeres	Strangford	Workington	Thomas
48		7 Sep. 1614	*Trynity* of Kirkcudbright – 20 tons	John	Boyde	Strangford	Workington	Thomas
49	f. 5	8 Sep. 1614	*William* of Ardglass – 10 tons	Peter	Roney	Ardglass	Chester	Patrick
50		9 Sep. 1614	*Jelliflower* of Ayr – 18 tons	John	Blacke	Strangford	Chester	Thomas
51		10 Sep. 1614	*Jonas* of Ayr – 16 tons	John	Barry	Strangford	Workington	John
52		14 Sep. 1614	*Peeter* of Largs – 6 tons	Thomas	Blealicke	Ardglass	Kirkcudbright	Thomas
		23 Sep. 1614	*Speedwell* of Liverpool – 10 tons	Thomas	Ferrell	Dundrum	Liverpool	Thomas
		25 Sep. 1614	*Trynity* of Ardglass – 10 tons	John	Flynne	Ardglass	Chester	John
		30 Sep. 1614	*William* of Ardglass – 10 tons	Peter	Roney	Ardglass	Chester	William
		18 Apr. 1614	*Katherine* of Strangford – 20 tons	John	Hugheson	Tenby	Strangford	John
Ingates	f. 2v	25 Apr. 1614	*Speedewell* of Liverpool – 10 tons	Thomas	Farwell	Liverpool	Strangford	Thomas
	f. 3							

Merchant Surname	Where Merchant is from	Goods	Total Value	Tax	Notes
Speres		14 fat beeves – £14.	£14	14s.	
Nicholson		20 fat cows – £20.	£20	£1	
Mc Aniske		23 cows – £23; 8 cwt wool – £12 16s.	£35 16s.	£1 15s. 10d.	
Thomas		11 fat cows – £11.	£11	11s.	
Nicholson		9 fat beeves – £9.	£9	9s.	
Thomas		27 cows – £27.	£27	£1 7s.	
Hunter		24 fat cows – £24.	£24	£1 4s.	
Mullinaxe		40 bal oats – £26 13s. 4d.	£26 13s. 4d.	£1 6s. 8d.; 6s. 8d.	
Done		15 fat cows – £15.	£15	15s.	
Blealicke		30 bal oats – £20.	£20	£1; 5s.	
Mc Anesk		40 bal oats – £26 13s. 4d.	£26 13s. 4d.	£1 6s. 8d.; 6s. 8d.	
Mc Cullin		12 fat cows – £12.	£12	12s.	
Nicholson		52 bal oats – £34 13s. 4d.	£34 13s. 4d.	£1 14s. 8d.; 8s. 8d.	RJH has note – tonnage left blank.
Pemberton		16 fat cows – £16.	£16	16s.	
Boyd		18 fat cows – £18.	£18	18s.	RJH has note – tonnage left blank.
Hueston		40 bal oats – £26 13s. 4d.	£26 13s. 4d.	£1 6s. 8d.; 6s. 8d.	
Blealick		20 fat cows – £20.	£20	£1; 5s.	
Thomas		6 cows – £6; 10 bal wheat – £10.	£16	16s.	
Houghton		16 fat cows – £16; 10 cwt tallow – £20.	£36	£1 16s.	
Houghton		16 cows – £16; 3 horses – £40.	£56	£2 16s.	
Meale		27 fat cows – £27.	£27	£1 7s.	
Scotte		15 fat cows – £15.	£15	15s.	
Barry		8 horses – £106 13s. 4d.; 16 cows – £16; 18 stones tallow – £3 12s.	£126 5s. 4d.	£6 8s. 8d.	
Blealic		18 cows – £18.	£18	18s.	No more individual numbers from here.
Ferrell		40 bal barley – £26 13s. 4d.	£26 13s. 4d.	£1 6s. 8d.; 6s. 8d.	
Flynne		11 cows – £11.	£11	11s.	
Pemberton		15 fat cows – £15.	£15	15s.	
Hughson		Salt – £8.	£8	8s.; 2s.	Names as given.
Farrewell					
		3/4 cwt hops – 15s.; 3500 spike nails – £1 6s.; 12 spades – 6s.	£2 7s.	2s. 4d.	

Number	Folio	Date	Ship	Captain – Forename	Captain – Surname	Place – From	Place – To	Merchant Forename
	f. 2	26 Mar. 1615	*Sondaye* of Ardglass – 16 tons	John	Flynne	Ardglass	Workington	John
		26 Mar. 1615	*Peeter* of Dunadee – 6 tons	Henry	Johnson	Dundrum	Irvine	John
		28 Mar. 1615	*Henry* of Ayr – 7 tons	Herbert	Maxfeild	Ardglass	Ayr	Herbert
		10 Apr. 1615	*Speedewell* of Strangford – 16 tons	Robert	Speares	Strangford	Irvine	Robert
		12 Apr. 1615	*Katherine* of Ardglass – 15 tons	Edmund	Mackaniste	Ardglass	Ayr	Patrick
		12 Apr. 1615	*Trynnity* of Ardglass – 14 tons	Peter	Roney	Ardglass	Workington	Thomas
		12 Apr. 1615	*Michaell* of Ardglass – 13 tons	William	Mackeniske	Ardglass	Ayr	William
		18 Apr. 1615	*Jelliflower* of Irvine – 15 tons	John	Boyde	Strangford	Parton	Peter
	f. 2v	18 Apr. 1615	*Jonas* of Largs – 10 tons	John	Blacke	Killough	Largs	John
		20 Apr. 1615	*Gifte of God* of Killough – 9 tons	Edmund	Duffe	Killough	Wales	Edward
		26 Apr. 1615	*Trynnity* of Wyre – 20 tons	Gowen	Dannson	Ballintogher	Wyre	Robert
		26 Apr. 1615	*Henry* of Wyre – 20 tons	John	Fisher	Ballintogher	Wyre	Robert
		28 Apr. 1615	*Margaret* of Holywood – 9 tons	James	Hogges	Killough	Workington	Jeffry
		3 May 1615	*Jonas* of Largs – 10 tons	John	Saunderson	Ardglass	Ayr	Thomas
		6 May 1615	*Peeter* of Glasgow – 8 tons	Robert	Kenningham	Strangford	Glasgow	Robert
		15 May 1615	*Katherine* of Ardglass – 15 tons	Edmund	Mackeniste	Ardglass	Parton	Thomas
		20 May 1615	*Trynnity* of Ardglass – 14 tons	Peter	Ronney	Ardglass	Kirkcudbright	Patrick
	f. 3	9 June 1615	*William* of Glasgow – 8 tons	John	Pibbells	Dundrum	Glasgow	John
		9 June 1615	*Margarett* of Largs – 7 tons	James	Bradshawe	Dundrum	Largs	Robert
		13 June 1615	*Margarett* of Ardglass – 8 tons	Patrick	Flynne	Ardglass	Glasgow	Thomas
		28 June 1615	*Sondaye* of Kilclief – 9 tons	Patrick	Mackcreery	Strangford	Isle of Man	William
	f. 3v	7 July 1615	*Trynnity* of Wyre – 20 tons	Gowyn	Dannson	Ballintogher	Wyre	Robert
		12 July 1615	*Vallentyne* of Liverpool – 16 tons	Silvester	Starkey	Strangford	Liverpool	Thomas
		16 July 1615	*Henry* of Wyre – 20 tons	John	Fisher	Ballintogher	Wyre	Robert
		24 July 1615	*Trynnity* of Ardglass – 14 tons	Peter	Roney	Ardglass	Workington	Patrick
		16 Aug. 1615	*Michaell* of Ardglass – 12 tons	William	Mackeneste	Ardglass	Workington	Patrick
		18 Aug. 1615	*Roberte* of Ayr – 12 tons	Robert	Kenningham	Strangford	Workington	Sawnder
		22 Aug. 1615	*Jelliflower* of Irvine – 15 tons	John	Boyde	Ballintogher	Workington	Thomas
	f. 4	30 Aug. 1615	*Jonas* of Largs – 12 tons	Robert	Maxfeilde	Strangford	Parton	James
		7 Sep. 1615	*Sondaye* of Ardglass – 15 tons	John	Flynne	Ballintogher	Workington	Thomas

Merchant Surname	Where Merchant is from	Goods	Total Value	Tax	Notes
Flynne		80 bal wheat – £80.	£80	£4	
Steward		20 bal barley – £13 6s. 8d.	£13 6s. 8d.	13s. 4d.	
Maxfeild Euston		50 bal oats – £33 6s. 8d. 100 bal barley – £66 13s. 4d.	£33 6s. 8d. £66 13s. 4d.	£1 13s. 4d.; 8s. 4d. £3 6s. 8d.; 16s. 7d.	
Mease		80 bal barley – £53 6s. 8d.	£53 6s. 8d.	£2 13s. 4d.	
Bleylicke		70 bal barley – £46 6s. 8d.	£46 6s. 8d.	£2 6s. 4d.	
Mackeniske		60 bal oats – £40.	£40	£2	
Maggee		80 bal oats – £53 6s. 8d.	£53 6s. 8d.	£2 13s. 4d.; 13s. 4d.	
Blacke Oxewicke		60 bal oats – £40. 80 bal wheat – £80.	£40 £80	£2; 10s. £4	
Nicholson		60 bal wheat – £60; 20 bal oats – £13 6s. 8d.	£73 6s. 8d.	£3 13s. 4d.	
Butteler Wrayye		80 bal oats – £53 6s. 8d. 60 bal oats – £40.	£53 6s. 8d. £40	£2 13s. 4d. £2	
Blealicke Kenningham		60 bal barley – £40 40 bal oats – £26 13s. 4d.	£40 £26 13s. 4d.	£2 £1 6s. 8d.; 6s. 8d.	
Blealicke		66 bal barley – £44.	£44	£2 4s.	
Meagh		40 bal barley – £26 13s. 4d.; 20 bal oats – £13 6s. 8d.	£40	£2	
Pibbelles		46 bal barley and oats – £30 13s. 4d.	£30 13s. 4d.	£1 10s. 8d.	
Greerey		40 bal barley and oats – £26 13s. 4d.	£26 13s. 4d.	£1 6s. 8d.	
Blealicke		40 bal barley – £26 13s. 4d.	£26 13s. 4d.	£1 6s. 8d.	
Lyle		9 horses and mares – £120.	£120	£6	
Nicholson		10 bullocks – £10; 1 horse – £13 13s. 4d.	£23 13s. 4d.	£1 3s. 8d.	
Horton		18 horses and mares – £240.	£240	£12	
Butler		8 bullocks – £8; 5 horses and mares – £66 13s. 4d.	£74 13s. 4d.	£3 14s. 8d.	
Connar		14 bullocks – £14.	£14	14s.	
Canne		15 bullocks – £15.	£15	15s.	
Gowen Rande		10 bullocks – £10. 8 bullocks – £8; 4 horses – £53 6s. 8d.	£10 £61 6s. 8d.	10s.; 2s. 6d. £6 1s. 4d.	RJH has noted that the total is an error in the customs' calculation.
Hueston Scotte		15 bullocks – £15. 9 horses – £120; 2 bullocks – £2.	£15 £122	15s.; 3s. 9d. £6 2s.	

Number	Folio	Date	Ship	Captain – Forename	Captain – Surname	Place – From	Place – To	Merchant Forename
		25 Sep. 1615	*Mathewe* of Wyre – 14 tons	Thomas	Brittayne	Ballintogher	Wyre	Robert
		25 Sep. 1615	*Mathewe* of Wyre – 14 tons	Thomas	Brittayne	Ballintogher	Wyre	James
		25 Sep. 1615	*Mathewe* of Wyre – 14 tons	Thomas	Brittayne	Ballintogher	Wyre	Richard
Ingates	f. 3	11 June 1615	*Vallentyne* of Liverpool – 16 tons	Silvester	Starkey	Liverpool	Strangford	Thomas
		11 June 1615	*Vallentyne* of Liverpool – 16 tons	Silvester	Starkey	Liverpool	Strangford	Edward
		26 July 1615	*Gifte of God* of London – 40 tons	Robert	Randall	London	Ardglass	Robert
	f. 3v	2 Aug. 1615	*Steephen* of Isle of Man – 12 tons	Silvester	Stephenson	Isle of Man	Portaferry	Silvester
	f. 4	10 Sep. 1615	*Sondaye* of Kilclief – 9 tons	Patrick	Mackreery	Isle of Man	Portaferry	Richard
		14 Sep. 1615	*Mathewe* of Wyre – 14 tons	Thomas	Bryttayne	Wyre	Ballintogher	Robert

Merchant Surname	Where Merchant is from	Goods	Total Value	Tax	Notes
Nicholson		40 bal wheat – £40.			
Carre		1 cwt linen yarn – £3 6s. 8d.			
Rose		500 sheepskins – £3 15s.	£47 1s. 8d.	£2 7s. 1d.	
Haughton		3 shortcloths – £20.			
Ellis		Sundry small wares – £15; 36 lbs tobacco – £18.	£53	£1 13s.	
Randall		1 cwt pewter – £3; 5 cwt hops – £5; 1 cwt sugar – £3 6s. 8d.; 2 cwt brass kettles – £7 9s. 4d.; 3 cwt prunes – £1 10s.; 2 cwt raisins of the sun – £1 16s.; 8 lbs tobacco – £4; tonnage of one tun of sacke – £3.	£29 2s.	£1 9s. 1d.	
Stephenson		9 cows – £9.	£9	9s.	
Gattenby		40 bal malt – £26 13s. 4d.	£26 13s. 4d.	£1 6s. 8d	
Nicholson		2 shortcloths – £13 6d. 8d.	£13 6s. 8d.	13s. 4d.	

Index of People

Index to Londonderry Port Books

Abercorn, Earl of, 7, 11, 13, 15, 17, 29, 47
Allison/Ellison, Alan/Alen/Allen, 26, 27, 38, 39, 46, 47, 50, 51
Andrew, John, 47

Baker, Giles, 11, 41, 51
Balie, John, 9
Ballentine, Hugh, 2, 3, 6, 7, 12, 13,
Ballentine, William, 30
Banckes/Bankes, John, 5, 9, 11, 13, 31, 45, 51
Barkeley/Barkely, John, 24, 37
Barran, David, 26, 46
Barrow, William, 41
Bartley/Bartly, John, 33, 45, 53
Baudie, John, 39
Bawby, John, 29
Benson, Peter, 41
Berne, Robert, 6, 7
Berriman, Thomas, 40, 41
Berrisford, Tristram, 19
Bersban, John, 29
Beton, John, 31
Betson/Bettson, John, 10, 16, 17, 53
Bias, Mr, 5
Bibbie, John, 29
Blacke, Robert, 8, 9, 38, 39
Blanne, John, 4, 5
Bleare, James, 32
Bohell, Hugh, 2
Boid/Boide/Boyde, John, 2, 3, 8, 9, 42, 43, 48, 49
Boide, Ringing, 9, 11
Bonde, John, 26
Booke, Robert, 25
Booke, William, 35
Borroughs, Raphe, 7
Boulton, William, 11, 17, 51, 53
Bourne, Robert, 20, 21, 30, 31
Boyles, John, 3
Bradshawe, James, 8
Bride, John, 10
Brookes, Giles, 14, 15
Brookes/Brooks, Martin, 4, 8, 10
Browne, John, 30, 31, 32, 35, 42, 48, 52
Browne, Thomas, 51
Burne, Robert, 3, 4, 5, 6
Byas, Robert, 5

Cambell, John, 6, 7, 23, 31, 49
Cambell, Patrick, 8
Canning, Thomas, 37
Carter, Henry, 43
Chillin, Josp, 11
Chohone, Robert, 32
Cirkwood, David, 30, 31
Cobereth, Patrick, 48
Coborne, David, 14
Coen, Hugh, 29
Cohone, Andrew, 31
Cohone, Hugh, 11
Cohone/Cohoone, Robert, 2, 3, 6, 8, 10, 22, 34, 35, 50
Cockran/Coheran/Cokeran/Cokran, Andrew, 4, 5, 6, 12, 13, 16, 17, 20, 21, 28, 29, 30, 31, 32, 33, 34, 38, 39, 40, 44, 45, 48, 49, 50, 51

Cressy, Roger, 42, 43
Crookewood/Crookwood/Crookwoode, David, 18, 24, 25, 28
Cuningham, Robert, 6, 7
Cuningham/Cunningham, William, 3, 7, 53
Curethe, William, 38

Dalbye, Moses, 15, 17, 39
Davis, John, 43, 53
Deene, John, 36, 37
Deloppe, Alan, 44, 45
Denall, William, 35, 51
Dicker, Alexander, 44, 45
Dickes/Dikes, Andrew, 3, 5, 11, 21
Donnell, Peter, 2, 3, 4, 5, 14, 15, 16, 20, 38, 39, 46, 52, 53
Downe, Foulkes, 29
Dunkenson, John, 51
Dutton, John, 37

Ellis, Henry, 4, 5
English/Englishe/Inglishe, Ninian/Ringing/Ningen, 5, 13, 53
Enry, John, 18, 19, 28
Euen, Saunder, 38, 39, 46, 47, 52, 53
Eury, James, 22, 23, 24, 36, 37, 46, 47, 48, 49
Eury, John, 19
Evans, David, 27
Evans, Thomas, 16
Even, Alexander, 8
Even, Saunder, 27
Evine, Robert, 5

Farroll, George, 2, 3, 4, 5
Felles, Christopher, 3
Fittzimons/Fitzimons/Fitzsimons, Richard, 3, 53
Fitzsimmons, Thomas, 5
Fleming, John, 29
Fleming, Martin, 53
Fleming, Robert, 8
Fleming, William, 48, 52, 53
Folesdale, John, 8, 9
Forrester, Robert, 10, 11
Forsithe, Patrick, 25, 49
Foster, John, 8, 9

Gaie, James, 12, 13
Galte/Gaulte, William, 4, 5, 46, 47, 48, 49
Gardner, Robert, 38, 39, 52
George, Archibald, 42, 43, 48, 52
Gland/Glande, John, 2, 3, 14, 15, 38, 39, 52, 53
Glasse, William, 50, 51
Graisie, John, 53
Grave, Ringing, 47
Graves, Michael, 11, 19, 53
Greeneoake, James, 3
Gregge, William, 8, 9, 12, 13
Guye, James, 38, 39

Hamelton/Hamilton, Sir George, 7, 49
Hamelton/Hammelton, Hugh, 3, 17
Hamelton, John, 17
Hamelton, William, 7, 25, 31, 37, 51
Hamill, John, 25
Hamlet/Hamlett, John, 2, 3, 4, 10, 14, 16, 18, 24, 25, 26, 28, 32, 36, 38, 44, 50, 52
Hamond/Hamonde, Brute, 13, 17, 33, 37, 47, 51

Hamond, George, 5, 9, 11, 13, 15, 17, 19, 33, 37, 41, 43, 49, 51
Harbinson, Archibald, 21, 51
Hardy, Edward, 14, 15
Harvy, John, 24, 25
Hatton, John, 39
Haye, John, 9
Heade, John, 42, 43
Henry, John, 6, 7
Holland, Laurence, 39, 51
Homes, Gabriell, 50, 51
Hone, Gabriell, 32, 33
Horton, Patrick, 10
Hoy, Abraham, 2, 3
Hunter, John, 26, 27, 32, 48
Hunter, Ringen/Ringing, 12, 24, 25, 30, 31, 50, 51

Jackson, John, 2
Jackson/Jacson, Thomas, 6, 7, 26, 27
Jeffery/Jefferye, William, 32, 33, 40, 41
Jinningham, John, 2

Kaile, John, 6, 7
Kenedie, John, 35
Keningham, Sir James, 9, 15, 33, 49
Keningham/Kenningham, John, 2, 25, 29, 49
Keningham/Kenningham, Robert, 2, 36, 37
Keningham/Kenningham, William, 9, 17, 23, 33, 35, 39, 47
Kile, James, 47
Knockes/Knox/Knoxe, Adam, 36, 37, 48, 49
Knockes, Andrew, 30, 31

Lan, Thomas, 32, 33, 49
Lanckforde/Langford/Langforde, William, 15, 19, 27, 31
Land, John, 2, 3
Landlers/Landles, Robert, 32, 33, 48
Larriman, John, 8, 9
Leach, John, 27, 47
Leate, Nicholas, 43
Leather, George, 25
Lee, Humphrey, 15
Leeche, William, 14, 15, 16
Legate, Michael, 6, 7
Leycocke/Lucoppe, James, 36, 37, 50, 51
Linseie/Linsey/Linseye, Mathew, 15, 16, 17, 20, 21,
Linseie/Linsey/Linseye, Robert, 4, 12, 13, 14, 28, 29, 34, 35, 46
Lion/Lyon, James, 8, 9, 11, 46, 47
Lion, John, 10
Lion, Robert, 38, 39
Lion, Thomas, 8, 9
Locon, Saunder, 12, 13
Lodimer, Adam, 6, 7, 8, 9
Lodimer, John, 8
Loggie/Luggie, John, 25, 29, 33, 41, 49
Lon, Thomas, 48
London, City of, 9, 15, 41
London, City of, 15
Long, John, 37
Long, Thomas, 36, 50, 51
Love, John, 42, 43, 50

McBourney, Thomas, 49
McKenny, Hugh, 47
McKenny, John, 50, 51
McMare, Thomas, 29
Mallon, James, 50
Mason, James, 51
Mather, William, 7

Mawberrey, Thomas, 10, 11
Mellin/Melon, James, 28, 34, 36
Mencriffe, David, 21
Miller, John, 44, 45
Moderell/Moderwell/Motherwell, Adam, 2, 3, 4, 5, 8, 12, 20, 21, 30, 31, 34, 36, 37, 44, 45, 48, 52, 53
Moderill, John, 34
Montford/Montforte, Thomas, 10, 11, 12, 13
Mordach/Mordocke, Patrick, 12, 44
Morison/Morrison, Robert, 6, 7, 24, 25
Morrison, David, 23, 52, 53
Morrison, James, 24, 25
Morrison, Thomas, 32, 33
Motherwell, Edward, 2, 3
Mullan, David, 4, 5, 12, 13
Murdach, Patrick, 30

Nelson, Hugh, 5
Nisbett, William, 2, 3, 19
Noble, Henry, 17
Nunne, Robert, 11

Ogle, Adam, 6
Oldfers/Oldphers/Alpherte, Wibrand/Wybrand, 2, 3, 7, 8, 9, 12, 13, 14, 15, 16, 17, 30, 31, 32, 33, 38, 39, 44, 45, 48, 49
Onion, John, 45
Ore, John, 22, 23, 30
Ore, Walter, 30
Ormes, Robert, 2
Orre, George, 21, 35, 49
Orre, William, 38, 39
Osbone, Henry, 37, 51

Parry, William, 5, 11, 15, 19, 27, 29, 43, 47
Pattison, William, 2, 3
Peate, Peter, 12
Penny, John, 32, 36
Piercson, Thomas, 10, 11
Pierson, John, 15
Pitts, John, 5
Poore, John, 3, 7, 9, 11, 13, 15, 21, 27, 43, 53
Porter, Robert, 33
Pyke, John, 6, 7

Redgate, Thomas, 29
Reimond/Reymond, Richard, 42, 43
Rider, William, 34, 35
Robinson, Henry, 28, 29, 44, 45
Robinson, John, 48
Robinson, Robert, 32, 48
Rogers, James, 34, 35, 38, 39
Rogers, William, 27, 31, 35, 47
Rosse, Francis, 12, 13
Rowley, John, 17, 27
Royle, Robert, 45
Russell, Archibald, 5
Russell, Robert, 5, 13

Sadler, Henry, 3, 5, 7, 11, 15, 17, 29, 31, 41
Sadler, Richard, 19, 29, 33, 37, 45, 49
Saunderson, Thomas, 34, 35, 50
Scot/Scott, John, 13, 48
Shaw, Robert, 4
Simple, Duncan, 20, 21, 30, 40, 52
Simple, John, 8, 9, 16, 17
Simson, Humphrey, 8, 9
Simson, William, 50, 51

Slois, John, 6, 8, 10, 12
Slone, John, 20
Smitar, Thomas, 4
Smiter, Theophilus, 22, 23
Smith, John, 13, 30, 31
Smith/Smithe, Jesse, 7, 11, 13, 15, 17, 19, 27, 31, 33, 37, 39, 41, 43, 45, 53
Smithe, John, 4, 5, 8, 9, 22, 23, 28, 29, 44, 45, 52
Smithe, William, 8, 9, 10, 11, 38, 39, 50
Snap/Snape, William, 12, 13, 52, 53
Somerell, William, 29, 50, 51
Stanton, Richard, 15, 27, 45, 53
Steward/Stewarde, Alexander, 7, 21, 31, 33, 49
Steward/Stewarde, James, 17, 41, 49
Steward/Stewarde, John, 2, 4, 5, 10, 16, 20
Steward/Stewarde, Sir John, 15, 35, 47
Steward, Saunder, 5
Steward/Stewarde, Walter, 2, 3, 34, 35
Steward, William, 14, 15, 19, 49
Stewarde, Sir William, 35
Steynings, Alexander, 7
Stobone, Thomas, 48
Stocton, John, 7
Strong, John, 19, 23, 29, 35, 47, 49
Sunter, Thomas, 12, 13, 14, 34
Swetenham, George, 41, 53

Thomas, John, 4, 5
Thompson/Tompson/Tomson, Hugh, 3, 9, 13, 21, 43, 49, 51
Thomson, John, 35
Tiling, Nicholas, 51
Tomson, Matthew, 41
Tomson, Robert, 43, 49
Trafforde, Harry, 37
Tuckey, Walter, 35

Van de Leure, Maximilian, 3
Verchilde, William, 18, 28

Walt, William, 20
Walter, Mr, 3
Warden, James, 48
Warden, John, 34, 35
Watson, James, 47
Watson, John, 41
Watt, William, 29, 35, 49
Wemes, David, 27, 47
Williams, John, 42, 43
Williams, Thomas, 37
Williamson, Peter, 10, 14, 22, 42, 46, 50
Wilson, Edward, 38, 39, 48
Wilson, John, 9, 10, 11, 13, 18, 19, 30, 31, 34, 35, 36, 52, 53
Wilson, Matthew, 24, 25
Woodroofe, George, 32, 46, 48
Woodroofe, Robert, 19
Woolle, Robert, 49
Wray/Wraye, James, 36, 37, 50, 51

Yeonen/Yeoven/Yeven, Saunder, 8, 9, 10, 11, 14, 16, 17, 26

Zacharie/Zachary, John, 8, 40, 42, 52

Index to Coleraine Port Books

Alche (see also Leach), Duncan, 64
Aldersey, John, 71, 87

Allenson, Andrew, 68
Allises, Andrew, 64
Allson, Alan, 62
Allson, Alan, 68
Andersonn, Ringin, 74, 75
Andiose, Renninge, 84, 85
Androse, Henry, 72

Barraine, Davie, 86
Barrow, William, 79
Bepell/Beple, John, 76, 86
Beresford, Tr[istram], 63
Berres, Robert, 62, 64
Betsonn, John, 70
Blacke, Thomas, 84
Blage, John, 74, 75, 82, 83, 84, 86
Blaick, James, 72
Blaier/Blare, James, 82, 83, 85
Bockes, Robert, 84, 85
Booth, James, 82, 83
Borne, Robert, 64, 68
Boulton/Bowlton, William, 71, 79, 87
Brasiar, Paul, 59, 61, 63, 67, 69
Breddy, John, 83
Breddy, William, 83
Brene, John, 74
Brenson, Davy, 75
Brocher, James, 66
Browne, William, 66

Canning, George, 79
Casie, Thomas, 63
Catar, Henry, 65
Cockerryn/Cougharen, Andrew, 58, 62
Cogan, Peter, 77, 87
Corphed, Davy, 68
Costardyne, George, 83
Creeley, Patrick, 84

Downe, Fulke, 67, 71

Egerton, Thomas, 63
Evans, Thomas, 68, 70

Farrall, George, 58
Fitchsimons/Fitesimons/Fitsimons, Richard, 63, 71, 85, 87
Flud, John, 69
Follarton, Adam, 84
Forrest, Robert, 78, 82, 84, 85
Fusher, James, 64, 75
Fyar, Richard, 58

Gage, William, 86
Garnere, Robert, 86
Garvan, Andrew, 82
Gaulte/Gawlt/Gawlte, William, 64, 68, 70, 71, 72, 73, 82, 83
Gawlton, William, 64
Gefferey/Jeffery, William, 66, 70, 74
George, Archebell/Archibald, 73, 83
Gill, Nicholas, 75
Goodchild, John, 71, 77
Gouse, John, 68
Gove, Thomas, 68
Gragke, William, 76
Grege, William, 62
Gresson, William, 84
Grill, Nicholas, 63

Haiward, Edmond, 73
Halton, John, 85
Hambleton, William, 82
Hammond, Brute, 77
Hamond, George, 71
Harton, Patrick, 56
Harvie, John, 84, 85
Hatton, John, 57, 59, 61, 63, 67, 69, 77, 79
Haward, Edmond, 57, 59, 61, 63, 71
Hellman/Helman, Thomas, 71, 85
Helpe, William, 84, 85
Hill, Davie, 84
Hillman, Thomas, 65
Hilton, Raph, 87
Holeston, Robert, 60
Howe, James, 62, 76
Howe, John, 76
Hunter, John, 70, 84

Ingman, William, 65, 69, 71

Jackson, Henry, 65, 75, 79
Jackson, John, 82
Jackson, Thomas, 68, 72, 73, 74, 75
Johnson, Thomas, 62

Kile, John, 60

Larkmor, John, 62
Lawramor, John, 66
Leach/Leche/Lecth/Leech, Duncan, 64, 68, 72, 74, 82, 83, 86, 87
Lee, Humphrey, 73
Longe/Longhe, John, 56, 62, 78

Maccon, John, 74
Maddrell, John, 68
Mane, John, 72, 74
Markemack, Licktower, 75
Marsonn, John, 84
Mellar, Andrew, 84
Mellen, Davie, 64
Mellenton, John, 70, 71
Michell, Andrew, 62
Millar, John, 78
Modwill, Adam, 86
Morrishe, John, 64
Morrison, John, 82
Mullen, Davi, 70

Norton, William, 68

Ormesonn, Robert, 58
Overry, John, 78

Parry, William, 67, 87
Parsonn, Thomas, 68
Perrie, William, 61
Pett/Pitt, Richard, 60, 81, 87
Portar, Robert, 84
Power, John, 87

Rabon, Lawrence, 85
Raye, James, 74
Reede, John, 86
Renkeyn, John, 66
Rixon, Robert, 75
Robarsonn/Robartsonn, John, 76, 84

Robinson, George, 63
Robinson, John, 84
Robinson, Steven, 84
Rooe, James, 86
Rowley, John, 87
Rowley, Ralph, 69

Sadlar/Sadler, Richard, 86
Sadler, Henry, 56, 58, 60, 62, 66, 74, 84, 85
Sampsonn/Semson/Somson, William, 64, 74, 86
Samreste, John, 87
Sempell, John, 68
Shen, Robert, 56
Smith, Steven, 85
Snape, William, 76, 86
Som'er, Peter, 83
Somerll, William, 66
Sommaran, John, 83
Sparrow, John, 71, 75
Stanton, Richard, 87
Stente, Walter, 64
Steven, Walter, 84, 85
Stevensonn, Robert, 73
Steward, Alexander, 65
Suntar/Sunter, Thomas, 62, 86
Swetnam, George, 81, 87

Taylor, John, 64, 66
Taylor, Phillip, 65
Tenkell/Tenkoll, John, 78
Tirlaigh, Nicholas, 71
Townesend/Townsend, Davie/Davy, 71, 75, 77, 79

Wallton/Walton, John, 59, 65, 71
Warden, Humphrey, 74
Watson/Wattson, Edward, 71, 87
Welles, Thomas, 71
Wheett/White, Steeven, 72, 82
White, John, 74, 84
Wiatt, John, 76
Willstone, John, 60
Willstone, Robert, 61
Wilson, John, 84
Wise, James, 60, 62, 64
Wright, Henry, 75
Wright, Robert, 75

Zacarie/Zacary, John, 56, 58, 64, 66, 68, 78, 80, 82, 86

Index to Carrickfergus Port Books

Anderson, Jacob, 92, 96, 97
Armoulde/Arnowld, William, 90, 96

Barwicke, Richard, 91, 93, 95, 97, 99
Beande/Beane, Thomas, 90, 91, 92, 93
Bowche, Anthony, 95
Bowllton, Thomas, 94, 95
Brasier, Richard, 99
Brooke/Brookes, Richard, 95, 97
Brookes, John, 97
Browne, John, 92, 98
Burton, John, 94, 95

Care, John, 94, 95
Cater, Henry, 97

a Conlon, John, 98, 99
Conway/Conwaye, Sir Fowcke/Fowlke, 93, 99
Cooper, Thomas, 97
Cooplande/Copland, William, 92, 94, 96
Cowlty, Christopher, 98, 99
Crofer, Murtha, 98

Davis, William, 94, 95, 98
Dawson, Thomas, 90, 94, 96
Denwell, William, 95
Dobbine, William, 93

Fane, John, 94
Farrell, George, 96
Farrer, George, 94
Farry, Thomas, 96
Fletcher, William, 93, 95
Freaue, John, 97

Gardner, John, 93
Goste, Robert, 98
Gravan, John, 94, 95
Griffen/Gryffen, Richard, 90, 92, 96
Gylpatricke, Thomas, 91

Hall, Edward, 93, 97, 99
Harris, William, 91, 97
Hill, William, 99
Holland/Hollande, Laurence, 91, 93, 95, 97, 99
Hollcott/Howlecott, Henry, 95, 99
Horseman, Ingram, 99
Hunter, John, 94

Johnson/Johnsone, Bartholemew, 93, 95, 97, 99
Jurdayne, John, 98

Keale/Keele, John, 92

Lanckeforder, Hercules, 95
Lauerance, Nicholas, 99
Lawrenson, Thomas, 92, 96, 98
Leamon, Peter, 98
Loddener/Lodener, Adam, 92, 93
Lookeuppe, James, 90, 91, 96, 97
Louerance, Michael, 93
Lucas, Andrew, 95, 99
Lucas, Francis, 99

Madrell, Adam, 92, 93
Makan/McCan, Arte/Arctt, 94, 96
Marshe, Mathew, 91, 93, 97
Mase, George, 97
Murden, John, 96
Murdoe, John, 90
Murfey/Murfyn, John, 94, 98
Murphy, James, 93
Murto, Edward, 94

Nicholls, Francis, 94
Nichollsone/Nicholson/Nicollsone, Edward, 90, 91, 93, 94, 97

Oxwicke, Thomas, 97

Peterson, Debut, 98
Picke/Pike/Pyke, John, 92, 96, 97, 98
Predis, William, 93

Randall, George, 91, 95, 99
Rayman, Richard, 92
Richardson, Simon, 99
Robbynson, John, 94
Ryman, Richard, 90, 94, 96, 98

Slater, Edward, 98
Smyth, William, 98
Smythe, John, 90, 91, 92, 96
Smythe, Stephen, 99
Spenser, Henry, 97
Stephenson, Silvester, 90, 91, 94
Steward, Henry, 90
Stribbell/Stribble, Samuel, 92, 98
Sum'erwell, Rowland, 92, 93

Wallche/Welche, John, 94, 98
Wattson, Gregory, 90, 96
Wattson, James, 95
Wattsone, Robert, 94, 95
Wells, Aunsell, 96
White, John, 94, 95
White, Michael, 95, 97
Wildes/Wyldes, Mathew, 91, 92, 97
Willes, Adam, 96
Willkenson/Willkinsine, Edward, 93, 97
Willy, Adam, 92

Index to Lecale Port Books

Allyson, Michael, 102
Aniskey/Aniskye, Mack/Macke, 106, 107

Barry, John, 108, 109
Blacke, John, 108, 110, 111
Blealic/Blealick/Blealicke/Blealike/Bleylicke, Thomas, 102, 103, 106, 107, 108, 109, 111
Boomer, John, 106, 107
Boyd/Boyde, John, 102, 103, 108, 109, 110
Bradshawe, James, 110
Brafford/Brafforde, George, 102, 103
Braye, Robert, 103
Brittayne/Bryttayne, Thomas, 112
Browne, John, 102, 103, 104, 105
Butler/Butteler, Robert, 111

Canne, Patrick, 111
Carre, James, 113
Clarke, Saunder, 106, 107
Connar, Patrick, 111
Coulter, Christopher, 102

Dannson/Daunson/Dawson, Gowen, 102, 110
Dawson, Thomas, 102, 103
Dobb, Richard, 107
Dobb, William, 107
Done, Patrick, 108, 109
Duffe, Edmund, 110
Dungelson, Thomas, 103

Ellis, Edward, 113
Euston, Robert, 111

Farrewell/Farwell/Ferrell, Thomas, 108, 109
a Felyn, John Boye, 106, 107

Fisher, John, 110
Flynne, John, 102, 103, 108, 109, 110, 111
Flynne, Patrick, 110

Gattenby, Richard, 113
Gowen, Sawnder, 111
Goyne, Alexander, 103
Greerey, Robert, 111
Gunnell, William, 103

Hamblett, John, 106, 107
Hamelton, John, 102, 103
Haughton, Thomas, 107, 113
Hewston, James, 103
Hewston/Hewstone/Hueston, Robert, 103, 106, 107, 108, 109, 111
Hewston/Hewstone, William, 106, 107
Hogges, James, 110
Horton, Thomas, 111
Houghton, Thomas, 109
Hugheson/Hughestone/Hughson, John, 106, 108, 109
Hughson, Robert, 106, 107
Hughson, William, 106, 107
Hunter, John, 108, 109
Hunter, William, 106, 107

Jackson, Richard, 102, 103
Johnson, Henry, 102, 103, 110

Kenningham, Robert, 110, 111

Lawtham, Thomas, 102, 103
Lyle, William, 111

Mc Anesk/Mc Aniske, Rowland, 106, 108, 109
Mc Aniske, William, 106
Mc Cullin, Saunder, 108, 109
Mackaniste/Mackeneiskey/Mackeniskey/Mackeniste/Mc Aniske,
    Edmond/Edmund, 102, 106, 107, 108, 110
Mackcreery, Patrick, 110
Mackeienkyn, John, 106, 107
Mackeneste/Mackeniske, William, 110, 111

Mackreery, Patrick, 112
Mage, Patrick, 106, 107
Maggee, Peter, 111
Maxewell/Maxwell, Herbert, 106, 107
Maxfeild, Herbert, 110, 111
Maxfeilde, Robert, 110
Maxwell, John, 106, 107
Meagh/Meale/Mease/Meaughe, Patrick, 103, 107, 109, 111
Moore, James, 106, 107
Moresey, Peter, 103
Mullinaxe, John, 109

Nicholson, Robert, 102, 103, 107, 108, 109, 111, 113

Osborne, Henry, 102
Oxewicke, Edward, 111

Pemberton, William, 108, 109
Pibbelles/Pibbells, John, 110, 111

Randall, Robert, 112, 113
Rande, Thomas, 111
Roney/Ronney, Peter, 106, 108, 110
Rose, Richard, 113

Saunderson, John, 110
Scotte, Thomas, 109, 111
Smythe, John, 102, 103
Speares/Speeres/Speres, Robert, 102, 106, 107, 108, 109, 110
Starkey, Silvester, 110, 112
Stephenson, Silvester, 112, 113
Steward, John, 111

Thomas, John, 108, 109
Thomas, Walter, 105, 109
Thomas, William, 108, 109

Wilson, William, 104
Wrayye, Jeffry, 111

Younge, Henry, 102

Index of Ships

Londonderry ships

Blessing, 4
Blessing of [blank], 2
Blessing of Burntisland, 26, 38, 46
Blessing of Glasgow, 20, 30, 40, 52
Blessing of Leith, 26
Bonadventure of Largs, 8
Bride of Hilbre, 2, 4, 6
Bride of Londonderry, 10, 14, 16, 18, 26, 28, 32, 36, 38, 44, 46, 48, 50, 52

Carvaile of Coleraine, 10, 16
Consent of London, 16

Daisie of Barnstaple, 40
Daniell of Leith, 36, 50

Edward (*Edwarde*) of Hilbre, 24, 26, 32
Elizabeth (*Elizabethe*) of Londonderry, 2, 4, 10, 20, 32, 36
Elizabethe of London, 10

Faulcon of Barnstaple, 42

George of Renfrew, 8, 10
Good Fortune of Ayr, 6, 8, 10
Good Fortune of Irvine, 44
Grace of Chester, 8, 10
Grace of God, 2, 4
Grace of God of Ayr, 52
Grace of God of Burntisland, 2
Grace of God of Dumbarton, 2
Grace of God of Greenock, 26, 32, 48
Grace of God of Irvine, 34
Grace of God of Largs, 8
Grace of God of Rothesay, 14
Grace of God of the Wemyss, 6
Greyhounde (*Greyhound*) of Londonderry, 4, 6, 8, 10, 12, 20, 30, 44
Guifte of Dumbarton, 4
Guifte of God, 10
Guifte of God of Ayr, 12
Guifte of God of Burntisland, 52
Guifte of God of Clyde, 48
Guifte of God of Dumbarton, 4
Guifte of God of Glasgow, 30, 52
Guifte of God of Irvine, 4, 36, 48
Grace of God of Largs, 48
Guifte of God of Saltcoats, 8, 12, 28, 38
Guifte of God of Strabane, 12, 14, 16, 20, 34, 46

Harry (*Henry*) of Ayr, 34, 36, 50
Henry of Londonderry, 28, 44
Hope of Dublin, 2
Hopewell (*Hopwell*) of Ayr, 12, 24, 36, 52
Hopewell (*Hopwell*) of Dumbarton, 8, 10, 14, 16, 26, 38, 46
Hopewell (*Hopwell*) of Largs, 12, 24
Hopewell of Leith, 14
Hopewell (*Hopwell*) of Renfrew, 26, 42, 48

Isable of Glasgow, 12
Isable of Greenock, 10

Jennet, 2, 6
Jennet of Ayr, 48

Jennet of Glasgow, 34
Jennet of Greenock (small boat), 48
Jennet of Irvine, 20, 30
Jennett of Mongavlin, 6, 30, 36
Jennet of Renfrew, 30, 36, 48
Jennet of Saltcoats, 6, 8, 12
Jennet of Scotland, 4
Joane, 2
Joane of Renfrew, 24
John of Dumbarton, 8, 14, 16, 20, 22, 28, 30, 38, 46, 48, 52
John (*Jhon*) of Glasgow, 20, 28, 34, 44, 52
John of Plymouth, 6
John of Renfrew, 2, 4, 8, 12, 14, 20, 30, 32, 34, 36, 48
Jonathan of Largs, 42
Jonathan of Saltcoats, 32
Jones of Fairlie, 8

Katherine, 2
Katherine (*Katherin*) of Renfrew, 2, 6
Katherine (*Katherin*) of Saltcoats, 6, 8

Man of Dumbarton, 2
Margaret, 2
Margaret of Ayr, 42
Margaret of [blank], 18
Margaret of Barnstaple, 28
Margaret of Bristol, 4
Margaret of Clyde (a small boat), 24
Margaret of Irvine, 2, 24
Margaret of Kirkcaldy, 2
Margaret of Largs, 8
Margaret (*Margret*) of Renfrew, 18, 22, 24, 28, 36, 46, 48
Margaret of Southend (Kintyre), 28, 30
Margerie of Chester, 2
Margret of Greenock, 10
Martine, 4
Mary and James of Dartmouth, 14, 34
Mary Grace of Burntisland, 30, 42, 52
Mary of Neston, 34
Mayflower of London, 12
Michaell of Parton, 34, 50

Peeter, 2
Peeter (*Peter*) of Londonderry, 8, 12, 14, 16, 30, 32, 38, 44, 48
Post (*Poste*) of Leith, 2, 10
Poste of Londonderry, 4
Providence of Dumbarton, 38

Robarte (*Roberte*) of Dumbarton, 2, 6, 8, 10, 14, 22, 32, 34, 50
Robarte (*Roberte*) of Renfrew, 32, 48
Roberte of Greenock - 50

Salamander of Irvine, 42
Sara of Chester, 42
Seaflower of London, 8, 40, 42, 52
Sondaie of [blank], 10
Speedwell of Liverpool, 4
Steven of Liverpool, 14
Stone of Renfrew, 4
Swallow of Dumbarton, 10, 14, 22, 42, 46, 50

Thomas of Clyde, 32, 48
Thomas of Greenock, 50
Thomas of Renfrew, 26

Thomas of Saltcoats, 6
Trinitie of Chester, 42, 48, 52

Unicorne of Chester, 38, 50

Vangarde, 2

William, 6
William of Clyde, 38
William of Dumbarton, 26, 46
William of Northam, 32, 40
William of Renfrew, 4, 12, 16, 20, 28, 30, 48, 50

Coleraine ships

Blessing of Coleraine, 70
Blessing of God of Burntisland, 86
Blessing of God of Shoreham, 72, 74
Bride of Hilbre, 56, 58, 60, 62, 74, 86
Bride of Londonderry, 66, 84, 86

Cathren of Ayr, 60
Cathren of Carlingford, 82
Cathren of Glasgow, 62
Clemott of Scotland, 84
Consent of London, 68, 70

Dove of London, 60, 62

Edward of Hilbre, 72
Enera of Resa, 56
Elizabeth of Derry, 56
Elizabeth of Glasgow, 82
Elizabeth of London, 68
Elizabeth of Scotland, 86

Fyall of Scotland, 84

Genett of Greenock, 60
Genett of Scotland, 84
Gift of God of Burntisland, 86
Good Fortune of Irvine, 82
Grace of God of Burntisland, 62, 70, 86
Grace of God of Saltcoats, 82, 86
Grace of God of Scotland, 74, 84
Griffin of Drogheda, 84
Guifte of God (*Gifte of God*) of Irvine, 64, 70, 72, 82

Hopewell of Larges, 70
Hopewell of Scotland, 70

John Dumbart of Scotland, 68
John of Renfrew, 86
John of Saltcoats, 84
John of Scotland, 76, 82, 84

Kathrine of Glasgow, 56

Mathew Margerett of Coleraine, 62
Margery of Hilbre, 58
Margett of Dumbarton, 86
Mary Grace of Burntisland, 74
Mary of Barnstaple, 76, 86

Pellican of Coleraine, 60, 62, 64
Perdew of Scotland, 74
Poote of Londonderry, 62, 64

Robert, 76
Robert of Irvine, 82

Salamander of Irvine, 72, 82
Saray of Hilbre, 76
Seaflower (*Sea Flower*) of Dover, 56, 58, 64, 66, 68
Seaflower of London, 78, 80, 82, 86
Spedewell of Liverpool, 58
Sundoay of Scotland, 56

Thomas of Glasgow, 72, 74
Trenyty of Chester, 86

Unicorne of Chester, 84

William of Barnstaple, 70, 74
William of Northam, 66, 70
William of Renfrew, 58, 62

Carrickfergus ships

Anne of Parton, 90, 92
Anne of Workington, 94, 96

Blessing [of] Ayr, 92, 96

Creason of Le Croisic, 94
Cuthberte (*Cuttbert*) of R. Alt, 92, 98

Daniel (*Daniell*) of Leith, 90, 96

Elizabeth of Liverpool, 92, 96, 98

Faulkon of Liverpool, 90, 94
Fortune of Chester, 98
Fortune of London, 90, 94, 96, 98

George of [blank], 98
George of Carrickfergus, 96
George of Douglas, 94
God before Maste, 94
Golden Grey of Liverpool (*Goulden Gray*) of Liverpool, 94, 98
Guifte of God (*Gifte of God*) of Carrickfergus, 92, 94, 96
Guifte of God of Croston, 98
Guifte of God of Isle of Man, 90, 94
Guifte of God of Glasgow, 90, 92, 94, 96
Guifte of God (*Guyfte of God*) of Parton, 94, 98

Haucke of Muscoovia (*Haucke of Muscovye*) of Amsterdam, 94, 98

Jennett of Ayr, 90
Jennett of Largs, 92
Jennitt of Saltcoats, 92
John of Carrickfergus, 92, 96, 98
John of Plymouth, 96
John of Renfrew, 92
John of Saltcoats, 94
Joseph of [blank], 96

Margett of Glasgow, 92, 96
Margett of Parton, 94
Margett of Saltcoats, 92
Martin (*Martyn*) of Chester, 90, 94, 96
Moises of Carrickfergus, 98

Peter of [blank], 98
Peeter (*Peter*) of Ayr, 94, 96

Robert, 92
Robert of Saltcoats, 94

Sara (*Sarah*) of Chester, 90, 92, 94, 98
Sarah of Weymouth, 90, 96
Speedwell (*Speedewell*) of Beaumaris, 90, 92, 96
Speedwell of Liverpool, 96
Sunday of Ardglass, 94

Trinitie of Ardglass, 98
Trynitie of Liverpool, 94, 96
Trynnitie of Parton, 90

Unicorne of Chester, 98

William of Northam, 92, 98

Lecale ports ships

Anne of Parton, 102

Blesseinge of God of Killough, 108
Blesseinge of God of Wyre, 108
Blessinge of God of London, 104
Blessinge of London, 102

George of Ardglass, 106
George of Isle of Man, 102
George of Lancaster, 102
George of R. Wyre, 102
George of Ribble Water, 106
Gifte of God of Killough, 110
Gifte of God of London, 112
Gifte of God of Strangford, 108
Grase of Strangford, 106
Gufte of Strangford, 106

Henery of Carlingford, 104
Henery of Kirkcudbright, 106, 108
Henry (*Henery*) of Ayr, 102, 106, 110
Henry of Wyre, 102, 110
Hope of Kinghorn, 106

James of Ayr, 106
Jelleflower of Fairlie, 102
Jelliflower (*Jelleflower*) of Ayr, 108
Jelliflower (*Jelleflower*) of Irvine, 102, 110

Jonas of Ardglass, 106
Jonas of Ayr, 106, 108
Jonas of Largs (Larges), 106, 108, 110
Jonas of Rosses, 106
Julian of Strangford, 106

Katherine of Ardglass, 102, 106, 108, 110
Katherine of Strangford, 106, 108
Katherine of Whithorn, 102

Mariegould (*Marygould*) of Strangford, 106, 108
Margaret of Holywood, 110
Margarett of Largs, 110
Marygould of Ballintogher, 108
Mathewe of Wyre, 112
Michaell of Ardglass, 110
Michaell of Largs, 108

Peeter of Dunadee, 110
Peeter of Glasgow, 110
Peeter of Irvine, 102
Peeter of Kirkcudbright, 106, 108
Peeter of Largs, 106, 108

Roberte of Ayr, 110

Sondaye of Ardglass, 102, 110
Sondaye of Kilclief, 110, 112
Sondaye of R. Wyre, 102
Speedwell (*Speedewell*) of Ardglass, 106, 108
Speedwell (*Speedewell*) of Liverpool, 108
Speedwell (*Speedewell*) of Strangford, 102, 110
Speedwell of Wyre, 102
Steephen of Isle of Man, 112
Stephen of Wyre, 102
Swifte sure (*Swyfte sure*) of Wyre, 102

Thomas of Kirkcudbright, 106
Trynitie of Wyre, 102
Trynity (*Trynitye*, *Trynnity*) of Ardglass, 106, 108, 110
Trynity of Kirkcudbright, 108
Trynnity of Wyre, 110

Vallentyne of Liverpool, 112
Violett of Liverpool, 108

William of Ardglass, 106, 108
William of Glasgow, 110

Map Section

Continental European ports mentioned in the Ulster Port Books

L = Londonderry
Ck = Carrickfergus
Co = Coleraine

Norway

Amsterdam (Ck)

Dieppe (L)
Rouen (L)

La Rochelle (L, Ck)

Bilbao (L, Co)

Londonderry: places mentioned in the Port Books

Plain text e.g. Rothesay = Port of origin.

Bold text e.g. **Greenock** = Port of origin and trading port.

Italic e.g. *Workington* = Trading port only.

Coleraine: places mentioned in the Port Books

Plain text e.g. Dumbarton = Port of origin.

Bold text e.g. **Greenock** = Port of origin and trading port.

Italic e.g. *Islay* = Trading port only.

Carrickfergus: places mentioned in the Port Books

Plain text e.g. Glasgow = Port of origin.

Bold text e.g. **Ayr** = Port of origin and trading port.

Italic e.g. *Barnstaple* = Trading port only.

Lecale: places mentioned in the Port Books

Plain text e.g. Glasgow = Port of origin.

Bold text e.g. **Irvine** = Port of origin and trading port.

Italic e.g. *Workington* = Trading port only.